WHAT IS PROFESSIONAL
SOCIAL WORK?

Malcolm Payne

VENTURE PRESS

Published by
VENTURE PRESS
16 Kent Street
Birmingham
B5 6RD
Tel: 0121 622 3911

British Library Cataloguing-in-Publication Data.
A catalogue record for this bo

ISBN 1 873878 17 6 (paperb

Printed in Great Britain

Cover Design by Western Arts
194 Goswell Road
London EC1V 7DT

Foreword and Acknowledgements

I have written this book for three reasons, two reasonably creditable and one somewhat discreditable. A little while ago at a conference of the Association of Teachers in Social Work Education, David Jones, then General Secretary of the British Association of Social Workers (BASW), argued that people were increasingly returning to a need to see social work as a 'profession' with standards of conduct. By implication, this movement was towards people accepting 'professionalisation' in social work. I wondered at the time what conceptions people might have of social work as a professional activity as they began to move into the twenty-first century - social work's second century. I thought it might be a rather different view than those traditionally associated with professions. David's speech stimulated me to think some more about this and it is one of the origins of this book.

I had previously written a book, *Modern Social Work Theory: a critical introduction* (Payne, 1991), in which I had included some material about the nature of social work and professionalisation. Because of the needs of the publisher, however, this had been truncated in the published version, and I nursed the wish to be able to give full rein to a dicussion of this subject. This is the second origin of my wish to write this book.

The more discreditable and most immediate origin of this book lies in a lunch with Venture Press's publisher, Sally Arkley, when I was unwise enough to mention my doubts about David's ideas on the comeback of professionalisation and my view that this was an important issue to be reviewed. Somehow this led to a oral agreement. The rapidity with which this was followed up by a written contract left me unable to resist.

The approach of this book is humanistic exploration in the territory of the discourses of social work. I have myself set out on an expedition among writings on the nature of social work as a profession. Any practitioner, student, manager or academic in any field of endeavour needs to make such a journey. In fact, we inevitably do so as part of learning and doing our jobs. I have reviewed, as part of my expedition, what others have said about these topics and tried to draw together views about them. In doing this, I hope my own exploration might assist others in making their own journeys. In particular, students may find this account useful in starting out on their own pathway to being a social worker. It will be obvious from the text that I do not think there will or should ever be a final answer about these issues. They are, however, always worth setting in the context of experience in each generation, and I consider it a privilege to be given a chance to make a contribution to wider debate about them.

I wish to acknowledge the contributions of colleagues who helped me develop some of the ideas in this book:

- in my own Department of Applied Community Studies at the Manchester Metropolitan University. The theoretical approach of this book stems from the ideas they have got me to think about.

- in the Department of Applied Social Studies of Hong Kong Polytechnic (now Hong Kong Polytechnic University) which invited me to give some seminars on social work theory, and responded to my ideas so critically and thoughtfully, and their Head of Department, Professor Diana Mak, who enabled me to use their Library;

- Gerd Hagen of the Norwegian College of Public Administration and Social Work, Oslo (NKSH), now part of the Oslo College, who invited me to give a seminar on the analysis of social work activity to staff from NKSH and the Diakonhjemmets Høgskolesenter Sosialhøgskolen. They also asked a lot of difficult questions;

- members of the Oxfordshire Branch of BASW, who similarly invited me to give a presentation on social work principles;

- Anne Parmley, who provided me with information about nursing ethics and principles and supplied up-to-date documents from the United Kingdom Central Council;

- Annette Blampied and Mike Harnor, colleagues in the Faculty of Community Studies, Law and Education at the Manchester Metropolitan University, who provided me with information about counselling and teaching;

- Gurid Aga Askeland, who read an early draft and made many perceptive and helpful comments;

- Dr Shulamit Ramon, the Russian Ministry of Higher Education and the Soros Foundation who invited me to give two papers on the nature of social work in Moscow,

- and many colleagues too numerous to mention who have discussed some of the points in this book at conferences and meetings that we have attended together over the last two years. It is better for what I have learnt from them, though they are not to blame for my inadequacies: I keep learning more and keep wanting to rewrite it.

But Sally has waited long enough for the outcome of that lunch.

Malcolm Payne
Edgworth
1995

Other books by Malcolm Payne:

Power, Authority and Responsibility in Social Services: social work in area teams (1979)
Working in Teams (1982)
Social Care in the Community (1986)
Modern Social Work Theory: a critical introduction (1991)
Linkages: effective networking in social care (1993)
Social Work and Community Care (1995)

Contents

Page

List of Figures and Tables

Figures

Tables

Chapter 1
Introduction: Starting Points and Pathways

Starting points and pathways

I can remember the occasion when I took the decision which was to lead me into social work. I was gazing unseeingly at the notice about the new course in social work in the darkened, pine-clad corridor of one of our new universities. I decided to go for it, in that corridor, not knowing what it would mean. It was the start of a pathway into and through a career in social work. Through my experiences on that pathway, I have formed conceptions of myself as a social worker. Everyone arrives, similarly, at their own view: of themselves within their occupation and of the occupation they follow.

Our occupational self-concept is not entirely personal, however. When I started out in the social services world, I acquired some ready-made concepts of what social work was about from the people who introduced me to their work. My social work degree provided an intellectual and academic basis for understanding the nature of social work and of my contribution to it. Both of these have been refined and developed by experience and learning throughout my career. So, my view of social work reflects and reacts to shared conceptions. These have come from social workers and others directly involved in the social services, and broader conceptions reflected in the news and entertainment media.

Any understanding of social work, therefore, is personal but the 'personal' reflects, and is mainly built up from, social constructions of social work. This book aims to review:

- constructions of the nature of social work, and

- ways in which and the extent to which it may be considered a profession, and in so doing

- to help readers in making their personal exploration of the issues reviewed here.

There are implications in taking this view of understanding the nature of social work. I accept that there are different conceptions that cannot be simply subsumed within each other. Neither can one or the other be found dominant. My view is that an understanding of the nature of social work must accommodate various visions but must provide a framework for seeing the visions as related to one another. If they were unrelated, they would not be relevant to a central concept: social work.

Many writers (eg Mullaly, 1993) identify only two visions: competing traditional and radical views of social work. Throughout this book, I identify three *general perspectives* on social work around which I argue visions of social work coalesce. These are:

- *Individualism-reformism.* This view focuses on the role of social work as an aspect of welfare services to individuals in societies. The main purpose of social work, in this view, is to meet individuals' needs, but there is also a role to improve services of which social work is a part, so that social work and the services can operate more effectively.

- *Socialist-collectivist.* In this perspective social work is part of a system which seeks to promote co-operation and mutual support in society so that the most oppressed and disadvantaged people can gain power over their own lives. The role of social work is to empower, facilitate and take part in a process of learning and mutual co-operation which creates institutions which all can own and participate in. Thus, an alternative form of society can develop. Elites who accumulate and perpetuate power and resources in society for their own benefit, leading to the oppression and disadvantage that others suffer, would be supplanted by a more egalitarian set of relationships among people.

- *Reflexive-therapeutic.* In this view, social work seeks to achieve the best possible well-being for individuals, groups and communities in society, by promoting and facilitating their own personal growth and self-realisation. They do so in a constant process of interaction with others, which modifies their ideas, and allows them to influence others - reflexivity. In this way, people gain power over their own feelings and way of life, and through this personal power are enabled to overcome or rise above suffering and disadvantage.

I contend that all visions of social work contain these three elements in various combinations and in tension with each other. The fundamental debate about the nature of social work is about how we may judge correctly the influence of each of these visions in the creation of social work as a whole.

An approach and a method

The idea of exploring an area of understanding implies a starting point and a *pathway* through the subject matter. We need to have a methodical way of carrying out our exploration. In this section, I explain how I shall approach the issue of trying to understand social work and the methods by which I shall work.

First, I make a distinction between social work:

- as an *activity*, something that human beings do, and
- as a *profession*, a particular kind of occupational group.

We can talk about and try to understand social work in either or both ways. In the end, they are inseparable, but distinguishing them at the outset helps us to analyse different aspects of social work more clearly.

In both cases, however, I see social work as a social phenomenon. That is, it is an activity which human beings carry out in relationships with one another. Some interactions are understood by the people involved and by observers as 'social work'. People may not define it explicitly. They may carry on without being clear about the nature of what they do. What they do, then, is socially constructed: what they *do* or what they *are* in society says to us what social work is.

How can we know what that social construction called 'social work' actually is? There are three ways of knowing. The first is by reference to authority, tradition and belief. This may sound a bit medieval. It is like the faith in God or Allah which we associate with religion. The scientific revolution of the sixteenth- and seventeenth-century enlightenment supplanted this way of knowing. It is not completely unrealistic as a way of knowing about everyday social work. Obviously, most social workers follow conventions and beliefs about social work most of the time and it works well enough. It does not help us, however, to respond to a sceptical critic who does not believe in our traditions.

The second way of knowing is associated with the scientific exploration which came out of the enlightenment. It is sometimes called rationalist or modernist. These ideas assume that there is a real world which can be explored and understood through observation, experiment and logical argument based on observations. We should observe what social workers do, distinguishing them from what other similar but different people do. Then we should construct a series of ideas or theories which describe the basic principles of social work. Trying these out in practice would enable us to say whether our description and theory did distinguish social work from other activities or occupational groups. Such an approach would give us evidence about what people think social work is, but it presents certain problems. It has been successful as a way of understanding the world, through scientific method. It has led to industrialisation and scientific advance which have changed our world for the better. The problems with it are that it is not very easy to come up with a final and definitive statement about the nature of a complicated social phenomenon. Because social work is a social construction, it might easily be changed by people doing other things in other social situations different from those we observed.

The third way of knowing is sometimes described as post-modernist. This is partly because it questions the universal validity of the modernist, scientific approach to understanding the world. It is also a way of thinking that has grown up after the period when modernist ways of thinking were dominant in creating industrialised urban societies. It says that all the theories and explanations that we have about the world are expressed in words and ideas created by human beings. Therefore, these ideas do not have any existence in reality; they are symbols of people's understanding of the world around them. We can only understand them by referring to the different ways in which human beings interpret these ideas. In the end, our understanding will be a mosaic of different interpretations set against each other.

The distinction between modernist and post-modernist ways of thinking originates in architecture. An analogy with the designs of buildings might help to explain the difference between these two ways of thinking. The design of the ideal modernist building derives from the function that it has to perform. Rooms are grouped together according to their purposes and shaped according to the most efficient way of organising the space required. So, modernist office blocks tend to be square and spare. Some pick out the pipes and structural steel and concrete so that you can see how the building is designed to meet its functions and the functions are made clear and explicit. Post-modernist buildings are designed from the point of view that they should be interesting and attractive according to the people involved in them. They might have many different roof and window shapes and different-shaped corners and pieces sticking out in a variety of colours. Different historical building styles and decoration are used, so there may be black-and-white Tudor gables with small-paned Georgian windows in the same building. They are in this way eclectic, perhaps to a modernist fragmented, in their style, rather than seeking to make everything consistent with one overall ideal of purpose. Also, they are concerned with the inner workings as well as the outside appearance . Applying this to social work, we might see ourselves as concerned with how the hidden world of ideas and social structures influences and is influenced by the evident aspect of practice and action.

None of these ways of thinking excludes the others. It is useful to collect evidence and assess arguments stringently, in the rationalist or modernist way. Belief sometimes helps us to retain a focus in a diffuse, complex situation such as social work. It may be very important to those who act from faith or are motivated by meeting spiritual or moral needs. But post-modernist thinking alerts us to the fact that any social reality is likely to be complex and ambiguous, because the complexity and variety of human beings and their ideas make it so. Rorty (1989) argues that there cannot be one universal set of ideas or words that can guide us, either towards general social purposes or towards private goals. Each of us has our own 'final vocabulary' which represents our own set of ideas. Our own sets of ideas cannot be any better at describing the world than any other.

All ideas are not, however, entirely relative; that is, the same as each other or as completely acceptable as each other. Post-modernist thinking requires us to evaluate the range of ideas that exist about a particular notion. There may be something to some, many or all of them. Some techniques exist for doing so.

One technique is the idea of *deconstruction*. This proposes that when we look at an idea presented by an author, we should explore what may lie behind its surface presentation. The author might take for granted a particular point of view which is not explicit in their argument. For example, an argument which may be familiar to social workers is the following. It is sometimes said to be wrong for social workers to argue for a change in policy. This is because they are employees of an agency which incorporates political objectives. Therefore, they should not as part of their work pursue political objectives contrary to the policies of their employers. If we look behind this point, however, we can argue that declining to pursue a change is as much a political act as pursuing one. It is as political to prefer the *status quo* as to seek change. People who argue this way sometimes forget, ignore or reject that.

Often, authors of ideas are participating in debates about issues. Deconstructing what they say from their point of view allows us to identify the debate with which they are involved. This takes us into the ideas of *discourse* and *discursive formation*. There are two related but separate ideas in this notion. Discourse analysis as a research technique involves identifying the detailed points made by a writer or speaker and how they contribute to the argument. We might look at how they phrase or order arguments, for example.

More generally, the idea of discourse claims that the nature of a body of social actions and debates such as social work is formed by people rubbing up against one another, acting together in concert or opposition and sharing or disputing their ideas about what they are doing and thinking. Their discourse forms the nature of the thing itself. Thus, the discourse 'social work' is formed by the actions, understandings, thoughts and arguments of the people involved in it.

In this usage, the idea of discourse comes from the work of Foucault (1972). Most statements can, on examination, be seen to imply a position in an underlying discourse. So, for example, those who argue that social workers should desist from seeking social change are not just giving guidance about the appropriate behaviour of an official or of an employee. They are taking a position about the political role of social work. They imply a position about social work as a contributor to maintaining social order rather than promoting social change. Because we can identify these positions as part of discourses, we can identify the authors of them as politically conservative in their view of social work. Alternative views exist. This analysis, then, helps us to be critical of ideas that we are trying to understand.

An important idea about discourses is the view that debates about the nature of things are debates about different people's or groups' representations of reality. Arguing about those representations is an attempt to gain dominance for one view of the world rather than another. If one side of the argument can gain acceptance for their view, they gain power over the world because their view has been adopted. Control of knowledge, then, gives control or power over the world, because it pushes other people into seeing things our way rather than in some alternative way.

This idea that gaining acceptance of our representation of reality allows us to control knowledge which in turn gives us power is important to the issues considered in this book in two ways. First, social work as an activity uses words and knowledge in an attempt to influence clients, the users of social work services. This is the focus of Chapter 3. Inherently, then, social work is about using power, and much of this book (especially Chapter 6) is concerned with where that power comes from and how it is used. Second, a profession, among other things, often seeks control over the knowledge and ideas which contribute to success in its activity. So in trying to understand social work as a profession, we are exploring how social work seeks to control knowledge and ideas and thus gain power over its area of activity. This is an important focus of Chapters 4 and 7.

I have emphasised ambiguity, uncertainty and fragmentation (Parton, 1994a), but because I intend an exploration of a professional and academic field, I must obviously claim that the field is capable of being known and understood. Everything is not relative and ultimately incapable of being captured. However, we cannot say that the evidence for deconstructing ideas and discourses is something called reality. Among the basic assumptions of understanding things in these ways is that we can only deal with human *representations* of reality, because reality can always be argued over. The representations that we use are, therefore, *texts* and *narratives*. These are the written down or spoken representations of reality. Narratives are sequences of description or argument where there are connections between the various events or things described or points made in the argument.

The approach and methodology of this book, therefore, are to consider two different types of text and narrative. The first type is direct accounts of social work as an activity. Each chapter contains some anecdotes which form a narrative about some social work activities, from which points are drawn which contribute to the starting point of the argument. I use these because I argue that all understandings of social work ultimately come from social workers' own experiences of the activity and the profession. These are mine, and you are helped to know how I am thinking by examining my narratives and the limitations and opportunities they offer to people trying to understand social work.

The second type presents social work indirectly, and therefore can only rely eventually on narratives about work practice and the profession. These are texts drawn from accounts of aspects of social work. I have selected from a range of such texts. I have chosen texts which have:

- wide currency as introductory statements, such as textbooks used in training students of social work which have had several editions,

- authoritative status, having been adopted by official organisations or governments, or

- currency as part of recognisable discourses in the social work literature.

A personal starting point and pathway
Having said something about my methodology, I give some examples by continuing with the narrative about my personal starting point and pathway. This is not only to give an example of a narrative. To judge my arguments and my narratives, some knowledge is needed of the personal viewpoint and experience that forms my own construction of social work. This is important even though, as is my wont, I shall try to convey fairly neutrally different constructions and viewpoints.

I have said something about my own starting point above. When I decided to join a social work course, casework from a psychodynamic perspective was the main form of social work which was studied academically. Social policy assumed a welfare state and a steadily improving range of services concerned with the welfare of those in need. Medical, psychiatric social work, moral welfare work with unmarried mothers and their illegitimate children were practised in separate agencies. Within local government there were children's departments, fairly newly established mental welfare departments and welfare departments providing services for elderly and disabled people. In criminal justice, there was a probation and aftercare service. The prison welfare service was being merged with it. Each of these groupings had its own professional associations. There was a generalist association for people who believed that social work was generic rather than wholly subsumed by these client- or service- based specialisms. Education for each of these groups was different, and my university had to gain separate approval from various authorities for recognition of its course for each specialism. Students had to choose one, and were not regarded as qualified in the others.

Five important contexts
An entirely personal description of a starting point is inadequate, and we need also to give an account of the context of social work within which we start. The contexts included in my account are:

● *Theories and conceptions* of social work.

● *Social policies* on the nature of social welfare in society, including the law which in many societies provides an important basis for social work decisions and actions (Ball *et al.*, 1988; Braye and Preston-Shoot, 1992; Vernon *et al.*, 1990).

● *The organisation of social services* within which social work is practised.

● The organisation of the occupational and *professional groupings* within social work.

● The organisation of *education* for social work.

This list of contexts identifies useful factors to explore when we are trying to understand social work. The first two are particularly the focus of Chapters 2-4. The third is covered in Chapter 5. Chapters 6-8 focus on the final two. Chapter 9 is an attempt at summing up. We can look at narratives and see whether they cover these points. So, we can evaluate the adequacy of narratives and texts that we are using partly by what contexts they are dealing with. We might conclude that a particular text is only partial or flawed if it fails to deal with a relevant context.

Alternatively, that area of debate may only be relevant to certain parts of social work, not all the contexts that we might consider. A text or narrative might raise additional or different issues. We might relate such issues to these contexts, or see them as a separate and innovative point in our discussion.

We can characterise our starting points and their context under each of the headings listed above. This permits us to reflect on something of our personal inheritances. Personal starting points reflect who you think you are. However, if it is some way in the past, considering differences in present and past views is useful.

Changes on our pathways
For example, if I were to describe my starting point as I conceive it now, I would comment that I came from a white, skilled working class family. Before my sociology course, however, it would not have occurred to me to think of my family in terms of class. Also, I had never met any black people, so being white was the only social context that I knew. It would not have occurred to me that it was important to characterise my family background as white until well into the 1980s. At that time, I realised that I could not regard being white as the normal state in Britain, with being black somehow not normal and therefore worthy of comment. Clearly both are in fact worthy of comment in understanding starting points

My first job was as a probation officer. Then when the Seebohm reorganisation took place, I followed my commitment to genericism by moving to a social services department. I carried a completely generic caseload. At the same time, I moved from the National Association of Probation Officers to the newly established British Association of Social Workers, following the same generic commitment. Involvement in 'radical' social work ideas of the early 1970s changed my original perspective on social work. I gained some experience of welfare rights work through my membership of the Child Poverty Action Group. Discussing new socialist theories through a local discussion group was also an important experience. After some years' practice, I was promoted to be a team leader and then area officer. Thus, I moved into social services management. Later, I moved into an academic job. After some years, I moved to manage a local community development agency in the voluntary sector. Then, I did policy work and developed new projects for a national mental health charity.

I regard all these jobs as being in social work. This narrative implies claims that being involved in education and management, being in the voluntary and statutory sectors and doing community, policy and development work can all be regarded as social work. People might disagree with this position, however. These claims can thus be seen as already part of a discourse on the nature of social work. I am taking a position and making a claim about what social work is by presenting this narrative in this way.

How can we understand the different conceptions of social work which my narrative implies? In some way we must conceive of social work as a collection of related activities, in different sorts of agencies, in different sectors of social life. The voluntary, public and academic sectors were mentioned: I could potentially have included the private sector. In the final section of the Chapter, I want to use the idea of networks as a way of understanding and exploring social work and its context.

Social work in context - networks

We have explored ideas of starting points and pathways. I have suggested that we start from outside social work and follow a pathway of experience through social work. Early on, we saw that, in my experience pathway, I moved to and across the borders of what some people might call social work. I suggest that other people do that too, in all the contexts that I identified. People move between:

- Different conceptions and theories of social work. I moved from psychodynamic theory to a radical view at first, but now would take in other concepts.

- Carrying out different social policies and legal roles. I started with a focus on criminal justice, moved to personal social welfare and at various times contributed to mental health work and to social security through welfare rights work

- Different organisational contexts. I have worked from a fieldwork team, in residential care, and in a variety of sectors and types of agency.

- Different occupational groupings. Some people come from nursing or the police into social work, moving on to being a psychologist or counsellor.

- Different forms of education. I started in social science. Others come from health care or education into social work. Some people move on from social work to gain specialised qualifications in family therapy or child protection, or move on to other forms of training.

If we put all the possible pathways for a group of social workers or for all social workers together, these pathways form a huge network of possible movements.

Some of those pathways will be well trodden. Many nurses or social science graduates might be coming into social work. Others will be overgrown and leafy; there might be few bank managers for example.

I owe to N. M. Tsang the idea that we can see social work (or any other occupation) as the place where a convergence of pathways forms a nexus of ideas. There people interact more closely and see themselves as 'together' in their work. They have been incorporated and socialised into social work. Each of them will have converged on that point; some will stay there; others will diverge towards other interests. They become more specialised, diverse or may modify their conception of social work or reject it altogether.

He drew a diagram which I have adapted (Figure 1.1) to show this description of social work as a profession or occupational group. The dotted circle in the middle of the diagram represents a conventional boundary for social work. Many people would define people within this boundary as social workers. They might be less sure of people just outside the boundary. The further a person has to travel to enter this boundary, the less sure we would be of calling them a social worker.

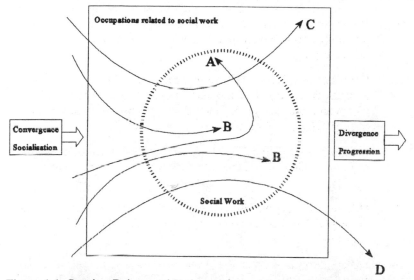

Figure 1.1 Starting Points and Pathways in social work (source, Tsang, personal communication)

Someone who has taken up volunteer work last week can barely be described yet as a social worker, though their pathway may take them there. A former social worker who runs the personnel department of a bank can barely now be described as a social worker though they have passed that way and taken something from it. The path of person A through social work moves from outside any relevant occupation, through a related job into the centre of social work and then away again to something, still in social work but a bit more peripheral, perhaps as a counsellor in a youth centre. The two people who followed paths shown as B moved more or less to the centre of social work and stayed there, say in social services departments. C moved through social work and ended up in an occupation related to it, perhaps they are now clinical psychologists. D left the field altogether.

Ramsey (1987) presents a similar analysis applied to social work as an activity, in his systems analysis of the interaction between clients and social workers. They meet together, each following their pathways, as, for the time being, part of agency, personal, occupational and social networks. Their interaction brings together those particular networks for a while. Then their pathways diverge again.

One way of seeing social work, then, is as part of a network of services and agencies. It has an interface with clients and the complex environment which surrounds us. Trying to understand social work as part of those networks seems useful, therefore. Such networks are very complex. They might best be understood by looking at social work in each context that I have identified, and then putting these together as in Figure 1.2. Let us look at each area in turn.

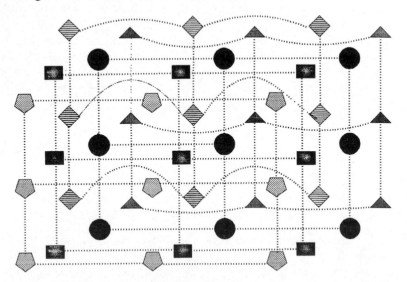

Figure 1.2 Networks with social work contexts (for key, see text)

Figure 1.2 could contain in each circle a theory of practice in social work; the diagram shows that there will be some connections between them; but not all - you might be able to find a gap. A social worker might be trained at the outset in one or more of these. Later, they might take up others during a career, as their ideas and the needs of clients developed. The squares set out social welfare policies and legal definitions of social work which might be available in any society. Again, a worker might start, say, in helping schoolchildren with welfare problems, move to mental health work as an approved social worker, thence to housing advice, and so on. Similar points might be made about the network of social services organisations in which social workers might work (triangles), the network of links among occupational groups with which social workers have contacts (diamonds) and among types of professional training (pentagons). So, we have different networks for each of the five contexts: theories, policies, services, occupational groups, and types of education. They all interlink in a complex pattern.

We have been looking at movements within the networks identified. These are serial movements, they take place over time, one after the other. Now, let us see how the networks might interlink. Take the example of someone who trained in social work, and later took an interest in family therapy. Some family therapy practice might be possible in a social services area team, given the right support and facilities. However, the worker might prefer a social work job in a psychiatric hospital with more opportunity to develop such practice. This worker moves between organisations, while remaining a social worker by profession and by training. The personal social services would still employ the worker, but he/she would be moving towards the health service as a setting for practice. If there were further training, an occupational shift towards family therapy, psychotherapy, counselling or psychology might occur.

Links may be seen, then, between different contexts as people move on their pathway through social work. This may become important for a variety of reasons. For one thing, movements within the networks might support or conflict with one another. Someone trained as a social worker, doing child protection casework in a social services area team is strongly a social worker. Someone trained as a social worker doing family therapy in a multi-disciplinary hospital team is less clearly a social worker. They may have moved on or, more likely, they will experience conflicts between different contexts as they try to do their job. For example, their manager from social services may make demands for practice which is inconsistent with their wish to do family therapy, and they may be supported in that wish by colleagues in the multi-disciplinary team. Generally, the further workers move away from complete consistency between the five contexts, the more conflict they will experience about the nature of what they are doing.

Connections between these different networks might strengthen its identity. For instance, psychodynamic theory is strengthened in social work by the fact that it has a strong place in social work theory, there are multi-disciplinary agencies where it may be practised and in concert with other professionals working with and trained within that perspective (Payne, 1992). The networks support each other. Cognitive theory, say, suffers because it is less developed in social work theory, there are few specialist agencies and it is used actively mainly by psychologists. The mutual support among the networks is less strong.

Looking at a more finely divided network might offer clues about the perception of boundaries between different occupations. Let us take the example of family therapy again. We can see it as a social work method where a social worker practises forms of it with other social workers in agencies which social work dominates. Very often, however, the facilities and multi-professional support of a multi-disciplinary agency which specialises in family therapy offer a more productive setting. In some areas, family therapy is practised in a multi-disciplinary agency with specialist facilities. This defines it more as a separate method of practice, bordering on a newly developing profession. Associations and specialised journals develop. We can regard these as part of the development of an autonomous profession.

Constantly changing boundaries and links
This network approach suggests that there is a pattern of potentially changeable boundaries between different occupational groups and theoretical ideas. People in one occupational group might move into settings where other groups are dominant. They might take up theoretical approaches to be shared elsewhere, and develop training or expertise which takes them into other occupational groups. They experience conflict between different aspects of the contexts which affect them.

When substantial changes of this kind take place, affecting many people within an occupational group, we may see changes in the recognised boundaries between groups. Domains are claimed by occupational groups, may emerge to be claimed or may lie unclaimed (Waring and O'Connor, 1981). For example, when I trained in social work, there was a view that the governor grade in the British prison service was akin to social work. Qualifications and training in either group were considered relevant to the other. This view has disappeared as the custodial role in prisons has become more complex. Also, the prison welfare service was taken into the probation service and evolved a stronger welfare role, taking this on from the governor and assistant governors. Social work training strengthened its focus and prison department training became more specialised. Similarly, over time, health visitors have moved out of the orbit of social work to reaffirm their health service location and nursing professionalism. In the mid-1990s, the probation service in the UK may be moving from the province of social work. As in the USA, it may be shifting more clearly into the judicial and criminal justice system. This has been debated for many years, but is happening because of a political impetus.

Occupational boundaries are unclear. Each of our five contexts contains overlapping and possibly conflicting boundaries. Groupings change and develop constantly, as each of the five contexts I have identified pushes people in different directions and has consequent effects on links between the different contexts. Individually we move through our own personal pathways in this complex of networks. Social work as an activity and as an occupational group moves along equally complex pathways in a constantly changing world. The aim of this book is to identify some of the factors which help to make sense of it.

In Chapter 2, attempts at defining social work show how the three general perspectives on social work, discussed above, interact with each other in views of social work. Chapter 3 examines accounts of social work as a personal and interpersonal activity, and Chapter 4 discusses the values which are said to inform that activity. These chapters identify the basic approach at the interpersonal level as reflexive-therapeutic, and how the two alternative conceptions of social work attempt to modify or disclaim that approach. We are looking at these aspects of social work because understanding the nature of social work requires us to understand what social workers say they do - we have to understand their representations of social work as an activity.

Chapter 5 is a bridge between the discussion of social work as an activity and as a profession. It shows how social work practice is affected and constructed by the fact that it is practised in agencies and how that fact characterises and constructs the nature of social work as a profession. I argue that it is crucial to an understanding of social work to see how it is practised in, influenced by, and affects, the agencies in which it is practised. Chapter 6 takes this discussion further. Social work practice involves using interpersonal power and in doing so may oppress groups of people in societies on behalf of the élites which construct social agencies as part of the apparatus of the State and other social structures. The dominant perspective in this aspect of social work is individualist-reformist but, again, we see how attempts have been made to modify or attack the dominance of this perspective in this area of debate. Understanding social work requires us to understand where it fits in power relations among the oppressed, disadvantaged people with problems that it seeks to serve, and others, including powerful élites, who are stakeholders in the provision of services to clients.

Considering the exercise of power in Chapter 6 prepares for the examination in Chapter 7 of debates about social work as a profession. Chapter 8 completes this discussion by examining social work as a worldwide phenomenon.

In these chapters, I examine the extent to which we can see social work as a profession - a special kind of occupation - in Western societies, where it was first constructed and then in different societies worldwide. To see whether and in what ways social work may be regarded as a profession, we have to explore in this way its characteristics and organisation as an occupational group. Chapter 9 attempts a review of the three general perspectives on social work. It considers social work as a personal, interpersonal and political activity and argues that as a profession it must incorporate all three. Our understanding of the nature of social work must therefore include elements of all three general perspectives. Any individual's view, therefore, will comprise a balance of these views, in which one or the other might be dominant.

Chapter 2
Definitions of Social Work

A conflict about social work

Intake teams receive, investigate and try to resolve problems which arrive in social work agencies. If they cannot do so, they pass on the work to long-term teams which provide more extensive help over a longer period. The B Area intake team had run into relationship problems with its long-term child care team. The complaint was that important child care work was closed down with only cursory assessment and without giving priority to the best interests of the child. It looked like a typical conflict of attitude between teams of these types. Intake teams get into the habit of looking for ways to deal with things quickly. They often dislike giving up work they have started. Long-term teams, on the other hand, look for broader and deeper issues. They are often slow to take on work. So, intake teams get in the habit of closing cases and holding onto work to keep the waiting list down. Then, when there is space, all the long-term work seems impossible to transfer, or it has vanished through interim measures.

On investigation it turned out that the teams had completely different views about working with 'at risk' children. The intake team had a policy of helping parents to deal with practical problems to relieve stress on them. Abuse had to be gross and obvious before they would act to remove the children. They described the long-term team as 'child-snatchers'. The long-term team thought that indications of abuse should be referred immediately to them. This was necessary because they would need specialised, long-term work. The children, for their own safety, should be removed immediately, while an investigation took place. An apparently commonplace dispute, about an intake team not being prepared to give up work, turned out to require a detailed analysis and resolution of attitudes to social work and child care practice.

Most of the time, everyday practice does not require us to think about and define the purposes of social work. We can take a rough approximation for granted. Sometimes, as in the intake and long-term dispute, this take-it-for-granted approach comes adrift and we find we really are talking about different things. Social work therefore occasionally faces practitioners with the need to review their ideas about the nature of their activity, and to see what underlies taken-for-granted daily assumptions is useful. This is one purpose of this Chapter.

Another purpose is to review texts which define social work, to identify the characteristics of those definitions. To try to define something is a modernist project, because it presumes that there is a reality which needs to be made explicit. But definitions enable us to understand from a variety of interacting texts different views of the nature of social work. Sometimes there is agreement, sometimes debate. Studying debates about definitions of social work identifies some of its discourse. We can see the interaction and attempts to demonstrate the influence of the three general perspectives identified in Chapter 1 directly in looking at definitions. This is because in debate about definitions, we are seeing explicit attempts to construct social work as a whole, rather than discussion about aspects of it or commentary which can avoid the issue of its nature altogether.

Issues of definition
What is a definition? In science, definitions specify in a short compass the nature of an object or phenomenon so precisely that there can be no doubt about what is being observed. In social affairs, things cannot be so precise. Human beings can create many possibilities in a social interaction. Definitions tend to identify the main characteristics of a social phenomenon, the essence. This helps to limit the complexity of the matter being discussed rather than capturing everything about it. The further a phenomenon moves from the essence of social work as described, the less it can be seen as social work. Alternatively, they seek to define boundaries like the dotted line in Figure 1.1. The boundary may be crossed, but inside it we can describe most activities as social work. Outside it, they are not, or are less likely to be, seen as social work.

Definitions of social work can never be divorced from the purposes for which they were written. Among these purposes, they often seek to make claims for particular points of view. For example, Collins and Collins (1981, p1) wrote a book about social work as an instrument for achieving change, so their definition is relevant to this:

> *Social work may be defined . . . as a process of helping people to cope better with problem situations. This will usually involve a change in some aspect of the situation; perhaps the client, possibly some other person or element concerned, or some combination of these.*

This view has elements of the individualist perspective, since it sees social work as being about problem-solving in society, but it is fundamentally reflexive-therapeutic since it eschews helping with a problem (individualist) in favour of 'helping people cope better . . .' and thus moving towards (personal) change. However, it avoids the collectivist, because it focuses on situation rather than broader social purposes. The aim of this, as with all definitions, is to make claims about social work in order to construct the prescriptions in the book as appropriate to, and likely to be successful in, social work (of the kind assumed in the book).

The discourse on definitions
Some issues of history

We can see social work as a product of industrialisation in the nineteenth-century in Britain, other European countries and the USA. However, the social service developments of that period originated in medieval legislation and services, or reacted or responded to the inadequacies of earlier provision and ideas. The rapid development in the nineteenth-century can be seen in this earlier context. Ideas of Christian and Jewish charity can be traced as part of nineteenth-century development back to the period of the Roman empire and beyond. The development and geographical expansion of the Christian Churches provide organisational and ideological links over the whole of this period.

However, such ideas are ethnocentric since they concentrate on developments in the largely white Western democratic communities and their social institutions. They are also limited in political analysis since they concentrate on the caring, charitable aspect of social work, rather than social control and social action.

Not all social developments derive from this tradition, even where there are similarities. Midgley (1981) has warned of the tendency for inappropriate Western conceptions of social work to be imported into countries where other cultures are dominant. Historical accounts relying on Christian philosophies tend to underplay the importance of social work origins in public services set up to control potentially difficult populations. One stream of social work development in British social services departments, for example, comes from the Poor Law and from work in the asylums and colonies for people with mental illnesses and learning disabilities in the nineteenth-century (Payne, 1979, pp 20-1). A more recent example appears in Gargett's (1977) pre-independence account of the development of official social welfare provision in Zimbabwe (then Rhodesia). He shows how social work provision arose from the needs created by urban settlement by Africans from rural areas. The initial impetus was a probation and school attendance service, to help control delinquency in a troublesome population. Broader concerns took time to develop. We cannot see social work as wholly charitable and caring when we examine the reality of these sorts of historical origins.

Debates about the nature of social work lie firmly within the Jewish and Christian, Western democratic framework. The previous diversion into some wider perspectives should make us cautious about accepting them as the only relevant debates. None the less, they are well documented and have substantially influenced the social work discourse.

Rooff (1957) argues that the organised Church in Britain stood aloof from active caring work, leaving the field clear to 'men and women of religion' to organise practical voluntary action. We usually trace the origins of social work as a profession to the Charity Organisation Societies (COS) of Britain and America. They promoted 'friendly visiting' by the well-intentioned in place of giving alms. One purpose was to prevent disorganised charitable giving (Woodroofe, 1962, p26). The philosophy of the time supposed that, in the words of a leading figure, Octavia Hill, '. . . without strong personal influence no radical cure of those who have fallen low can be effected' (quoted by Woodroofe, 1962, p58). The method was one of moral influence on people who had fallen into difficulties, through no fault of their own. Those who took no personal responsibility were consigned to the rigours of the Poor Law. Organised charity and Poor Law oppression were thus two sides of the same controlling philosophy. An alternative, Fabian, view that social conditions should be improved and proper income maintenance made available to support people through unexpected difficulties competed with the COS view (Jones, 1976, 1979).

These continued to have influence in British social work, in early accounts of social work as having a social reform role. One example is Attlee's (1920) discussion of the social worker as 'agitator'.

In these early stages of the development of social work, therefore, we can identify both social control (individualist) and caring, charitable (reflexive-therapeutic) roles of social work. They were counterposed but also in alliance as part of the same social processes. One strand of thinking was also concerned with social reform (socialist-collectivist). It opposed social work accepting controlling functions on behalf of dominant social philosophies in society.

Development of social work purposes
From the idea that charitable work should be organised and efficient came an attempt to establish social work as a discrete area of activity and as a profession. Part of this process led to a formalisation of ideas about it. There was also debate about its role in society. For example, Richmond (1917, p357) developed the view that 'social diagnosis' was at the centre of social work practice. It needed to 'make as exact a definition as possible of the situation and personality of a human being . . . in relation to the other human beings upon whom he in any way depends or who depend upon him and in relation also to the social institutions of his community'. Subsequently, she defined social casework as consisting of 'those processes which develop personality through adjustments consciously effected, individual by individual, between men and their social environment', (Richmond, 1922, p99). This is, evidently, a reflexive-therapeutic view.

In this kind of statement, priority is given to meeting individual needs for help with adjusting to the community or helping the community adjust to individual needs. The moral purpose of nineteenth-century charity is now missing, but is being replaced with a concern for personal development. Some might see this as clothing moral purposes in intellectual guise.

Representatives of American agencies met together in the Milford conference which defined social casework as dealing with 'the human being whose capacity to organise his own normal social activities may be impaired by one or more deviations from accepted standards of normal social life . . .' (quoted by Cannon, 1928, p 17). Cannon goes on to argue that this definition must lead to indistinctness because we cannot say what accepted social norms might be. This is an early example of the debate between those within social work who assume an accepted social order (individualist-reformists) and those who acknowledge potential differences in interest in society (socialist-collectivists).

In a famous paper, Lee (1929) drew attention to the dichotomy between 'cause' and 'function' in social work. He argued that as social work struggled to become a profession, it was moving away from being a *cause* ('a movement toward the elimination of an intrenched evil' p22) and towards becoming a *function* ('an organized effort incorporated into the machinery of community life in the discharge of which the acquiescence, at least, and ultimately the support of the entire community is assumed' p23). By becoming institutionalised and part of community life, it was in danger of losing its focus on the social changes needed to remove major social ills. This was one of the earliest commentaries that institutionalisation and professionalisation of social work would ally it with power élites.

These early writers on social work were writing as though social work was becoming an organised and recognised occupational group. They present the reflexive and possibly individualist objective of caring services deriving from altruistic concern for disadvantaged people. A socialist-collectivist critique complains about the loss of a focus on social change.

In the 1930s, psychoanalytic thinking began to affect social work ideas. Such ideas were sometimes presented with a reflexive-therapeutic perspective less committed to psychoanalysis itself in definitions like the following:

Social work concerns itself with human beings where there is anything that hinders or thwarts their growth, their expanding consciousness, their increasing co-operation. Social case work is that form of social work which assists the individual while he struggles to relate himself to his family, his natural groups, his community . . . we shall use no methods that in themselves hamper the growth of the human spirit (Reynolds, 1935, pp136-7).

Collectivists committed to a social change view of social work have always disputed such views. This was particularly strong at the time of the recession. Lurie, famously in the 1930s (Schriver, 1987), maintained a consistent critique. He focused on the tendency to use psychological techniques to exclude promoting practical help from the community:

The concrete value of the social case worker in the past has been the possibility of using available resources in the community . . . Helping individuals to obtain relief, to register for and obtain employment . . . to obtain health, educational and recreational services on some decent level have been important contributions made by the social agency to social welfare. At present, we must recognise the fact that all of these services, economic, vocational, health and cultural, are less and less available in relation to the needs of the masses of the population . . . with the depression there are evidences that they are deteriorating in quality (Lurie, 1935, p617).

This view, while collectivist in its concern for 'the masses', has elements of individualism in its emphasis on practical help for individuals.

Both in the USA and in Britain, we can exaggerate the influence of psychoanalysis in everyday practice (Lees, 1971; Alexander, 1972). It was heavily used in a few élite agencies and in training courses which few took. Elsewhere people were more pragmatic. In Britain, the influence was two decades later in the 1940s and '50s (Yelloly, 1980). Butrym (1976, pp2-3) argues that it was the continuing role of statutory responsibility in British services which prevented workers from having the professional independence to follow such trends. This represents a view that individualist-reformist State provision is likely to restrict wholesale influence for reflexive-therapeutic ideas. In the USA, the élite voluntary-sector family service agencies incorporated psychoanalytic enthusiasm more freely. However, it is the élite which writes the definitions, and psychoanalytic views of the world became routinely incorporated into accounts of social work. It thus became strongly reflexive-therapeutic in character, particularly when we focus on the individual level of work. This view is also dominant in agencies which are able to maintain independence from pressures to be more pragmatic and convert therapeutic personal growth into individualised service provision.

The assumption that social work is reflexive-therapeutic in character also has a period flavour. We can see it particularly in definitions of the 1940s and '50s, quoted below. Another important definitional development came with the explicit statement of the major principles of 'diagnostic' casework, the dominant casework theory of this period:

> *Social work rests ultimately on certain assumptions . . . without which its methods and goals can have no meaning. The axioms are, for example: human betterment is the goal of any society; . . . the general standard of living should be progressively improved; education for physical and mental health and welfare should be widely promoted; the social bond between man and man should lead to the realisation of the age-old dream of universal brotherhood. The ethic derived from these and similar axioms leads to two nuclear ideas which distinguish social work as one of the humanist professions. The first is that the human event consists in person and situation . . . which constantly interact, and the second that the characteristic method of social work incorporates within its processes both scientific knowledge and social values in order to achieve its ends (Hamilton, 1951, p3).*

In this important definition, individualised, psychologically-orientated work becomes the dominant focus of the definition. This is set in a context of concern for social objectives. There is an assumption of a flow of social progress of which social work's positive objectives are part. Such a construction may be contrasted with socialist-collectivist views that there is a conflict about social values between élites with the State representing them and groups who produce most clients of social work.

An influential statement in Hamilton is the identification of 'person' and 'situation' and this terminology has, with developments, continued as the basic focus of social work practice. It only follows Richmond's adjustments between 'man and his social environment' quoted above. Hollis, in a later influential definition, states:

> *The major system to which diagnosis and treatment are addressed is the person-in-situation gestalt or configuration. That is to say, to be understood, the person to be helped - or treated, if you prefer - must be seen in the context of his interactions or transactions with the external world; and the segment of the external world with which he is in close interaction must be understood (Hollis, 1970 pp35-6).*

The NASW (1981) 'Working Statement' on social work, for example, says: 'Social workers focus on person-and-environment *in interaction*'. This basic idea that social work is concerned with the interaction between people and their environment has, therefore, been current since the 1920s.

Some accounts of casework in the 1950s retain the reformist idealism of the earlier definitions, but with a clearer focus on the personal. The major British text of the period, published at the same time as Hamilton, says:

> *The basis of all case work is the natural human response of one individual to another in some need which he cannot meet alone. . . If the starting point is [this] . . . either because society has not allowed for provision for his wants or because he himself cannot make use of the provision offered, then the simple elementary process of social work is to give the individual's need an individual remedy; and similarly to help such other individuals as may subsequently happen to be in the same straits. Sometimes the difficulty is seen to beset, not one solitary individual at a time, but such a number of people and in such a manner that collective action is necessary and the appropriate activity to meet it can only be social reform. In some cases, again, it begins to appear that the individual is suffering not from any single need that can be supplied separately but from a poverty of social life, the lack of opportunity for certain social experience . . .; and the remedy is then by means of group or community work. . . There is the fundamental unity of one whole process underlying all these different activities, springing from the natural human situation and the natural human response to it in which it all originates (Cormack and McDougall, 1950, pp16-17).*

The grandiose statement of social purposes is there, but the area claimed for casework is a limited one. One significant point is that social work is described as a formalisation of a 'natural' human response to personal and social need. This incorporates the idea that social work is really some form of organised altruism on behalf of society in the form of the State. Moreover, the altruism is assumed, whereas some would say that human beings are essentially egotistical and tend not to help others naturally. Cormack and McDougall's definition thus represents a more individualist-reformist position than the more reflexive-therapeutic view of the American definitions considered. I would argue that this comes from the position of social workers in Britain during this period as functionaries of the new Welfare State. Therapeutic ideals were less capable of implementation, but were an ideal to be reached in a much more pragmatic, individualist form of state social work. This is much more typical of continental European social work than the therapeutic American definitions referring to practice in a few élite agencies.

An important American text of the 1950s proposes similar limited aims, however, and perhaps we can see the advance of the sizeable, even if residual, welfare state in the USA too:

> *Social casework is a process used by certain human welfare agencies to help individuals to cope more effectively with their problems in social functioning. . . The nucleus of the casework event is this:*
>
> **A person with a problem comes to a place where a professional representative helps him by a given process** (Perlman, 1957, p4, original emphasis)

So far, we have been exploring definitions which arose from early debate which occurred as part of an attempt to establish social work. This continued in a stream of definitions written since the 1950s. These sought to assert and seal commitment to the coherence of social work and to make claims for its professional status. Often, they were written immediately after major changes in the organisation of the professional groups in social work or in education. The following are some well-known examples.

Specialist social work professional bodies in the USA merged into one association (the National Association of Social Workers, NASW) in 1955. In 1958, the 'Working Definition of Social Work Practice' appeared. It was longer than three closely printed pages in Bartlett's (1970, pp221-4) reprint. It covered the 'constellation of value, purpose, sanction, knowledge, and method' typical of social work. However, the statement of purposes in this definition has been influential and is still quoted (Morales and Sheafor, 1992, pp13-14; Compton and Galaway, 1994, p5). It is as follows:

> *The practice of social work has as its purposes:*
>
> *To assist individuals and groups to identify and resolve or minimize problems arising out of disequilibrium between themselves and their environment.*
>
> *To identify potential areas of disequilibrium between individuals or groups and the environment in order to prevent the occurrence of disequilibrium.*
>
> *In addition to these curative and preventive aims, to seek out, identify, and strengthen the maximum potential in individuals, groups, and communities.*

The American association responsible for control of social work education (the Council on Social Work Education, CSWE) was established at much the same time. It also devised a definition:

Social work seeks to enhance the social functioning of individuals, singly and in groups, by activities focused upon their social relationships which constitute the interaction between man and his environment. These activities can be grouped into three functions: restoration of impaired capacity, provision of individual and social resources, and prevention of social dysfunction (Boehm, 1958).

NASW adopted another interim definition nearly twenty years later:

Social work is the professional activity of helping individuals, groups, or communities enhance or restore their capacity for social functioning and creating societal conditions favourable to that goal. Social work practice consists in the professional application of social-work values, principles, and techniques to one or more of the following ends: helping people obtain tangible services; counselling and psychotherapy with individuals, families, and groups; helping communities or groups provide or improve social and health services; and participating in relevant legislative processes. The practice of social work requires knowledge of human development and behaviour; of social, economic, and cultural institutions; and of the interaction of these factors (NASW, 1973, pp4-5).

The reason for this definition was the need to incorporate social change objectives more explicitly into a definition. This move responded to the development of radical perspectives on social work in the 1960s and '70s. Including these perspectives into the accepted statements about social work was an important move to seal this major change in perspective into formal statements of social work. The balance of definitions thus included a more-socialist-collective perspective than previously.

Similar efforts have achieved similar results in the UK. A working party of the British Association of Social Workers (BASW) included the following 'working definition' in a report on 'the social work task'. This is another example of bringing together different specialisms in a merged association.

Social work is the purposeful and ethical application of personal skills in interpersonal relationships directed towards enhancing the personal and social functioning of an individual, family, group or neighbourhood, which

necessarily involves using evidence obtained from practice to help create a
social environment conducive to the well-being of all (BASW, 1977, p19).

This definition is, however, still primarily reflexive-therapeutic rather than collectivist. At much the same time, a working party of the Central Council for
Education and Training in Social Work (CCETSW) was set up shortly after its
establishment. It produced the following, again termed a 'working definition':

Social work is a form of social intervention which encourages social insti-
tutions to respond to individual needs, enabling individuals to use their
resources and in turn to contribute to them. It holds that the capacity and
dignity of the individual are enhanced by participation in the life of the
community. To achieve this end, it contributes to adjustments in the distri-
butions of power and resources and attempts to help people, whether as
individuals or groups, to have sufficient control over their lives to increase
their opportunities for personal choice and self-realisation (CCETSW, 1975, p17).

Much of this is still reflexive-therapeutic in emphasis focusing as it does on personal choice and self-realisation, but it does contain, in a balanced way, a socialist-collectivist acknowledgement of the importance of power relations.

When social work education in Britain was reconstructed in the late 1980s,
CCETSW produced a further formal definition:

Social work is an accountable professional activity which enables individu-
als, families and groups to identify personal, social and environmental diffi-
culties adversely affecting them. Social work enables them to manage
these difficulties through supportive, rehabilitative, protective or corrective
action. Social work promotes social welfare and responds to wider social
needs promoting equal opportunities for every age, gender, sexual prefer-
ence, class, disability, race, culture and creed. Social work has the respon-
sibility to protect the vulnerable and exercise authority under statute.
(CCETSW, 1991, p8; original edition, 1989).

This is a heavily individualist-reformist definition. Almost all aspects of personal
growth have disappeared. However, although individualist in its focus on
accountability and in the largely controlling actions envisaged, there is a socialist-
collectivist recognition of the importance of acting on power relations. So, this
definition almost sets up two opposing positions, which are both incorporated
together. The inconsistency between controlling responsibilities and protecting
vulnerable people is simply accepted by its incorporation in the final sentence.

A further NASW Working Definition appeared in 1981 identifying, again with a reflexive-therapeutic focus, the purpose of social work as being

> *... to promote or restore a mutually beneficial interaction between individuals and society in order to improve on the quality of life for everyone.* (NASW, 1981).

Some definitions offer descriptions of the characteristics of social work activity, rather than trying to describe its essence. They include material about the objectives, methods, values, the type of person helped and the settings in which social work takes place. These are some examples from introductory textbooks, one British:

> *Social work is a form of human activity, in which certain members of society, paid or voluntary, intervene in the lives of others in order to produce change. . . The aims of man in society are also the aims of social work insofar as its central concerns are the basic necessities of life and the regulation of behaviour, but the means employed by its practitioners are influenced by their values and beliefs, which tend to place limits on the methods they use, excluding, for example, warfare and repression. Social work may be said to spring from those means of interaction between human beings designed to bring about change through caring and concern . . . it has a special interest in those members of society who may be deemed to be disadvantaged in some way, in broad terms those who are handicapped either mentally, physically or socially* (Haines, 1975, pp1-2).

and one American:

> *Social work may be defined as an art, a science, a profession that helps people to solve personal, group (especially family), and community problems and to attain satisfying personal, groups and community relationships through social work practice, including case work, group work, community organisation, administration and research. Social work practice today is often generic, involving all three of the traditional methods. The major focus is on reducing problems in human relationships and on enriching living through improved human interaction* (Skidmore, Thackeray and Farley 1994, p8).

All these writers want to point up the special nature of social work practice in their different ways. Haines indicates that ethical limits on practice methods exist. He wants to show how social work values focus attention on particular kinds of method. Skidmore *et al.* stress the technical and scientific nature of practice. They soften it with the word 'art', thus raising and avoiding a longstanding social work debate about its scientific or artistic character. The American text takes for granted that social work is a profession, an assumption that would be strongly debated in the UK. Haines, on the other hand, focuses on social work as an activity, avoiding comment on its institutional or professional position.

Individualist and radical criticisms

The focus of much analysis of the nature of social work in recent decades is reflexive-therapeutic, although there have been, as we have seen, various attempts at balancing this with other perspectives. We can therefore see much debate about definition as being attempts to assert the countervailing importance of alternative perspectives. Individualists say that because they make claims for a professional and intellectual territory reflexive-therapeutic definitions can seem pompous, excessive or mystical. Enthusiastic embrace of psychoanalysis in the 1930s produced mystical statements such as that of Marcus (1935, p126):

> *After Mary Richmond came a psychiatric deluge. It overtook case work from without in the shape of theories about human development, explanations of human behaviour and relationships, and methods for changing human feelings and conduct. . . New material was brought into use, this time material more directly and authentically related to psychoanalytic experience and knowledge. The observations of case work were noticeably sharpened and deepened by attention to data the significance of which had been established by psychoanalytic enquiries. The findings of case work were subject to improved understanding supplied by psychoanalytic discoveries about the structure, development, and functioning of the human psyche. The case work method of study and treatment underwent inner corrections inspired by psychoanalytic experience with methods of studying the mind.*

This quotation shows how, in those who were so inclined, the new ideas offered by psychoanalysis were accepted relatively uncritically. Note, for example, 'authentically' and 'corrections' as examples of acceptance of these ideas. Such claims led to Wootton's (1959, p271) famous attack:

> *. . . modern definitions of 'social casework', if taken at their face value, involve claims to powers which verge upon omniscience and omnipotence. . .*

And:

It might well be thought that the social worker's best, indeed perhaps her only, chance of achieving aims at once so intimate and so ambitious would be to marry her client (Wootton, 1959, p273).

Wootton, and other individualist-reformist critics, accept that social work focuses on individuals, and either ignore social change altogether or see it as a matter of reform or improvement of the existing system. She argues for restricting social work to practical advice:

The range of needs for which public or voluntary services now provide, and the complexity of the relevant rules and regulations have now become so great, that the social worker who has mastered these intricacies and is prepared to place this knowledge at the disposal of the public, and when necessary to initiate appropriate action, has no need to pose as a miniature psychoanalyst or psychiatrist: her professional standing is secured by the value of her own contribution (Wootton, 1959, p296).

One example of a modern individualist-reformist is Davies (1994). He has a clear view that the nature of social work is '. . . *maintenance:* society maintaining itself in a relatively stable state by making provision for and managing people in positions of severe weakness, stress and vulnerability; and society maintaining its own members, without exception, by a commitment to humanist endeavour.' (p40, emphasis original). In saying this, he is engaging with at least three debates. First, he responds to critics that social work claims too much. He purposely plays down the claims of social workers to achieve miracles of social and personal change.

In doing so he is, second, engaging with the therapeutic literature (such as Collins and Collins, quoted above) which focuses on personal change as an objective in social work. Social workers may contribute to change, but only by maintaining the capacity of society and individuals to respond to each other. Maintenance can subsume change.

Finally, third, he is engaging with the radical or socialist theorists who would claim that social work is most valid when it seeks to achieve permanent change in society. Davies says that it is unrealistically uncomfortable for an employee of official agencies to take such a view. Anyway, occasional personal interventions are unlikely to achieve such results in an apparently stable society. Also, political action is not the central function of social work. The clarity and power of Davies's view can only be understood fully by seeing it as part of the discourses in which he is engaged. Those discourses are about the social and political role of social work rather than its definition as such, but we can understand his definition from his debate about the issues that concern him.

Individualist-reformists reject or limit the importance of therapeutic objectives. They would say that we are unlikely to get personal psychological change from social work interventions. Therefore, the daily usage of social work should not seek such objectives. The institutional position of social work is emphasised: what the agencies are there for, and what they want to do, is considered the most important determinant of the nature of social work. Individualists say that this limits the freedom to be therapeutic and to seek social reform.

There are two perspectives on that limitation. Individualist-reformists emphasise social work's social control role. They argue that this inhibits a therapeutic approach within many relationships. It also aligns social work with current power structures rather than enabling it to reform them radically. We shall meet this argument again in Chapter 6 on power in social work.

However, reflexive-therapeutic definitions of social work often assert strongly their viability against individualist-reformist critiques. Writers from this position reject technological, scientific conceptions of social work. Personal and interpersonal helping relationships and the associated values of respect for others and caring should be at the centre of social work. So Wilkes (1981) argues that an essential feature of many of the people social workers help is that they are undervalued by society. Social work primarily aims to increase their valuations of themselves, by acting intuitively, and seeking meaning within their lives as part of valuing them. This view plays down the importance of service provision or social change in favour of emphasising the mutual interaction and influence of worker and client (hence reflexivity) and personal growth objectives. Krill (1990) argues that we should concentrate on subjective experience. Weissman (1990, p63) argues that social work can be creative if it is more 'playful', in a serious way, by relaxing rules and conventions. In this way, workers and clients are enabled to cross boundaries which limit their creativity. This involves using our thoughts and responses to what we experience, trying to understand what is meaningful for people and for ourselves. England (1986), recognises the difficulties of trying to define social work's claims, as would a post-modernist. Although they can all be criticised, they reveal something of the nature of social work because:

The source of social work's potential strength . . . is the very fact that it does not separate the world experienced by those in need of help into component segments. Such experience is always a complex, composite experience, it is always a unique synthesis; yet it cannot be impossible to construct such a synthesis, because the client - and everyone - does so all the time. The strength of the able worker lies in his ability accurately to join the client in the construction and experience of this synthesis. It is only through such sharing that people sometimes say to others (and should say most often to social workers) 'you seem to understand' - and we know that to be understood by others is a necessary and a therapeutic experience (England, 1986, pp6-7).

Brandon and Jordan's account of 'creative social work' lies in this radical, but therapeutic, tradition. It gives some idea of what this view of social work consists of. First it rejects the institutional pressures on social work:

Powerful social forces push social workers into restricted roles. There is a strong public expectation that they should be nicely and inoffensively helpful, never angry and disturbing. Some clients paralyse social workers' imagination and creativity with threatening and disruptive demands, but most see them as low-ranking officials of whom little is to be expected (Brandon and Jordan, 1979, p1).

Second, it identifies qualities which characterise 'good' creative social work:

. . . self-confidence . . . of the kind that comes from security of identity, from knowing one's own boundaries and limits as a means of recognizing and respecting others'. . . positive use of feelings he previously feared as damaging and destructive, and to rely more on intuition. . . Closely linked with greater trust of self is an increased respect for clients . . . enjoy his contacts with most clients, to like them better and so share more of himself with them . . . enter into more of a partnership with clients, recognizing their strengths and developing them . . . sharing, sometimes to the point where there is a kind of fusion between client and social worker . . . the importance of flexibility in what they are as well as in what they do . . . respond less predictably to clients' needs . . . a substantial element of self-discipline . . . (Brandon and Jordan, 1979, pp3-4).

The other kind of dissent from the individualist assertion of the central role of services and agency definitions of social work comes from socialist-collectivist positions. We have seen already that social change objectives contesting the acceptance of social order and smooth social progress have always been present in social work writing.

Fook (1993, p7) identifies five major themes of this perspective:

- A structural analysis (see Mullaly, 1993). Causes for the personal problems that social workers deal with are identified within social and economic structures of society. We can, as a result, avoid labelling and stigmatising clients with blame for their problems.

- Continual analysis and attempts to avoid the adverse consequences for clients of the social control functions of social work.

- Continual analysis and criticism of social, political and economic factors which are causing problems for clients.

- Trying to protect clients against oppression by more powerful people, groups and social structures.

- Seeking to promote personal liberation and empowerment and social change which benefits clients.

In this last respect, and in the sense that radical social work claims '. . . that it questioned conventional practice in terms that pushed the interests of the client to the fore. . .' (Langan and Lee, 1989, p7) it has affinities with the personal growth perspective. However, it has a stronger focus on the structural.

Conclusion
This chapter reviewed definitions of and debates about social work throughout the twentieth century. Within the discourse, individualist-reformist views emphasise caring, altruistic concern for individuals within a context of seeking social improvement. They accept that social work takes part in social control. In later definitions this is an explicit purpose. This position emphasises social provision and claims that social control excludes significant commitment to social change or reflexivity and therapy. Its emphasis is on the role of social work with individuals. The two alternative general perspectives emphasise the social change purpose of social work (socialist-collectivist) and the personal growth objective (reflexive- therapeutic). They would argue that the role of social work should balance these purposes more strongly against control and individualistic provision.

We shall meet these three positions about social work again. I argue in the next two chapters that because of the way social work *as an activity* is constructed the reflexive-therapeutic perspective is strongly present, although in some cases an individualist position is equally viable. However, it is seen as more pragmatic and dominated by general social interests, rather than the personal needs of clients. It is not until, later, we come to look at social work *as a profession* that wider social purposes are at issue, and the debate between individualist-reformist and socialist-collectivist perspectives comes to the fore.

Chapter 3
Social Work as Personal and Interpersonal Activity

The Screaming Woman

When people ask me what social work is like, I often tell them the narrative of the screaming woman. Many social workers have similar anecdotes about their practice. Explaining what we do usually reflects the personal and interpersonal activity that we undertake, rather than anything else. It is the most easily explained and understood aspect of social work. Personal activity is also what social workers observably do. So, it is central to the experience of social work and developing the experience and identity of social workers. Other aspects of the nature of social work are more the product of analysis. The personal aspect contains the daily experience of social work. Our early pathway through social work usually involves integrating our experiences of social work as a personal activity. Narratives like that of the screaming woman codify and classify the important parts of social work as a personal experience.

I was on standby duty overnight for a social services department. The phone call from the police, asking if I was covering mental health emergencies, came at ten o'clock. 'We've got a problem here: there's this screaming lady.' 'How do you mean "screaming"?' I asked. 'Well she's screaming. You'll see when you get there.'

The estate of public housing, on the edge of the city, was arrayed down a hillside, and I entered the estate from the top. Laid out below was a wide sweep of low-rise housing, encasing several blocks of flats surrounded by tatty lawns. I could see the centre of a disturbance. Around the entrance of the most-distant block was a crowd of fifty or sixty people, with a police car parked nearby. As I drove down the hill, through the window piercing screams were coming from one flat. A young and very anxious police officer emerged from the crowd and came across.

'It's this Mrs Woods,' he explained, 'she's just sitting up in bed and screaming.' Another screech rent the air. Answering my questions, he said that, aside from the name, he could find out little about her. She did not have many dealings with the neighbours; there was a husband, but he was absent. Neighbours had tried to get her to stop screaming; he had tried reasoning with her; all useless. We began to push through the growing crowd and, as we did so, the police officer concluded his account of the situation by saying: 'She's hysterical.'

My mind was already racing and the event was so unusual that I can still remember how my thoughts picked up on his comment. As a technical diagnosis of mental illness, the police officer's comment was inaccurate: hysterical behaviour refers to avoidance of reality by unconsciously mimicking behavioural or physical symptoms.

Also, it was probably a sexist comment, attributing emotional behaviour to irrational characteristics assumed to be associated only with women. Still, it set me thinking. At school I had won a prize. As one of the books I chose a study of hypnosis, which described how most people could be hypnotised, that is, put into a form of sleep. The person is relaxed through being spoken to slowly, calmly and monotonously. People are more or less suggestible; that is, more or less responsive to this technique. As I walked through the typical council flat into the bedroom where a late-middle-aged woman was sitting up and periodically letting out a loud scream, my mind leapt to the man who taught me psychiatry. He was a tall, black-suited beetle of a man, who smoked dark cheroots. Talking about people who exhibited hysterical behaviour (in the technical psychiatric sense described above) I remember him saying: 'They are very suggestible.' My mind made the connection. If Mrs Woods had been hysterical in the technical sense, she was likely to be suggestible, and therefore easily subject to hypnosis. The police officer's comment might be inaccurate psychiatrically, but his common-sense theory of her behaviour might offer a way of beginning. I was not about to try hypnotism as such (not having any need to or being remotely qualified) but I could defuse the immediate crisis by putting her to sleep.

I resolved on this and sat on the edge of the bed. I leaned across Mrs Woods and took her hand, so that she could see me and be in contact with me. I explained who I was and why this strange man was in her bedroom. She continued to scream. I then said, in a low, slow voice: 'You are feeling very tired, your eyelids are heavy, you want to go to sleep . . .' and she keeled over to one side and went to sleep. I was the hero of the hour. Within moments of entering the flat, the disturbance that had kept everyone excited for some while was resolved, as far as the neighbours and the police were concerned. The skills of social workers were at a premium that night; every previous effort had failed, and I had instantly succeeded. The officer started to disperse the crowd.

A more-complex narrative would include Mr Woods's return home from the pub. It would describe a history of domestic violence; of depression, anxiety and dread as a loved family left home and an empty old age loomed and of need for personal and family change to offer fulfilment again. These matters occupied the social services in the future as they dealt with Mrs Woods. However, this one brief and unusual incident contains many elements of all personal social work, as we often describe it:

- *Intervention* in the personal aspects of peoples' lives.

- *Human communication within a relationship* is the fundamental basis of social workers' actions.

- Social work is a *process*; that is, it is not a series of discrete events, separate from one another. All events in a social work activity are joined. A progression occurs from one point to another helped by the relationships which are established among the people involved.

- Specific *values* lie beneath all social work activities.

- I used *knowledge and skills* drawn both from my academic learning and from my personal experience and life interests.

- I used myself. The *use of self* in relationships within social work meant that my self-confidence in the face of demands from police and neighbours, my self-control in the face of anxiety about what to do, my mental energy in the face of an unknown situation, and my personality and ability to interact with a stranger in a personal way were all brought into play.

This chapter explores in greater detail accounts of most of these aspects of carrying out social work activities. One, the area of social work values, is so complex and important to an understanding of social work that it is reserved to the next chapter. This focus on activity, however, is a limited perspective. There is no mention in this list of characteristics of social work of social or environmental change, although some of the points may include this. Also, there is no mention of the agency or managerial control or political or community sanction for the work. So, while the personal and interpersonal aspect of social work is often the first we get involved with and describes well what social workers do on a daily basis, it emphasises the reflexive-therapeutic in social work, contains some element of the individualistic, but mainly excludes reformist and socialist-collective perspectives. However, as we shall see, there are alternative constructions of some of the most important aspects of personal and interpersonal social work which try to redress the balance of analysis in favour of these alternative perspectives on social work as a whole.

The narrative of social work as a personal and interpersonal activity, then, asserts a claim for social work. That is, the interpersonal aspect and whatever it achieves is worthwhile to clients as participants in the endeavour. This is so, even though, as I shall argue, other social purposes are fulfilled by social work activity and social work's presence in the world as a profession. The personal and interpersonal narrative attempts to provide a coherent analysis and valuation of a variety of aspects of social work. It forms the essence of the public and everyday understanding of social work as an activity. The additional aspects of social work both as an activity and as a profession require analysis and development from a basic understanding of social work in its personal and interpersonal form.

Intervention
According to the personal/interpersonal narrative, social workers intervene in other people's lives and social situations. The loose meaning of 'intervention' is virtually anything that a social worker does with or on behalf of clients. People using 'intervention' in this way (generally individualist-reformist in approach) accept that social work is an authoritative action in the client's existing state. A second, tighter, usage of 'intervention' focuses on activities intended to affect clients' lives. In the following account I give some examples of how the term is used in these different ways.

When he writes '[s]ocial work has now developed a range of methods of intervention . . .', Tilbury (1977, p4) uses the word to mean almost any activity that social workers undertake: he goes on to enumerate casework, group work and community work with a huge range of people's and social problems. Pincus and Minahan (1973, p15) classify the 'social functions' of social workers' 'intervention activities and tasks'. Similarly, Shulman (1991, p10) calls practice theories including '. . . constructs about clients that are closely tied to prescriptions for worker interventions'. And Wood and Middleman (1989, p35) claim that '[e]very instance of social work involves an intervention into the relationship between people and their social environment in order to improve the quality of that relationship'.

Compton and Galaway (1994, p427 emphasis original), provide an example of the more restricted use of intervention to describe ' . . . activities undertaken subsequent to the development of a service contract and directed toward the achievement of goals specified in the service contract.'

In this account, the intervention is by worker and client together into a problem. Doel and Marsh (1992, p21) make a similar point describing task-centred work as

'. . . an active intervention with an emphasis on the role of the client in negotiating and undertaking appropriate programmes of help'. However, this is not the only possible object of intervention in social work. Germain (1979, p8) argues for a wider conception of intervention, reviewing the development of social work ideas, culminating in an ecological perspective:

> In the ecological view, practice is directed toward improving the transactions between people and environments in order to enhance adaptive capacities *and* improve environments for all who function within them. To carry out the professional purpose requires a set of environmental interventions and a set of interventions into the transactions between people and environments to complement the sets available for intervening in coping patterns of people (emphasis original).

Here, interventions are formally stated sets of actions with environments, transactions and patterns of behaviour, and are what the *worker* does, rather than something which is shared.

One widely used theory of social work explicitly contains 'intervention' in its title: *crisis intervention*. One important account of this theory (Rapoport, 1970) rarely uses the word, however. She prefers 'crisis theory' or 'crisis-oriented brief treatment'. At one point, she makes a distinction between intervention and prevention: '. . . principles applicable to modes of intervention and prevention' (Rapoport, 1970, p269). Parad (1965, p1) makes the same distinction between preventive and crisis intervention in the classic book. He defines crisis intervention (p2) as '. . . entering into the life situation of an individual, family or group to alleviate the impact of a crisis-inducing stress in order to help mobilize the resources of those directly affected, as well as those who are in the significant "social orbit" . . .'. Brewer and Lait (1980, p121) apply the preventive/interventive distinction more widely in social work: '. . . evidence of the effectiveness of preventive casework is even more tenuous than in the case of intervention.'

Three points about intervention may, then, be made. It can be understood to mean anything that social workers do. Sometimes, it is limited to social work activity which is specifically designed to achieve change in clients or social situations. This second usage sometimes seeks to distinguish such purposive social work activity from work which aims to provide support or to prevent deterioration in a situation.

Two implications of the idea of intervention
Among the implications of seeing social work as an intervention is, first, that it asserts that social work tries to create a balance. The altruism of caring and helping is counterposed against the authoritative imposition of involvement against the conventions of the social worlds in which social workers act. In this way, the individualist requirement for invoking social control is incorporated into the basic reflexive-therapeutic approach of personal and interpersonal social work. Second, it makes claims for its scientific and authoritative nature. Such claims support social work against criticism of its invasive nature.

We can best see the first point from a striking representation of intervention in Morales and Sheafor (1992, p16). Their diagram (reproduced as Figure 3.1) shows the worker inserting a wedge in the social and personal environments of the client. The worker invades a part of their personal life-space, where the intervention takes place. Then, it affects clients personally and their world more widely. This presentation of intervention casts social workers as outsiders in the social situations where they help. Moreover, it implies action (Lewis, 1982, p189) rather than simply being present in the client's life, or being non-directive.

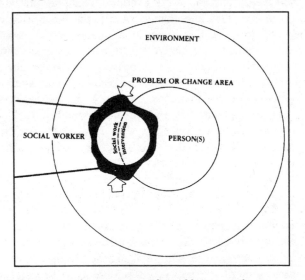

Figure 3.1 Diagrammatic representation of intervention.

From: Armando Morales and Bradford W. Sheafer *Social Work: a profession of many faces* (6th edition) Copyright © 1992 by Allyn and Bacon. Reprinted by permission.

Similarly, I argued elsewhere (Payne, 1992) that all involvements with other human beings or other organisations necessarily implied intrusion on those individuals or organisations, their freedom to act as they wished and their privacy of decision making. Workers create a balance of advantages between intruding too much and getting involved enough to have an effect.

These views imply that the normal situation where we give help is a closed social world in which official or professional helpers do not take part. Moreover, it sees social life as ordered. People go along in their social world until some invasion changes that. If we accept this as normality, seeking or receiving help from outsiders is a socially-less-preferred option than receiving help within the social circle. This conception of social work activity is not necessary, although seeing social work activity as intervention implies it. Socialist-collectivist views say that a better description of social life is of constant social change. Social work activities would then be one part of the continuing experience of change.

Focusing on social work as intervention has political and social implications. Politically, it implies that providing welfare services is not a natural way of providing help. So, for example, political assumptions that providing such help should be a normal role of the State in welfare societies might be questioned. Thus, seeing social work as intervention is a conservative or right-wing view which defines social work as an exceptional intervention rather than a proper role of the State or society. Socially, it places burdens on those who are seen as the natural carers within social circles: often we assume that these are women, or close relatives. Thus, the situation in which social workers are assumed to be outsiders also assumes a gendered order of caring and the role of families, communities and others in the closed social circle in the welfare of its members. Taking for granted that social workers intervene may carry many of these hidden political and social assumptions.

The second point, that using the term 'intervention' justifies social work's credentials for invasive activities, can be seen in the fact that its widespread use is only recent. Accounts of social work in the 1960s do not use the term. For example, Compton and Galaway's (1994) emphasis on intervention in a text focused on 'problem-solving' is not to be found anywhere in Perlman's classic text (1957), where casework is said '. . . to provide these two kinds of conditions: the resources and influences by which its client's social needs may be met and the modes which promote its client's personal and social effectiveness' (Perlman, 1957, p84). The collections of accounts of social work theories published by Roberts and Nee (1970) similarly mainly refers to treatment, although Smalley (1970, p80) criticises diagnostic theorists for seeing social work as a 'repertoire of interventive acts' applied to clients who are 'classified' according to the worker's preconceived ideas. The evident target for her comment, Hollis (1970 p36), describes casework, however, as '. . . a blend of processes directed as diagnostically indicated toward modification in the person or his social or interpersonal environment or both, and of the exchanges between them. Smalley (1970, p119) refers to '. . . the engagement of the other through the use of a relationship process . . .'; and Thomas (1970) focuses on behaviour 'modification'.

The importance of intervention
Why has intervention gained importance? Intervention is often particularly used in Britain to refer to situations where the social worker has legal responsibilities. Department of Health guidance on the implementation of the *Children Act 1989,* for example, and the *National Health Service and Community Care Act 1990* both use intervention as the model of what social workers do.

Not all modern accounts of social work use intervention as a term for describing social work activity. Davies's (1994) well-known text from an individualist viewpoint, for example, talks about neither treatment nor intervention but *maintenance*, through the exercise of skills and knowledge in relationships.

Intervention, then, is associated with reflexive-therapeutic views of social work, but as they have been adapted to respond to a technical-scientific conception of social work as concerned with knowing and purposeful action, instead of, as in the reflexive concepts, responsive and developmental processes. Johnson (1992, pp66-8) argues that it came into use in the 1960s as a replacement for the term 'treatment'. She associates it with theoretical and practice changes in social work citing:

- New practice theories which rejected the medical model, particularly shifts away from psychoanalytic theory.

- An emphasis on community and group work which did not use the idea of treatment so readily.

- The social systems theory emphasis on individuals as being within a social network. Social work moved from a focus on individual change towards wider activities in a personal network.

- Changes in the USA towards work with client groups, such as drug abusers, which required a more aggressive practice stance.

The view of intervention in narratives about social work presents social workers as 'outsiders' who invade the social territories of their clients. They have social, moral and political authority to act in relation to those clients. That authority reacts against alternative ways of providing welfare within families and communities. Social workers refer to intervention to claim technical competence for their invasion and to identify their social authority in acting in this way. However, this modern terminology replaces a 'softer' usage referring to therapeutic activities which imply a different form of authority and competence derived from knowledge and expertise. It is also an alternative to 'working with' clients, which implies a more co-operative and less invasive mode of practice. Thus, we can see the reflexive-therapeutic origins of this interpersonal practice, and how it has been adapted with individualist overtones to provide a more technical-scientific interpretation of social work activity thought to be appropriate for a modernist age.

Human communication within a relationship
However invasive it is, social work is always carried out by communication between the worker and others involved. The communication takes place within a relationship or relationships.

Communication conveys meaning between human beings by using symbols. A symbol is a device which 'stands for' something else. Sometimes the symbols are words, which may be conveyed in speech or writing or by sign languages. Sometimes the symbol is a piece of behaviour, such as touch, closeness or attitude. Sometimes the symbol is a situation or observation which may be interpreted in particular ways. Examples are where someone is disabled or possesses the characteristics of a particular ethnic group. The fact that social work communication takes place in a relationship derives from an assumption that social work is a process. It continues over time. Therefore, the people involved have a period of continuing contact. The social work narrative is that the relationship does two things:

- Its special emotional nature has the capacity to 'move' and therefore influence the client.

- It creates an atmosphere of co-operation between worker and client. This forms the instrument through which communication takes place. The communication is also a factor in the worker's influence.

43

Merely attaining effective communication is not enough to achieve changes in clients. It must be specially directed or organised to have its effects. Theory and research into social work, and the knowledge- and skill-base of social work, discussed below, often focus on what communications might be effective to achieve which results.

This traditional formulation of the use of relationship is represented best in Perlman's book on the subject:

> *Relationship is a human being's feeling or sense of emotional bonding with another (p23). '[It is] an* **emotional** *experience. We are* **moved** *when our emotions are touched,* **motivated** *by the push and pull of feeling.' (p51) . . .* **A professional relationship is formed for a recognised and agreed-upon purpose . . . is time-bound . . . is for the client . . . carries authority . . . is a controlled relationship . .** (pp62-74) (Perlman, 1979, emphasis original).

These ideas are built up from two sources: the work of Biestek and Rogers and their colleagues. The classic account of relationship in social work is Biestek's (1961) book on casework. He explores seven basic characteristics of the casework relationship:

- *Individualisation* - Recognising and understanding clients' unique qualities; work is adapted to those qualities.

- *Purposeful expression of feelings* - Recognising clients' needs to express feelings, particularly negative ones, and listening purposefully to encourage that expression is essential to working on clients' problems.

- *Controlled emotional involvement* - Being sensitive to and responding appropriately to clients' feelings.

- *Acceptance* - Perceiving and acting towards clients as they are with their qualities and weaknesses. Through acceptance, workers may understand clients better, and free them from things which get in the way of dealing with problems realistically.

- *Non-judgemental attitude* - Conveying to clients a feeling that they are not blamed for causing their problems or needs.

- *Self-determination* - Acting in ways that recognise clients' rights to freedom in making choices and decisions within social work processes.

- *Confidentiality* - Preserving secret information revealed as part of the social work process.

Some of these principles are both ethical in character and practical. Biestek argues (pp120-1), for example, that confidentiality, while an essential value in professional practice, is also necessary to create trust so that worker and client can work together. Similarly, many of Biestek's principles set an atmosphere within which other aspects of social work might operate.

Rogers (1951) worked more widely than social work in many different forms of therapy. His account claims that three aspects of relationship are necessary to provide successful therapy:

- Clients must see that workers are *genuine and congruent* in the relationship, so what they do and say reflects their real personality and is not 'put on'.

- Workers have *unconditional positive regard* for their clients. This is similar to acceptance and a non-judgemental attitude.

- Workers have *empathy* with clients' views of the world.

These have been developed subsequently by Truax and Carkhuff (1967) and Carkhuff and Berenson (1977) to ideas of honesty and genuineness, warmth, respect, acceptance and empathetic understanding.

Since relationship is both a means and a carrier of influence by communication, it is usually presented as positive, and assumed, from a therapeutic perspective, always to be so. However, some writers recognise tensions which derive from the attempt to gain influence. The ideas that social work relationships have purpose and involve the use of authority and power suggest that they are not wholly benign and congenial. It is more likely that their benignity is constructed to conceal the purpose and application of influence. Johnson (1992) and Compton and Galaway (1989) present similar accounts of relationship, drawing on each other. However, the way that they deal with influence and purpose marks a recognition in the latter of the tensions. Johnson, although she derives her account from theirs, presents a bland, wholly positive impression. For her, everything is something that the worker does or is and conveys to the client. She sees no problem with the worker's expectations or insistence of the client. Her purpose is known and accepted. Compton and Galaway recognise that using authority and power goes beyond having expectations, and purpose for them is a way of limiting the use of power.

Johnson (1992):	*Compton and Galaway (1989):*
authority and power - expecting that clients will work at their problems, expecting clients to go beyond present abilities and insisting that they do what they can for themselves.	**authority and power** - the use of workers' capacity to persuade and influence, using power derived from their position in the agency and as a professional and deriving from their expertise and skill.
purpose - the relationship has a purpose known to and accepted by both worker and client.	**purpose** - limits and focuses the relationship according to objectives and values, so that power is not used capriciously

In a later edition (Compton and Galaway, 1994) Compton and Galaway go further in exploring complex interactions between workers' honesty in using power and authority and their clients' respect for them.

Other formulations of relationship in social work present alternative views. Three views show alternative positions:

- Acknowledgement of *alternative bases for relationship* which are other than mutual trust and bonding.

- The socialist-collectivist view that relationships should be *dialogical*. That is, they should focus on debate between workers and clients which explores issues to enhance clients' understanding of social forces affecting them. They can then learn to become more active and in control of attempts to resolve better-understood social conflicts.

  This educational process is called *conscientisation* or consciousness-raising. The emphasis on dialogue rejects a relationship constructed for therapeutic purposes. Its authority and influence are seen as at least potentially oppressive. This view extends the concern about difficulties raised by these aspects of relationship in more-sophisticated mainstream accounts of relationship, such as that of Compton and Galaway, discussed above.

- A view which emphasises the *content* of communication rather than relationship as the medium of it.

An example of alternative bases for relationship is the account of Pincus and Minahan (1973). They propose that social work relationships contain three types of 'atmosphere' or 'posture'. These are:

- *Collaboration* based on trust and mutual agreement similar to the mainstream narrative.

- *Bargaining*, in which testing of the objectives of the parties involved and give and take between those interests occur.

- *Conflict*, in which disagreements and arguments occur.

This somewhat individualist-reformist account usefully acknowledges that elements of conflict and bargaining exist in all social work relationships. Also, in their view, relationships may exist with people other than clients, (eg other agencies and professionals) and need to be analysed in the same terms. This focus is largely absent from therapeutic social work thinking about relationship.

An example of the socialist-collectivist approach is:

Normalization, collectivization and redefining are the means of carrying out consciousness-raising. The medium within which each of these activities is carried out is dialogue, between the social worker and the service user and among services users. Dialogue is the vehicle for uncovering people's subjective reality and opening it to critical reflection (Mullaly, 1993, p173).

However, an alternative view of a radical social work relationship focuses on the explicit promotion of equality:

The main difference between a traditional and a radical casework relationship is that the latter places emphasis on equality and sharing, rather than the often unbalanced paternalistic style of many traditional workers . . . the radical casework and client relationship is best seen as one of joint learning through an exchange of impressions, rather than an imposition of one person's interpretations on another (Fook, 1993, p103)

These perspectives on relationship explicitly identify the political nature of the focus which mainstream social work writing places on relationship. Individualist-reformist accounts of relationship assume the worker's power and right to influence clients according to socially defined objectives, developed through agencies and social assumptions. Alternative accounts of relationship also alert us to the possibility of seeing relationship as less important than therapeutic accounts of social work imply: action, conflict and debate may be more important.

Individualist-reformist views also play down the importance of relationship in favour of the content of the communication between clients and workers. Davies (1994) focuses primarily on the socially-defined functions of social work and presents its major focus as the maintenance of social relations under stressful situations. While he acknowledges relationship as important in these activities, he does not give it a central place, focusing on skills such as interviewing to structure his account. He differentiates (pp163-70) between structured approaches to practice, used primarily in short-term interventions with specific purposes, and long-term relationships, used where long-term support and assistance are being provided.

Other writers concentrate on workers' roles within relationships, which are taken for granted in themselves. For example, Wood and Middleman (1989) discuss 'positioning' as the process 'intended to provide a social-emotional environment congenial to connection or rapport . . .' (p38). However, they describe this in technical communication terms, covering, for example, placing the worker in the room in relation to the client. Intervention is undertaken through four roles:

- The *conferee*, who debates with and advises clients.

- The *broker*, who links clients with others and arranges services.

- The *mediator*, who negotiates within the client's network to facilitate progress for them.

- The *advocate*, who puts a case for resources or social change on behalf of individual clients, or groups.

Whittaker and Tracey (1989) see social treatment as a framework for interpersonal helping. Workers with good judgement following relevant individual values use their self in carrying out similar roles. One characteristic of these accounts of social work is their emphasis on the negotiating and advocacy roles.

To summarise this discussion, individualist-reformist social work narratives concentrate on the personal and interpersonal helping and broking, and their treatment of relationship is an example of this. In doing so, they deny the political nature of the relationship created. This is because they exclude discussion of the direction of influence applied covertly by the creation of trust and empathy in the relationship. Individualist views concentrate on the purposes, roles and content of activity within social work rather than the medium of communication. Such views essentially deny the political nature of relationship. Socialist-collectivist accounts recognise the complexity which acknowledging the political nature of social work relationships brings to social work practice. They use the political nature of social work relationships for empowerment purposes. The fact that they do so emphasises the conservative political objectives concealed in the individualist-reformist narrative. The possibilities of a sharing or educational style of relationship and of developing greater equality in the relationship for its own sake represents a therapeutic conception of social work. England's (1986) self-actualisation view of social work as art, for example, concentrates on the use of the social worker's self to enhance coping and clients' valuation of personal meaning of their lives. However, this is not fully realised in practice and in many accounts of social work practice, because of influences from the individualist technical conceptions of social work activity.

Process
Seeing social work as a process is another crucial element in reflexive-therapeutic narratives about social work. The essence of the idea is that social work is not a series of discrete events. Instead, each interaction between client, worker and others is part of a social order. Each communication affects all the others to produce a flow of events. We saw earlier that intervention also assumes a continuing flow of life in a social order. By virtue of being in a continuing relationship with the participants, the social worker has the means to influence the sequence. More simply, some accounts describe process as a frequently occurring sequence of events. Group and community work views see understanding process as an objective in the work.

As with relationship, this narrative of process has two dissenting positions:

- The individualist-reformist position argues that social work activities are separate events given coherence by their relevance to an assessment of need.

- The socialist-collectivist position gives coherence to social work activity by reference to identified social objectives of the work.

The idea of process as a special feature of social work is associated historically with the functional school of social work theory. Functional theory is reflexive-therapeutic in that focuses on process by emphasising that personal growth as a human being is a central 'purpose' for people. Helping achieve this purpose gives direction to the services offered by agencies. So the client is not a static object to be classified. Workers do not select types of appropriate treatment to achieve their or the agency's preconceived ends (Smalley, 1970, pp80,96). Instead, social work must leave

> . . . *room for the emergence of the unknown, the unpredictable, for 'becoming' through the utilization of the immediacy of a continually shifting life situation. It calls for the development of a method which requires the social worker's engagement of the other in a relationship process through which that other may both discover and modify his own wanting and develop new power for satisfying his own wants.* (Smalley, 1970, p96)

This somewhat mystical, reflexive-therapeutic account claims 'process' as the nature of interpersonal social work activity itself. A similar approach is represented by proponents of 'problem-solving' such as Perlman (1957) and Compton and Galaway (1994). The argument here is that personal and interpersonal social work

> . . . *stems from a conception of human life being in itself a problem-solving process, a continuous change and movement in which the human being works on so adapting himself to external objects or them to himself as to achieve maximum satisfactions* (Perlman, 1957, p53).

A simpler individualist-reformist conception of process describes it as a sequence. Garvin and Tropman (1992), for example, describe beginning, middle and ending phases in helping individuals, groups and families, organisations, communities and societies to change. They divide these three basic phases in different and more-complex ways in each case, however. Wood and Middleman's (1989, p69) account of social work also identifies a sequence in social work. They distinguish understanding social work from doing it:

> *[O]ne must do it one step at a time. Therefore a second, complementary model is needed, a process model that indicates what to do first and what to do next, a process model that tells workers every step of the way what to ask themselves and what to do contingent upon the answers . . . a process model that translates principles and procedures . . . into sequential practice behaviour.*

The sequence starts with a contract phase, where workers and clients agree about the aims of the work. A task phase follows: various activities take place. In the termination or re-entry phase, work ends, or further aims are identified. A similar understanding of process is reflected by the more conventional Tilbury (1977 p177). He sees process as having four phases of intake and orientation, exploration and testing, problem-solving work and termination. However (p192) he does link process to 'progress'. The implication here is that seeing social work as a continuing sequence helps to identify improvements in clients. Process leads to or is (it is not clear which) progress to Tilbury.

In group and community work, process gains another important aspect, as an objective in its own right. Mondros and Wilson (1994), for example, discuss empowerment through social action work with community and self-help groups. They describe

> *[p]rocess goals [as] ... desired ends that focus on the process by which the organization becomes more and more able to effect its outcome goals. Long-term process goals go to strengthening the organization...* (Mondros and Wilson, 1994, p137)

In group work, Garvin (1985, p211) defines processes as '... those changes occurring in activities and interactions ... that are related to goal attainment ... and ... group maintenance'. In both these cases, processes are what goes on in the group or community organisation. Professional work with such organisations, however, has among its aims strengthening the capacity of the group or organisation to function to achieve its own objectives. One aspect of that capacity is the ability to create useful interactions within it. So strengthening process becomes a group or community work objective, and not, as in casework, a means to a therapeutic objective. It is still, none the less, reflexive or individualist in wanting a therapeutic aim rather than seeking to empower the group to achieve desired social change.

Seeing process as a sequence of activities is more limited in its claims about social work than Smalley or Perlman's ideas about personal growth or problem-solving being integral to human life. In these integral views, the focus of social work action should be an essential process within human life, rather than specific problems or tasks. This leads some to make links between social work and wider processes. For example, Askeland (1994) argues that social work interaction processes and problem-solving are analogous to the learning process in higher education. Social work processes can be understood by seeing parallels between the two. As with the integral position, group and community work views of process as an objective incorporate it as a fundamental part of human interaction. In the same way, it is argued that workers need to see process as a valid object of social work action in its own right. It is not merely as a means to action, as the relationship might be.

It is reasonable, then, to describe a focus on process as characteristic of a reflex-ive-therapeutic position. An example of the individualist-reformist position is Davies (1994, pp76-92). He identifies an eclectic selection of eleven strategies for change and a number of 'dimensions of practice'. However, these focus on the objectives that agencies might wish to attain, rather than attempting a coherent account of the nature of social work activity itself. For him, social work compris-es the role carried out in the agency and the methods used, rather than being a sep-arately identifiable activity.

Examples of socialist-collectivist positions are in the work of Rees and Fook. Rees (1991), developing ideas of empowerment, identifies a sequence of steps in empowerment, and in the focus within which skills are applied. He starts, conven-tionally, with preparation and assessment, going on to less-conventional skills of negotiation and advocacy. Fook (1993) is concerned to identify several strategies and techniques and to distinguish what activities and perspectives on practice might be considered radical rather than traditional.

Knowledge and skills
Social workers use knowledge and skills in their work. We often regard the knowledge and skill characteristic of an occupational group as marking it as a pro-fession, because, as we saw in Chapter 1, power over the social territory of an occupation often comes from control of knowledge. Bartlett (1970, p63) reports that an American committee on the nature of social work practice '. . . recognized that mature professions rest upon strong bodies of knowledge and values from which scientific and ethical principles that guide the operation of the practitioner are derived'. Knowledge has been valued from the earliest days of social work, when the attempt was being made to distinguish a defined activity which was dif-ferent from mere beneficence. Loch's (1883, p10) guide to 'charitable work', for example, says:

> *Two kinds of knowledge are required . . . : a knowledge of the social life of*
> *the class of which the person in distress is a member . . ., and a general*
> *knowledge of character - a discernment of the value of evidence, combined*
> *with a knowledge of the modes and possibilities of charitable assistance.*

Knowledge is about understanding, whereas skill is about capacity for doing. The connection between the two arises because social workers must have the capacity to use knowledge in practice, applying and adapting it to the particular situation which they face. The skill with which they can do so defines the validity of knowledge in a practical activity such as social work. The capacity to reason using knowledge is a crucial element of social work (Lewis, 1982). Knowledge which cannot be applied at best merely contributes to attitudes and contexts. At worst, it may not be useful at all. Skill which cannot use knowledge is less skilled than it might be. Judgements about how knowledge and skill should and should not be used is the province of values, considered in the next chapter.

What is knowledge?

Chapter 1 discussed different ways of knowing. Most accounts of social work knowledge are modernist and tend to lead to an individualist perspective on social work . That is, they assume that we should treat accounts of a real world supported by evidence as representations of reality on which we can act. This leads to certainty in action, and gives authority to act. Socialist-collective perspectives would take authority to act not from expert scientific knowledge but from collective support. Reflexive-therapeutic accounts focus on the ambiguity of knowledge - anathema to the believer in scientific knowledge of reality. Modernist texts tend to devalue beliefs and values as knowledge. Gordon (1964, p60), for example, uses 'knowledge' to mean

> an experientially based *picture that man has built up of the cosmos and himself in it - a picture of the way things are* as distinct from what he might wish or fantasy or think they *should be.* (emphasis original)

Examined more closely, much of this claimed knowledge, even when drawn from apparently scientific sources, is ambiguous. Many sources of valuable knowledge are not scientific. Gordon (1964) distinguishes direct knowledge acquired through our own senses from indirect knowledge gained through communications from others. Direct knowledge might be more reliable than indirect knowledge, but both may be ambiguous. Communications, through speech, writing, graphical representations, such as diagrams, through mathematics and statistics are through the media of symbols. Knowledge gained through our own senses may be mistaken, if the senses are misled through selective attention and misperception.

Knowledge comes from reasoning about evidence, including 'causal accounts' which contain social workers explanations (Bull and Shaw, 1992) and from the evidence itself. So, knowledge may be 'built up', as Gordon puts it, through argument and debate about evidence. CCETSW (1991, p14) argues that social workers '. . . must be able to conceptualize, to reflect, to analyse competing theories, ideologies and models of practice which will inform their work'.

Many conceptions of social work seek to promote scientific knowledge above all others. However, the essentially reflexive nature of social work reasserts itself in opposition to these views. Much social work literature identifies and accepts other kinds of knowledge, contrary to the strict scientific knowledge viewpoint. Davies (1994), for example, identifies four sources of knowledge:

- *Empirical evidence* - Some writers claim that only knowledge from empirical verifiable sources should be used. Davies (1994, pp92-3) points out that little social work knowledge is of this kind. He argues, though, that research encourages scepticism about managerial, political and professional claims. Feminist theory argues that rationalism reflects a male way of looking at the world, which denigrates the value of personal experience and feelings.

- *Practice theory* - Social workers draw upon experience and acquired and shared 'wisdom' about how to act. Modernists criticise reliance on such knowledge, since it has not been rigorously tested. However, there are other views about this. One, illustrated by the work of Krill (1990), argues existentially that knowledge can only be 'known' through the experience and self-testing of human beings. England (1986, pp34-8) argues that social work is characterised by being carried out by a group of people who have developed the capacity to explore and understand others and the complex interacting factors involved in human and social life. This is so complicated that empirical knowledge can never be sufficient. Instead, social workers have the skill of using whatever knowledge exists, gaining more, and applying it all to individual complex situations that come before them.

- *Conventional wisdom* - Davies (1994, p93) suggests that doing things the way they have always been done may be a powerful influence. Agencies' conventions, legal limitations and expectations are often influential in what social workers do.

- *Personal motivations and ideals* - Many social workers are guided by their personal beliefs (such as Christian, Muslim or other faiths, or political beliefs). Davies (1994, p93) argues that this helps them to accept the stresses of social work as a career.

A considerable force of argument exists in social work counteracting the assumption that scientific ways of knowing are the primary source of knowledge for practice. Goldstein (1988) proposes that in addition to the modernist approach to knowing, a humanist approach can be constructed. This relies on 'narrative' knowledge which tries to show how the human mind constructs its understanding of the world. Evidence includes artistic representations of the world which display something of the workings and understandings of the mind. Also, narratives and analyses of social work which emphasise understanding and process rather than outcome can contribute. Finally, clients themselves can express and demonstrate knowledge of worlds which is unavailable to the worker's personal experience. Witkin and Gottschalk (1989) argue that value issues are integral to scientific ways of understanding and are legitimate criteria for evaluating social work knowledge. Weick (1990) argues that intuitive ways of knowing should also be accepted within social work. Pieper (1989) proposes that a heuristic paradigm for knowing in social work is most appropriate. It accepts '. . . any problem-solving strategy that appears likely to lead to relevant, reliable, and useful information' (Pieper, 1989, p8).

The modernist claim that social work is or should be based on scientific knowledge can therefore be doubted. Sources of evidence are usually ambiguous and uncertain. Used in practice, they rely on argument and interpretation. Social work needs ways of knowing which deal with ambiguity rather than those which reject uncertainty in favour of the scientific. It thus maintains an essentially reflexive view of knowing. This has implications for views of social work as a profession, since, as we noted in Chapter 1, professions often seek control over areas of knowledge. If knowledge itself is ambiguous, such control is not easily asserted. This issue is explored further in Chapter 7.

Issues with social work knowledge

Widely agreed areas of social work knowledge cover understanding of the organisational and legal contexts of work, social scientific knowledge about human beings and their interactions, and social work practice methods (see Kadushin, 1964; Barker and Hardiker, 1981; Compton and Galaway, 1994; CCETSW, 1991; Johnson, 1992). Within these general groupings of knowledge, identifying more detailed accounts of knowledge is possible. The potential range is vast. This is dealt with in several ways:

- *Specialisation* - Social workers limit what they need to know to particular areas of concentration. The problem then is how they may define such areas of specialisation.

- *Genericism* - General principles are identified which might apply across a range of situations. This sometimes leads to problems in putting vague general principles into operation, or applying or transferring them from one area to another.

● *Limitation* - What is not directly useful is excluded from consideration. This has been the approach of CCETSW, the British social work education body, in its 1994 review of the British social work qualification. In one consultation, for example, it sought views on knowledge which might be considered desirable rather than essential, so that the merely desirable might be excluded.

The extent of social work knowledge raises issues of integrating:

● *Knowledge from different sources.* Theories or information about the same thing may compete or conflict. We have to decide between or select from them.

● *Items of knowledge with each other.* Even if knowledge is consistent, we have difficulty in fitting different items together to make an over all picture or symbol.

● *Knowledge with practice.* Although we may know something, using it in practice may not be easy.

The way in which the same knowledge might be used varies. Fook (1993, p44), for example, contrasts traditional social work conceptions with radical conceptions within the same area. A traditional (therapeutic) social worker might explore communication patterns or group of family norms, for example. Radical (socialist-collectivist) workers would look at social power imbalances or inequalities and dominant social ideologies about the value of particular social and group structures. Constable and Cocozzelli (1989) argue that all workers of whatever orientation have to focus their knowledge according to three main dualities. These are focusing on the person or their social relations, the problem or the person and individual adjustment or social change. These may be regarded as akin respectively to individualist-reformist, reflective-therapeutic and socialist-collectivists positions identified in this book.

Skills
Four ways in which social work skills are seen are:

● as *activities* in different phases of social work.

Pincus and Minahan (1973, p98) provide an example:

Eight essential practice skill areas can be differentiated: 1, assessing problems; 2, collecting data; 3, making initial contacts; 4, negotiating contracts; 5, forming action systems; 6, maintaining and co-ordinating action systems; 7, exercising influence; and 8, terminating the change effort.

●   as *personal capacities* of social workers.

An example is the CCETSW (1991, pp16-7) analysis of 'the core skills of social work' prepared as part of the reform of social work education in the late 1980s. It included cognitive skills of analysing, evaluating and conceptualising; interpersonal skills; decision-making skills; administrative skills and skills in using resources. A similar American document (CSWE, 1988) distinguishes cognitive and interactive skills, breaking them down more fully in detail. The Barclay Report (1982, p151) on the role and tasks of social workers also distinguishes three similar groups of skills: in human relationships, in analysis (assessing people, analysing situations and evaluating outcomes), and in effectiveness (doing what was planned).

Another similar example is Davies's text (1994, pp203-4), which refers to interpersonal skills, assessment skills, writing skills and workload management skills. He also (pp205-6) refers to qualities such as perseverance, skill in confrontation, ability to create action, assertiveness and self-confidence, ability to work with hostility, skill in working within time-limits and ability to work in stressful situations. Rosenfeld (1984) also presents two broad areas of expertise, in assigning priorities and in inventing interventions. In his (reflexive-therapeutic) view, the skill of social work lies in the capacity to be creative, rather than in explicit lists of competencies. Even when we examine the more detailed examples of what comes under each heading, such analyses do not help us to clarify or analyse the ability which is required to take action in social work situations.

●   as *roles* taken by social workers.

Some examples of these are considered below in relation to competences.

●   as *competences* involved in carrying out social work tasks.

These are derived from functional analyses such as the work of Teare and McPheeters (1970), Baker (1976), and BASW (1977). Such analyses break down social work roles into descriptions of specific activities with which a definable and testable skill can be associated (see Payne, 1982). These can then be integrated into different roles, according to the way in which an agency wants to organise its work. They can transfer skills more readily from one activity to another, because they have not been learnt as part of a large, complex activity. For example, a role such as social worker for a child in care might involve many of Teare and McPheeters's tasks including advocate, teacher, behaviour changer, caregiver, mobiliser of resources, administrator, evaluator and outreach from the agency into the community. BASW (1977) would also recognise roles like being an agent of social control, being an adviser, enabler and protector. The worker might see these as child care skills. If they were learnt separately, though, they could more easily be applied to the role of helping a mentally ill man's family support him. The same skills might be applied, using different knowledge, to deal with the problems faced by mentally ill people in this situation. Skill analyses may therefore be regarded as more generic than client-group specialisms. Different areas of knowledge allow us to apply skills differently. Thus, for example, CCETSW (1991, p16) refers to the interpersonal skill of recognising and working with feelings and their impact on themselves and others. This might equally be a cognitive skill, and be of use in decision-making, administration and using resources.

Shulman (1991, pp42-60) studied social work skills primarily for their capacity to help in developing and using a social work relationship. He divides these into two groups:

- skills which help clients manage their feelings, which lead to a feeling of trust

  - reaching inside silences
  - putting clients' feelings into words
  - showing that the worker understands clients' feelings
  - sharing workers' feelings.

- skills which help clients to manage their problems, which lead to a feeling of being cared for

  - clarifying the worker's purpose and role
  - reaching for client feedback on purpose
  - partialising clients' concerns (splitting them up, so that they are better understood and more easily worked on)
  - supporting clients in taboo areas.

This analysis is much more concerned than functional accounts of social work skills to analyse the detail of interpersonal interactions within social work activities. Lewis (1982) regards skill as containing elements of knowledge, action, values and style. In his view they are characteristics both of the worker and of social work as an activity.

A radical analysis (Fook, 1993) differs from this, because it requires different skills to act in a radical way:

- Dealing with bureaucratic organisations. This includes documenting and researching what the worker does, and analysing agency policy and practices constantly. Such activities help to find ways of opposing oppressive practices in the agency and among colleagues and of surviving excessive stresses in practice.

- Developing critical awareness.
- Advocacy.
- Empowerment.
- Relationship.
- Social education.
- Active use of resources.
- Social empathy.
- Social support.
- Evaluation of outcomes.

More restricted analyses, such as that of Compton and Galaway (1994, p428), include the roles of social broker, enabler, teacher, mediator and advocate. Whittaker and Tracy (1989, p102) describe five roles of therapist-counsellor, educator-skills trainer, broker of services-resources, advocate and network-system consultant. Compared with earlier work, such as that of Teare and McPheeters (1970) and Baker (1976), these have a stronger emphasis on social work's indirect roles. It indicates a broadening of approach and an acceptance of wider skills associated with working with other agencies and within the community.

In accounts of social work knowledge and skills, therefore, a variety of claims are made that we can specify such knowledge and skills. However, we have seen that much of what is claimed as knowledge is ambiguous and interpreted, and thus supports a reflexive-therapeutic view of social work. Analyses of skills vary according to the purposes for which they have been made. Functionalist analyses present a modernist account, claiming clarity, universality and transferability of their analyses, and implying an individualist conception of social work. Interpreted through radical accounts such as Fook's or individualist accounts such as Schulman's, however, we can see again that the same material might apply to different purposes and ways of understanding social work personal and interpersonal activity. Ambiguity and reflexivity are restored.

Use of self
The personal/interpersonal social work narrative claims that social workers use their own personality and self-understanding as part of what they do. Since social

work is *inter*personal, the personalities of workers *and* clients must both be involved in the relationship. The relationship must, as we have seen, be genuine and warm, so the worker must feel and convey these feelings. However, the relationship gives workers possibly covert power over the client through having a purpose. Therefore, the fact that it is not a friendly and loving relationship must also, for the sake of genuineness, be conveyed.What is meant by a 'self'? It relates to the notion of identity, since self means having a continuing character which we or others can identify. It means more than a name and more than a body, since it also implies established and characteristic ways of thinking and acting. Shaw (1974, pp19-20) summarises the idea of 'self' as follows:

> . . . *as a result of socialisation, an individual comes to take a partly conscious, partly unconscious view of his own totality. This structure consists of a set of attitudes towards, or beliefs about, one's own needs, goals, abilities, feelings, values, prejudices, self-characteristics and methods of relating to other people . . . . This structure, or self-view, operates at a number of levels; it acts as a filter through which experience is mediated; it acts as a framework by means of which meaning can be given to experience; it also acts as a guide to decisions, choices and selections of possible alternatives. Once the self-concept is formed it is very resistant to change and comes to constitute the basis on which future psychological development is likely to take place.*

The use of self within social work is often associated with:

● The aim of personal growth and self-actualisation for clients.

For example, Howe's account of social work theories says (1987, pp113-4):

> *To help her clients, the social worker must be able to make imaginative use of her own experience, particularly as it occurs in the immediate relationship. The 'use of self' defines both the social worker's practice knowledge and her practice behaviour. The worker must be aware of her own thoughts and emotions: if she feels hostile or protective towards the client, she must know this, note it and be prepared to use it . . . This intuitive feel of the other person and the effect on oneself produces an understanding which becomes an integral of the worker's self. Thus, the worker gains her understanding, not by a struggle to explore external issues but by articulating her own consciousness.The worker having self-awareness, including understanding and being able to accept and value what is found out about oneself.*

Johnson (1992, p82) puts it thus:

It has been said that the most important tool a social worker possesses is herself. To use that tool skilfully and knowledgeably, a worker must have considerable self-knowledge. This calls for an introspective stance that seeks to bring personal concerns, attitudes, and values into the area of conscious thought. It calls for a continuous search for self-understanding and for a reasonable degree of comfort with the discovered self.

●   Individuality and creativity in social work.

Davies (1994, p178) argues:

Each social worker is a unique being, and, since the use of self is one crucial part of her function, it follows that the development of self-confidence is an appropriate ambition in its own right. Social work is a creative job and artistry of the practitioner is a vital component once the other qualities have been mastered.

●   Intuition.

England (1986, p32ff) treats the two concepts as almost identical:

. . . this use of self extends far beyond the worker's emotional involvement and in fact determines the character of his professional knowledge and behaviour. Competence in social work therefore will be found not by seeking to avoid intuition, but by its recognition and development, by the creation of uncommon common sense. Social work is a matter of intuitive understanding, but it must be intuition which is unusually sound, unusually fluent and accessible and subject to unusually careful evaluation.

●   Worker style.

This is a characteristic way of acting which develops through workers training and experience. It may include the acquisition of a theoretical perspective, or with an eclectic self-developed amalgam of perspectives (Brown, 1977).

The idea of use of self presents serious problems. First, it implies that the workers' approaches to clients will be stable and unchanging. They will have a style, use their stable and continuing personality and respond consistently. This contributes to congruency, but detracts from the possibility of flexibility. Second, it might imply that workers do not take on new ideas and theories once their self has become established. Third, the eclectic and intuitive character which many associate with the idea of worker style raises all the problems of eclecticism: how are ideas selected and integrated? If this is only on personal preference, what is the justification for the selective judgements made? How can the worker know that they have selected from the widest possible range and most appropriate ideas? See Payne, 1991, pp47-51, for a longer discussion of issues about eclecticism. What actions and observations in the relationship and more widely lead to the particular intuitions which the worker feels? The conscious use of self in social work relationships implies that workers are constantly trying to bring intuitions into conscious thought to explore openly the evidence and justification for them.

All these ideas are directly associated with reflexive-therapeutic conceptions of social work. Probably because of that, writers on social work from other perspectives do not discuss the use of self directly. Radical socialist-collectivist theory, for example, focuses on dialogical relationships in which debate and understanding are the objective, rather than therapeutic change. Imbrogno (1993), in relation to social development, argues that such approaches can avoid the need to conceptualise problems, by allowing client and worker to arrive jointly at a consensus about value conflicts. As we saw when discussing knowledge and skill many modern accounts concentrate on processes such as advocacy, liaison and mobilising resources with and on behalf of clients. Task-centred social work, a strictly individualist construction, implies explicit definition of workers' and clients' activities. The mystical use of self has less of a place in such conceptualisations.

Davies (1994, p179ff), while emphasising the importance of the use of self, also points out that this and all personal aspects of social work discussed in this chapter, are only part of social work activity. In this way, he seeks to distance himself from the reflexive-therapeutic aspect of social work which is strongly apparent in accounts of personal and interpersonal social work. He says social workers also use external resources in group work, community work, by working with volunteers, in liaison and linking work and in providing residential, day and other forms of care service. Here, he is emphasising the individualist-reformist concentration on service provision.

Conclusion
Personal and interpersonal activity of social work with clients often seems to be the essence of social work. This was true both in my pathway through social work and in many narratives. In this chapter, I have tried to unpack such narratives to see what they mean and what implications they carry.

The personal/interpersonal social work narrative constructs a coherent account of interpersonal social work in which many features of its nature interlock.

Intervention, relationship, process, use of self, use of knowledge and skill intertwine in emphasising personal and interpersonal activities. The focus is reflexive-therapeutic views of social work. Alternative conceptions from individualist-reformist and socialist-collectivist positions avoid or reconstruct many aspects of this narrative. Such reconstructions provide alternative views of social work which deny or criticise the coherence and comprehensiveness of the narrative.

So, narratives treating social work only as personal and interpersonal activity are inadequate as a characterisation of the whole. The existence of individualist-reformist and socialist-collectivist positions identifies the political nature of accounts of personal/interpersonal social work as represented in the texts we have considered. The idea of intervention implies the imposition of help from outside normal social environments by using power derived from agencies whose objectives are defined by élites in society. Accounts of the use of self, knowledge and skill, relationship and process can be recast to different purposes other than the caring, congruent, interpersonal help model of the reflexive-therapeutic narrative.

Accounts of social work as a personal activity, while apparently simple and understandable, and possibly socially acceptable, are inadequate as full accounts of social work. They convey only part of the truth. Where does social, political and moral authority for this personal activity come from? In moving on to these areas of debate, it is important to re-emphasise the personal nature of social work. Whatever purposes may be found, they are implemented by workers engaging in interpersonal communication with members of the public. Hidden implications of the personal nature of social work raise the political and social issues which are integral to a full understanding of social work. The narratives of social work considered in this chapter, however, show us how in the reflexive-therapeutic narrative and its alternatives, social and political objectives are implemented. Social work always involves people meeting up and doing things with each other within their personal social arenas. We must understand how that takes place in order to understand social work. That is why I have placed it, as I experienced it in my personal pathway, near the beginning of my understanding of social work.

Chapter 4
Social Work and Values

Value debates from practice disputes

A doctor telephoned the area office to ask for Mr Cawson's compulsory admission to mental hospital. He had just made a serious attempt at suicide. A colleague visited his home and discovered that Mrs Cawson was away from work. She was prepared to stay with her husband all the time for a few days. The hospital would offer a psychiatric clinic appointment three days later for assessment and treatment. Mr Cawson would accept that, but he refused to be admitted compulsorily. He would attend a day centre, but none was available in the area. It was unfortunate, my colleague thought, that Mrs Cawson should have to stay at home because we had no day centre. However, since she could stay with her husband at least until he was seen at the clinic, he could not justify a compulsory admission. The doctor complained about the social worker questioning his judgement about his patient and that we might have put the patient's life at risk. We identified several points which potentially raised value issues:

- The conflict between the value of reducing or eliminating a serious risk of death to this client and the value of not restricting the liberty of the client by compulsorily admitting him to hospital.

- Disagreement which reflected adversely on the judgement of the doctor, a professional colleague.

- Compulsion was only considered, and professional activity interfering in the Cawsons' quiet enjoyment of life occurred, because we did not have adequate resources. A day centre would have prevented the issue arising.

- We relied on and applied extra personal pressure to Mrs Cawson as a carer to compensate for our inadequate services. This was another example of exploitation of conventional caring roles of women in place of providing adequate services.

- We were considering compulsion to prevent Mr Cawson committing an act which is legal and which he is free to commit. The mandate for our action comes from an assumption that those concerned for general welfare, and perhaps the State, have a duty 'to do the right thing' even when the object of our help does not want it.

In another case, I was the field worker responsible for Corinne, a fifteen-year-old young woman in care, who became pregnant. After some discussion, medical advice and investigation and subsequently specialised counselling, she decided to have an abortion. This was considered legally and medically appropriate. I arranged for it. However, the residential care worker responsible for her, to whom she had been close, objected on religious principles. She tried to dissuade Corinne, refused to help her prepare emotionally and practically for the admission for the abortion and was hostile to her when she returned. In this case the following issues arose:

- Corinne had been involved in an illegal act (sexual intercourse below the age of sixteen years) and was planning to do something which some people consider immoral.

- The residential care worker acted morally from her point of view, but contrary to Corinne's expressed wishes and intentions and the needs that normally the worker would have tried to meet.

In yet another case, Clive, a fifteen-year-old boy subject to a supervision order for some minor offences, was failing to attend school. The head teacher asked me to take him into care since he was setting a bad example to other boys in the neighbourhood. However, Clive's younger brother, on whom because of proximity he would have had most influence as a bad example, was not playing truant. I was prepared to apply pressure to attend, to help Clive overcome the problems of resuming attendance, and have him taken by car, but this was not enough. The head teacher made a complaint to the social services director about my refusal to act in this way. He said it was interfering with school discipline. In this case, the issues which arose were:

- Clive's failure to comply with his legal responsibility to attend school.

- The conflict between the need not to take excessively punitive action against Clive and the possible damaging effects on the school and upon others.

- In general the conflict between a punitive and a helping approach.

- The law imposes requirements on a child on the assumption that education has value. This conflicted with Clive's view that school conferred little benefit for the future or interest at present.

Looking at these cases together, different sorts of value issue arise:

- Conflicts about the value we attach to various objectives.

- Some value conflicts affect clients' behaviour, such as having an abortion, not going to school, committing suicide. Others are concerned with workers' or other professionals' behaviour, such as not co-operating with the doctor's or head teacher's professional needs.

- Conflicts between the principled and the pragmatic. Issues which are to some people matters of value are to others merely pragmatic responses. The residential worker's religious principles clashed with my wish to avoid disruption for Corinne. The head teacher's valuation of education, discipline and punishment clashed with my judgement about the effectiveness and worth of punitive actions.

- The source of principles of behaviour or permission to act, such as religion, law, professional convention, public expectation.

Conflicts of view among people involved brought these issues to prominence. Disagreement raises the possibility of alternative views. If most of the time we are not questioned, many actions are informed by unconsidered value judgements. As a result, we often do not deal adequately with the conflicts within clients' own minds. A wider public sanctions social work but is not aware of many doubtful decisions. We would also not have dealt with issues which might concern them. For example, Mr Cawson, Corinne and Clive had to wrestle with the moral issues of, respectively, committing suicide, having an abortion and committing an offence. Many members of the public would not accept the right to commit suicide, have an abortion or avoid school as readily as we did. Following the professional practice principle of acceptance (see Chapter 3) might lead social workers to accept behaviour too readily which the general public or political élites would reject. They pay for and sanction social work powers and responsibilities. Should their views be considered, and if so how might their views be known?

Value issues, then, are important to understanding social work in two different ways:

- They illuminate social work practice because they are distillations of hard cases which show how in practice social workers deal with difficult situations.

●   They illuminate social work as a profession, by showing us how social workers typically think about difficult problems.

For example, a study by Horner and Whitbeck (1991) in the USA showed that social workers, personal values differed from those in the general population because they assigned more importance to interpersonal relationships, service to others, open-mindedness and the self-concept. They perceived professional value as differing because social work gave more importance to equality, working for the welfare of others and open-mindedness. Some evidence is offered here which supports the narrative offered in Chapters 3 and 4 of the nature of interpersonal social work and its values.

However, consistent with the approach of this book, I argue that these conventions do not display absolute standards of what is right or wrong in social work practice. They represent the view arrived at for now of a suitable approach to practice. Moreover, if they are only views which have become the occupational convention for the present, they might change or be renewed. If so, what appears to be a clear standard hides the fundamental uncertainty of the discourse that it, for the moment, represents.

Values dualities - maps of the minefield of practice

Bartlett (1970, p63) distinguished knowledge and values. Knowledge, in her view, refers to 'verifiable experience' presented in objective 'rigorous statements'; values refer to what we regard as desirable, what we prefer. They are qualitative judgements, which we cannot prove empirically.

She argues that some values eventually become knowledge since they are really hypotheses about society which are as yet unproved. When we show them to be true, she says, they become knowledge. However, as we saw in Chapter 3, the distinction cannot be so easily drawn, since much social work knowledge is ambiguous, and the contention that rigorous scientific knowledge of practice is possible is contentious and outside the reflexive-therapeutic mainstream of accounts of personal and interpersonal practice. Moreover, conversion to knowledge is impossible for values: they are inherently disputable. One of her examples is the idea that individuals in society are interdependent. She claims that this is seen as a value, but is self-evidently true, so should be regarded as knowledge. However, while many societies attach value to interdependence, others assert that individualism and independence are more valuable. Bartlett's account, therefore, is ethnocentric. She is in fact making a value statement, and can only regard it as convertible to knowledge within her own culture. She raises a political discourse about individuals' relationships with societies. This is an example of a central point in this chapter. Value statements always represent dualities and imply debates between value statements and their alternatives.

This means that the sets of rules which exist in the form, for example, of codes of ethics, cannot be rules for all time and every situation, but represent an agreed contemporary position. Apparently clear value statements guiding practice conceal wide variability and the availability of alternatives. Approaching social work values as a set of rules leads us to this view: we state a rule and then the exceptions. Taking a dualities approach, though, does not view the guidance as a prescription for action. Rather, it draws attention to where social workers have found that there are often issues to be addressed. A code of ethics is a map of the minefield of practice. Each of its simple prescriptions identifies a duality. It presents the convention and implies the opposite. Thus, for example, the rule of confidentiality presumes that we must also know about and understand openness. However, a dualities view does not imply conflict. As Imbrogno and Canda (1988) argue, taking a holistic view of anything implies taking into account its opposites.

Taking some social work principles and evaluating the dualities identify actual or potential debates within social work values - the last, confidentiality, is dealt with at greater length and with more-detailed argument to provide a fuller example of the argument. Among easily identified dualities is:

- individualisation - collectivisation.

Issues of individualisation raise issues of shared concern among clients with mutual interests. An example might be people on a housing estate who want to change their environment and how repairs to their houses are carried out. Individualising such issues is often inappropriate. Often, social workers must question the extent to which the work should be done individually or collectively and whether problems are individual or social in character.

- acceptance - reject dependency.

Acceptance implies that the worker will not reject clients and will agree to work with their problems, however distasteful they find them. Yet workers must also move towards terminating their work, since social work always seeks to avoid making clients dependent on social work.

- non-judgemental attitude - critical evaluation.

Social workers must act non-judgementally, so that clients can be open about every aspect of their problems, however unpleasant. On the other hand, social workers must always make evaluations on behalf of agencies and society, for example when protecting children from abuse. They have to be prepared to help clients accept the realities of their life and sometimes confront them with their behaviour, rather than concealing unpleasant realities.

- anti-discriminatory approach - avoid labelling and victimising.

Social work should also act without prejudice and seek to break down barriers caused by longstanding aspects of social structures which prejudice the interests of entire social groups. At the same time, we should avoid people in minority or oppressed groups from feeling picked out, avoid their being pressed to take on battles that they cannot afford or cope with and avoid treating them as always the victims instead of having some influence and freedom of action. Yet taking an anti-discriminatory approach sometimes involves focusing on aspects of life which label and victimise. Clients and workers often differ about the value of expressing or avoiding difference as part of anti-discriminatory practice.

- self-determination - rule-following or interdependent.

Many social situations require people to be more autonomous, but many require interdependence. In social situations, everyone follows rules and conventions of behaviour to some extent: to be self-determining implies partly that one can choose whether or not or how to be rule-following. Social workers have to consider the extent to which self-determination, rule-following or being interdependent is appropriate in a situation or whether a balance between them is appropriate.

- respect for persons - respect for community.

We must have respect for the needs of individuals, but we also need to respect the value of community support and involvement. At times wider social networks take priority over individuals.

- confidentiality - openness.

Many situations require confidentiality, but many require openness. Social workers must consider the degree to which each is appropriate and protection for people when confidentiality may lead to risk for individuals or openness lead to distress.

It is a widely accepted convention that workers should keep secret matters which are imparted to them in confidence during their work. However, there are widely accepted exceptions to this convention. We can breach confidentiality when life is at risk or perhaps where it benefits the client. Usually, though, we would not do so without consulting them, unless the matter is urgent. We might not bother consulting them if an unimportant breach was to another professional who would keep confidentiality.

Exceptions to an apparently clear rule involve in real life many complex judgements. In different settings, different levels of importance might be given to injunctions and exceptions. For example, I am involved with a child advocacy service, which represents the views of young people to agencies who are responsible for caring for them. The service has a principle of not telling the agencies anything without the permission of the young person unless a life is at risk. This is because it is the service's job to represent, and therefore to be on the side of, the young person, and only the young person, and their views. The agencies have difficulty with this view because they are accustomed, being usually concerned with the child's 'best interests', to being told matters of concern by other professionals, without the young person being consulted. This example underlines the actual variability of the application of the confidentiality convention in everyday practice.

To go further, the confidentiality convention is a cultural assumption, based on the individualism characteristic of most Western societies. In many societies, the accepted approach to dealing with an individual's problems is to involve friends, neighbours and community in the resolution. Silavwe (1995) gives an example of this while discussing social work in Zambia. Helping with a family problem there, would involve relying on the extended family, the tribe and elders. This places the authority for intervention clearly with the people around the person or people affected. Sometimes, it places the worker in a position of, in effect, giving consultation to others who are working to resolve issues in their community - genuine community care. Western social workers also involve family members or neighbours in therapy or care for someone in need, but usually they negotiate the degree of openness required. Once others are involved, though, we move into an open rather than a closed situation. This might have gains, in strength of support and understanding, authority to act and in commitment. We must balance these against losses in privacy, unpressured self-motivation and freedom of thought and action for worker and client.

Why are values presented as rules?
Exercising values in social work, therefore, often means making complex judgements in ambiguous situations. This suggests that more complex or alternative

- Values statements come from practice issues which social workers typically face.

They therefore come to be expressed as conventions or guidelines about suitable approaches to that practice, in a way that arises from the political situation within the occupational group. Gill (1992) argues that there are 'moral communities' which have arrived at an agreed position about the approach that they will take to issues which involve ethical decisions. These positions derive from tradition and shared experience in that group. Thus, while we cannot arrive at a particular view about a situation which all people would agree with, it may be possible to recognise an 'occupational ethic' with which many social workers would agree. We noted some evidence, above, that social workers at least in one country do view the world differently from the general public and that form such a moral community.

Also, values cannot be represented unless workers have faced and appreciated the relevant issues. For example, greater priority was given to anti-discriminatory principles in the 1980s. Such principles are consistent with ideas of respect for persons and acting in an unprejudiced way, which might come from the sort of principles we have been discussing. They came to prominence in the 1980s because of larger numbers of minority ethnic groups in some important Western societies. There was also rising social conflict around gender and especially ethnic minorities in countries formerly assumed to be ethnically homogeneous. Thus an implied and assumed value becomes explicit, and then is refined and debated. Until it became an issue, however, it had no chance to develop as a value. Who knows what other important professional values are lurking, unthought of, awaiting their period of topical relevance? Who knows what groups of people are being oppressed and ignored because the profession has not yet faced an issue about them?

- They are used for socialising and educational purposes.

Most workers do not refer to values regularly, and are only introduced to them specifically when in training. Thus, the codifications or texts contain a statement about the nature of social work. This is because specifying a particular resolution of the conflicts directs neophytes faced with the complexity of the dualities in a particular, usually helpful, way.

- They are political documents in the public domain used to present or represent social work in the ways that it would like to be understood in public.

Often this means that codes of ethics are presented as conventional, acceptable guidelines, rather than representing the possible complexities. As Watson (1985) argues, they offer an opportunity to the public to test out social work actions. They also alert workers and clients to areas where they might make complaints, or where adjudication about issues is needed. These last two reasons refer to the effect of value documents being in the public domain. Both their educational and political purposes lead to simplifications. So, dualities are too complex to present to neophytes and unsuitably complex for public debate, so a more simplified guideline is presented.

Values and social work

Aspects of social work's professional ethic can be found in various documents about social work values. Different texts within social work illuminate the 'intrinsic' ethic, that is, one claimed by insiders to the occupation. I look at accounts of ethical principles first and then formal statements of social work ethics contained in codes of ethics.

Several texts identify social work values, and offer some account of agreed positions, which is individualist-reformist in approach, since it focuses on moral behaviour between persons. Many of these (eg, Horne, 1987; Timms, 1983; Tolfree, 1980; Butrym, 1976; CCETSW 1976) are explicitly based on Biestek (1961 - see Chapter 3, p39-60). Some writers do not accept his practice-oriented principles, purposeful expression of feelings and controlled emotional involvement, as concerned with values.

'Respect for persons' also appears in these texts, CCETSW and Tolfree regarding it as pre-eminent or overarching. Respect for persons seems to present a purpose (social work seeks to respect people) or a description of the nature of social work (it is a characteristic of social work that its practice respects persons) rather than expressing guidance about what social workers should do. Downie and Telfer (1969) argue that respect for persons is an attitude towards others which leads to ways of treating others. It implies valuing others because they possess the fundamental characteristic of human nature, a rational will. Consequently, they can be self-determining and rule-following, that is, they can decide to act on their own or to follow social or legal rules, rather than acting independently. We must therefore value that person's own ends and the expression of their personality through their actions. Utilitarianism, that is, seeking the greatest good of the greatest number of people, appears to respect others' ends. However, in a complex society where people's ends conflict, we have to amend it by concerning ourselves also with equality and liberty. This would avoid valuing one person's ends excessively over another and restricting one person or group unreasonably in favour of the interests of another. By taking other people's ends seriously, we have to accept their moral responsibility for their actions, their capacity to use their freewill and, if appropriate, to follow rules. We should act and treat others accordingly.

The idea of respect for persons is helpful in the sense that it gives some overall guidance for the ways we should behave towards others. As Ragg (1980) argues, it allows us to place a moral approach to other human beings at the centre of what we do. It is, he says, not an instrument of work, but a moral principle of it. However, he claims that it is wrong to place the responsibility of society in providing resources as an equally or more-important moral responsibility. This view neglects the importance of equality and freedom as balancing factors for respect for persons in a complex society.

The importance of equality and freedom as social values in the fundamentally individualistic ethic of respect for persons suggests that we should include notions of social justice among social work's objectives. Socialist-collectivist views of social work ethics emphasise collective rather than individual human rights. Accounts of rights and social justice include expressions of values which might have applicability to social work. For example, reviewing the law in freedom and individual rights, Robertson (1993) focuses on the right not to have personal liberty unreasonably restricted by improper constraints or by being forced to speak. Applying these ideas to social work, we might seek to prevent imprisonment of young, elderly or mentally ill people through social work powers or oppressive questioning of clients in child abuse investigations. Other rights concern the right to protest and complain (but not offensively), rights to privacy, to social workers not having unnecessary secrets from clients, being fair in their regulation of clients' behaviour (or of services, as when social workers inspect elderly people's homes) freedom of expression, of movement, from undue control and from discrimination. The Commission on Social Justice (1994) refers to positive rights: to have an investment in our education, to have opportunities to work and achieve other personal goals, to have security of income and if we are ill, and to accept responsibility for ourselves to others to whom we have a duty and more widely to having a 'good' society.

The individualistic moral principles derived from casework reflecting the importance of respect for persons do not, therefore, cover the wider social, collectivist objectives of social work. Possible issues which might be covered are considered below, in the section 'Wider social principles'.

However, individualistic and collectivist elements appear in formal statements of social work values contained in codes of ethics. Table 4.1 compares some different social work codes (in summary). The Table is based on the British Code (BASW, 1988) and the others are compared with it. The American Code (NASW, 1980) is much the most comprehensive, and also covers matters relating to private practice, such as setting fees, which reflects the practice situation in the USA. The Dutch Code (Netherlands Committee on Professional Questions Regarding Social Work, 1987) is given as a sample of European Codes. The Residential Care Association's Code of Practice (Beddoe, 1980) is included to give a comparison which focuses on the residential and group aspect of social work, even though it is not particularly widely disseminated and was devised for an organisation which has now broadened its focus.

Many aspects of these codes' statements reflect both interpersonal ethics and social objectives. These include injunctions against discrimination, and promoting advocacy or campaigning to inform governments of their 'contribution to hardship'. Positive objectives include increasing clients' choice, promoting diversity and helping clients obtain appropriate services. Also included are professional objectives such as continuing education and self-development and seeking agencies that allow ethical practice. Some guidelines are also offered to help in professional behaviour, such as requirements to co-operate with others, balancing duty to the agency against duty to the client and giving priority to professional over personal interests. These are very much more detailed in the RCA Code. There is a compromise between comprehensiveness and concision. If a code cannot cover everything, where is it best to stop?

Most of these codes express in greater or lesser detail the kinds of value commitments considered above. However, some are concerned much more strongly with the maintenance and protection of the profession: this is particularly so of the American Code. Only the Dutch Code deals specifically with the issue of the worker's religious or personal principles and the need to leave the client free to choose. Both these instances of difference derive from responses to needs in the particular countries. The American Code reflects a greater degree of private practice and independent accreditation of workers, while Dutch society and social agencies are rather less secular than British and American societies. Some differences result from the period in which they were written. The American and British focus on (respectively) 'diversity' or 'anti-discrimination' is a product of the concerns of the 1980s in Britain which affected the USA rather earlier. It had not yet had impact in Britain when the RCA Code was being written, even though this has the same date as the American Code.

Table 4.1: Social work codes of ethics compared

BASW (1988)	RCA (Beddoe, 1980)
6 value & dignity of human beings irrespective of origin, race, status, sex, sexual orientation, age, disability, belief, contribution to society; encourage self-realisation; 10iii no selective acts out of prejudice; no tolerance of discriminatory actions; do not deny difference	1i value and dignity irrespective of origin, status, sex, age, belief, contribution to society
7 enhance human well-being; relieve & prevent hardship, suffering; help individuals, families, groups, communities; operate services, contribute to social planning & action; practice based on systematic knowledge and experience	
8 use integrity, skill; increase own & professions knowledge, skill; evaluate methods & policies in light of changing needs; co-operate with other professions	3.1g honesty about own feelings, give time to discuss personal reactions; 3.2a form relationships so that residents can trust worker; b explain things to resident to develop understanding and self-control; c improve resident's self-esteem; d take interest in residents personal interests
9 bring to attention ways government, society or agencies create or contribute to hardship; balance duty to agency with duty to client; respect rights of powerless clients	3 1f promote group acceptance and understanding of agency aims

NASW (1980)	**Netherlands (1987)**
IIF3 do not condone, collaborate or facilitate in discrimination on . . . any preference, personal characteristic or status; VIP1 prevent and eliminate discrimination; VIP4 promote conditions which encourage respect for diversity	8 respect client; 10 equally willing to help any client
IC2 prevent inhumane or discriminatory practices; IIF1 serve with devotion, best possible skill; IIG foster client self-determination IIG3 do not violate or diminish clients' rights; IVL3 prevent and remove discrimination in agency's employment practices; VIP5 provide services in public emergencies	1 main duty is assistance to client; 9 offer help according to agency objectives and community needs
IA1 maintain high standards of personal conduct as worker; 2 do not participate in dishonesty etc; ID act with integrity and impartiality; 1 resist pressures against discretion and impartiality; 2; IIF2 do not exploit professional relationships for personal gain; 4 avoid relationships conflicting with clients' interests; 5 no sexual activities with clients; 9 end services no longer needed; 10 do not end services too quickly; 11 inform clients if services may be interrupted or ended; VO1 base practice on recognised knowledge; 2 examine and keep in touch with emerging knowledge. 3 contribute to knowledge; VIP6 promote change to improve social conditions, social justice; encourage public participation in social policy-making	6 work in best possible way
IVL stick to commitments to employers; 1 work to improve agency's practices and policies; 2 do not work for or place students with agencies in dispute with professional bodies; scrupulous with agency resources	2 contribute to fulfilling agency tasks; 21 loyal in acheiving aims and developing policy of agency; 23 justify actions to management if required

BASW (1988)	**RCA (Beddoe, 1980)**
10i contribute to policy; use knowledge, skills, experience for benefit of all; refuse dehumanising & discriminatory policies	1viii refuse abuse of skills; 1x develop better understanding of contribution of residential care;
10ii respect clients, safeguard dignity, individuality, rights	1iii recognise individuality; ensure clients receive basic human rights and justice; 3.1i, 3.2 develop and implement plan for residents bearing in mind agency's aims and group needs; 4.3a appreciate value of positive risk for clients; b take initiative in decision-making
10iv help clients increase choice and power	1ii self-determination, able to choose within the law and social norms; 3.1 provide stimulating environment providing care, nurture and promoting residents' well-being; a physical needs; b feeling of worth, dignity; c maintain and promote personal development; h develop involvement in group life; 4.3 stimulating environment means allowing choice and acceptance of risks
10v no rejection of client or loss of concern, even where protecting them or others	1iv accept and value client because of inherent worth; 3.1d professional accepting respectful relationship; e promote group acceptance of individual behaviour
10vi professional responsibility priority over personal interest	1vi balance needs of worker and residents

NASW (1980)	Netherlands (1987)
IIIJ1 cooperate with colleagues to promote professional interests and concerns; K1 do not solicit colleagues clients; do not take on professional responsibilities for another's client without consultation; 3 treat temporary or emergency clients the same as own clients; VN2 support policy change	22 notify management of data to inform policy
VM uphold and advance profession; 1 protect and enhance, responsible and vigorous in discussion and criticism; VN1 give time and effort to promote respect for social work	
	8 respect client's personality; 13 explain value base and leave client free to decide
VIP2 ensure all clients have access to required services; 3 expand choice and opportunity	14 always act with cooperation and knowledge of client; 15 if client unable to understand, justify actions
IC professional obligations primary; IIF primary responsibility to clients; III set fees fairly; 1 do not accept reward for making or receiving a referral	

BASW (1988)	**RCA (Beddoe, 1980)**
10vii continue education and training; responsibility for service	4.2c recognise own strengths and weaknesses and use team to support; g particpate in research and knowledge development; h pursue learning opportunities
10viii collaborate in clients' interest	1ix share relevant information with people who need to know; 3.2 implement plans in co-operation; 3.2 keep colleagues informed; 3.3 maintain and increase liaison with other agencies; a regularly; b value clients' family and friends; c support resident in family changes; d attend relevant meetings; e become involved with family and friends; f contact in resident's community; g contact with relevant official bodies; 4.3c,d keep colleagues informed where risk-taking occurs
	4 residential work is teamwork; 4.2a support colleagues and be supported; b participate in meetings etc; d openess about own and colleagues actions; 4.3e seek management approval and support where risk-taking occurs
	4.1 provide full information for applicants for posts; 4.2e use supervision, ask for help when needed; f participate in and learn from job appraisal
10ix make clear whether public actions are personal or for an organisation	

NASW (1980)	Netherlands (1987)
IB become and remain proficient; 1 accept responsibility only if competent; 2 do not misrepresent qualifications; IC1 retain responsibility for service.	8 worker responsible for choice of actions
IIIJ8 treat other professionals with same respect as social workers	4 understand, value other professions; 5 work with volunteers; 19 cooperate in clients' interests if not restrained by confidentiality
IIIJ treat colleagues with respect, courtesy, fairness, good faith; 4 findings, views and qualifications of colleagues; 5 act considerately for colleague whom worker replaces or is replaced by; 6 do not obtain advancement by exploiting colleague's dispute with employers; 7 seek arbitration where disputes between colleagues must be resolved	24 solidarity with professional colleagues
IIF9 use supervision in best interest of clients; IIIJ9 orderly and explicit arrangements for supervision; 10 fair, clear criteria if employing and evaluating others; 11 share evaluations with the person evaluated	26 offer knowledge and experience to colleagues; compare opinions with others
IA3 distinguish private from professional statements	
	7 avoid harming profession's image
VM2 act through appropriate channels against colleagues' unethical behaviour; prevent unauthorised and unqualified practice; 4 do not misrepresent qualifications or service	27 if serious concern unresolved about colleague's behaviour, complain to disciplinary committee

BASW (1988)	**RCA (Beddoe, 1980)**
10x help clients obtain entitlements in an ethnically & culturally appropriate service; promote diversity	3.2e promote participation by having clear agreements
10xi information given for one purpose not to be used in another; respect privacy	1v preserve secret information
10xii work for agencies which allow workers to accept ethical obligations	2 ensure agency has specific statement of aims which meets its responsibilities

Table 4.1 Codes of Ethics compared

NASW (1980)

Netherlands (1987)

IIF6 provide accurate and complete information about services available; 7 tell clients of rights, risks opportunities, obligations

11 explain methods and policies to client; explain refusal of service

IE4 discuss case or service research only with those entitled to know; 5 research information about individuals confidential; IIH respect privacy and confidentiality; 1 share confidential information without consent only for compelling reasons; 2 inform clients about limits of confidentiality; 3 when clients have access to records, protect confidentiality of others; gain informed consent before video or audio taping 3rd party observation; IIIJ2 respect colleagues confidence

3, 17 secrecy of information deriving from social work function, except to protect people; 18 client may not have sole right to permit disclosure; 19 only pass on necessary information; 20 if a witness in court of law, worker must decide what must be withheld

16 only gather necessary information

IIJ3 create and maintain conditions facilitating ethical and competent practice

IE study and research according to proper conventions; 1 consider human consequences; 2 consent; 3 protect subjects from harm; 6 take credit for work done, give appropriate credit

One alternative approach to presenting a code practice is Galper's (1975, pp224-7) attempt to create a Code of Ethics for radical workers. This focuses much more strongly than conventional codes on collectivist assumptions of seeking the general welfare, rather than that of individuals' and changing society in order to achieve it.

Ways of looking at values
So far, I have been examining social work values within one system of thought, which I might describe as secular logic. That is, the values are not based on religion, but come from rational argument and debate about the nature of society. These derive from social workers' experiences of the issues that they need to face in their occupations. We may also identify other ways of looking at different kinds of values. The CCETSW Working Party (1976, pp20-26), for example, explores cultural traditions which might influence views of social work values, including religious systems of thought like Christianity and Zen Buddhism, social theories and ideologies like Marxism and liberalism, psychological theories of human nature such as psychoanalysis and behavioural or mechanistic views and philosophical systems of thought such as existentialism. We could easily identify other possibilities, for example Muslim or Hindu traditions. Not all of these are monolithic. For example, within both Christian and Muslim philosophies fundamentalist and more liberal approaches to values exist, which would offer different views of value systems. Such systems of thought can influence whole societies and cultures and colour how people react to issues and social expectations. They can be important to particular groups and operate as a set of assumptions for a moral community, which others might not share or might even find difficult to understand. The CCETSW group, for example, argues that Zen Buddhism requires an approach to the development of consciousness which is antipathetic to Western culture and thus hard to appreciate for Western social workers.

Even within a secular view of ethics, there are a variety of views of the basis of ethical principles. Reviewing these while considering the needs of biomedical activities, Beauchamp and Childress (1994) identify eight different kinds of principles which might be the origins of relevant sets of principles:

- Utilitarianism - Is based on the consequences of our actions for others. The aim might be to achieve the most favourable outcome for the most people, or for the most important or highest priority people - 'the greatest happiness of the greatest number'.

- Kantianism - Is based on obligations to others. The aim is to meet promises that you make or reasonable expectations from others - 'do as you would be done by'.

- Character ethics - Identifies 'good' people as having the moral virtues of someone who acts from proper motives. Examples are: acting with respect, beneficently and with fairness. Ordinary standards set rules of obligation for most purposes such as truthfulness, confidentiality, respect for privacy and faithfulness. Exceptional standards set ideals of action which all might aim at but sometimes do not achieve, such as being truthful or always respecting confidentiality.

- Liberal individualism - Is based on individuals' rights to pursue their own interests and make claims on others. They follow systems of rules that allow us to be clear about what people's due is and to make the necessary claims. Rights are balanced by communal interests, and are usually associated with obligations, since if someone else has a right, we have an obligation to meet it. Our obligations vary: we do not have to meet all rights. Some, though, such as justice, are 'perfect' in the sense that we could not avoid giving someone justice, whatever the other consequences.

- Communitarianism - Relates to ethics based on the good of the community, social objectives, traditions and the idea that people should co-operate with one another. Giving importance to these ideas rejects individualism, autonomy and rights of individuals, focusing instead the value of a well-structured community life and the importance of social practices like good parenting, teaching and healing. Some would argue that these should always supersede individual rights or ethics based on individual need.

- Ethics of care - Derives from the idea that true ethics come from attachment to others in relationships, rather than detached assessmentsof benefits to society (communitarianism) or to other individuals (liberal individualism or utilitarianism). Ideas such as sympathy, compassion, fidelity and love bind us to act ethically in relation to other people in groups and individually. Such views are related to feminist analyses (eg Gilligan, 1982) which argue that women have a particular 'voice' in human relationships, persuing such ethics, which is lost in male analyses of rights and duties.

- Casuistic views - Casuistry argues that decisions can only be made pragmatically by a close examination of the particular circumstances and whom they affect. The approach is like that of the British and American Common Law which relies on building up a response to situations through understanding precedents and distinguishing the details of the present situation from what people have done in the past. This approach particularly rejects systems of rules or principles as the basis for ethical decisions. Rather, sets of principles might emerge from the consistent application of casuistry over a period. This is the way codes of ethics or professional standards of behaviour are built up.

● Common morality theories - Principles are checked against pre-existing 'commonsense' ideas of what is moral.

Social workers sometimes use or relate to each of these approaches to setting ethical standards, and combine them in different ways. Social work practice in Western countries often refers to individualism, because it seeks the best for individuals, and casuistry because individualisation requires it to distinguish every case from every other and come to the right approach for each. Because of its commitment to relationship as the basis for interpersonal work, social work ethics are particularly conscious of the ethics of care. Much idealistic social work writing assumes the emotional commitment to care and being a 'virtuous person' (Imre, 1989). It also values character ethics: reflexive-therapeutic and artistic approaches to social work particularly emphasise this ethical stance. On the other hand, we have seen that socialist-collectivist views of social work look to overall social purposes. This combines an approach to rights and obligations with social and individual equality and justice.

Combining such different ethical frameworks also leads to practical difficulties. This has led some writers to distinguish between rights to develop personal growth and rights to be treated equally with others. Weale (1978), for example, distinguishes between formal or procedural equality, where people are treated fairly, and substantive equality, where outcomes are fair. Thus Stevenson (1973) argues for social security claimants that they need, and should be entitled to receive, the highest possible allowance, should be helped by professionals to do so (creative justice), and should also be treated equally with others (proportional justice). Treating large numbers equally might make the system so expensive that the optimum allowance for some might be lost. On the other hand, giving a few very high allowances for meeting their needs might lead to wide inequalities of allowance. This sort of conflict is particularly likely to arise where limited resources or opportunities mean that not all needs can be met. So, as we have seen, where there is a market situation and rationing, creative or substantive justice may be impossible for most people because there are insufficient resources, but procedural or proportional justice will fairly distribute the inadequate resources.

Social work value systems contain many conflicting elements and principles, many of which cannot easily be combined into one general set of principles. I have argued that many of them are dualities, areas of debate which alert us to where issues exist for social work, rather than resolving those issues for us. How, then, should we regard the worth of the principles explored above as mainstream social work values? I argue that a wider range of alternative or different formulations is possible, and I do so from three points of view. First, I examine alternative types of philosophical principle which may be found in social work. Then, I explore systems of principle in areas within which social work operates. Finally, I look at ethical systems in related occupational groups: medicine, nursing, counselling and teaching.

Alternative philosophical principles

So far, I have been writing as though all values are of a similar kind. Generally, works on social work values concern themselves with moral values, that is, behaviour which we value because we see it as virtuous. However, we may recognise other possibilities. For instance, the CCETSW Working Party (1976, p14) comments: 'Although economic, aesthetic and other forms of value influence moral values, it was agreed that for our purposes moral values were the most important.' This priority might not have been so obvious after the 1980s, in which economic values gained greater political and social importance. Economic values represent a debate about what importance we give to needs for subsistence and ways of meeting those needs, whether by individualistic competition or by co-operation. At least some supporters of conservative Thatcherite and Reaganomic values might argue that economic value was a prerequisite to the pursuit of other values, since contributing to economic value within society is crucial to its continuance. Restoring the economic viability of an individual or family by providing or supporting someone in getting employment or achieving the highest level of income support is more important than welfare needs such as good parent-child relationships. Interpersonal welfare might follow from success in meeting economic welfare needs. This is the argument behind giving priority to basic human needs, through welfare rights services, or through alleviation of hunger and economic development in Third World countries.

Reamer (1993), reviewing the philosophical foundations of social work, identifies political and moral philosophy, logic, epistemology and aesthetics as relevant.

Political philosophy concerns issues such as the role and limitations of the State, government and the private and voluntary sectors in providing social welfare services. It also covers different types of fairness among people receiving services, their rights as citizens and consumers. These have practice implications, and decisions about them affect approaches to social work, but they are mainly concerned with the level of aims. Other aspects of political philosophy might equally well have relevance to the purpose, nature and activity of social work. Pursuing social welfare through such activities as social work might be seen as a very low priority or a subsidiary purpose to social objectives such as these. Discussing political philosophy in relation to social work helps us understand the nature of social welfare, justice and equality as objectives in social work. It also raises the issue of the role of social work in wider political objectives such as the pursuit of peace and law and order which might otherwise seem distant from daily social work practice.

Logic, according to Reamer (1993), is another important area of philosophy which has importance for understanding social work. It is concerned with ways of distinguishing good from bad reasoning. Social workers use reasoning all the time in their interpersonal activity. They try to understand complex social situations and the reasons for them, and apply interventions in ways which will lead to change. They identify appropriate evidence and reason from it what explanations of behaviour and situations might fit. Then they have to reason about which response to their understanding would achieve appropriate ends. Clear evidence about behaviour and social situations is often impossible to obtain, and arguments have to be concerned with possibilities and options. We might equally argue that they should learn the skills of rhetoric (presenting effective arguments) to help them use their capacity to think logically. Social workers are also concerned with the logic of their clients' behaviour. They might have to judge whether a client is telling the truth, for example, by judging their behaviour against what they say. In looking at communication in Chapter 3, we saw how selective perceptions and misinterpretation of communications can inhibit the effectiveness of communication. This is another situation in which logic is necessary to being able to judge, through illogical responses, when communication has gone wrong.

For related reasons, epistemology is also important. This is the study of knowledge and how it is acquired and communicated. How do we 'know' about clients and their situations, and how much is that knowledge or supposition? Social workers use observation, written evidence, judgements by others and many other sorts of knowledge, but may not be careful enough about judging the validity of the evidence produced. Often, for example, people give too much credence to written or documentary evidence when it conflicts with other information they might have.

Reamer (1993) and the CCETSW Working Party (1976) both propose aesthetics as a valid basis for values. This may seem surprising because we are accustomed to seeing social work as scientific and logical rather than as concerned with artistic judgement. However, many writers such as England (1986) and Munson (1993) have discussed social work as an art rather than as a science. Munson usefully points out that it is a calumny on the study of the arts to suggest that science has a monopoly of reasoned argument and the use of evidence. In fact, there are established rules for making judgements and having debates through criticism about what is 'good' and 'bad' art or literature. Referring to some of this literature, Reamer (1993, pp161-2) argues that art is a body of knowledge and skill which is organised to create changes in various media with an identifiable outcome. The complexities of the media (paint and canvas, stone, words in relation to a fictional theme, notes in relation to a musical theme) are the basis for the selection of various reactions by the artist to it which lead to the particular outcome, which is then subject to reactions by observers. The observers are themselves, together with the whole enterprise, affected by the society in which the artist, the art and the observation take place. I have rephrased this literature somewhat to show how similar this sort of account of art is to the accounts of social work which we have been exploring. As with art, a piece of social work might be, and sometimes is, criticised in relation to how social workers have responded to the media of the social situation they are dealing with - have they missed crucial points, for example? Equally, outcomes are criticised - is the new social situation after the worker's intervention to be valued?: and so are processes - did the social worker help the client to feel comfortable and secure in their interactions?

Social work is artistic in other ways than in making an analogy between art and social work activities as a whole. It could be argued that many judgements made by social workers are artistic in character. England (1986, p99) shows how social workers use such a term as 'beautiful' or 'pleasing' to describe successful pieces of work. Judgements about whether to act to deal with particular kinds of behaviour may be aesthetic. Unattractive behaviour in a mentally ill person or dribbling because of a disability may press us to deal with this as a problem, but it may only be a problem because the behaviour is unattractive to us and to others. Social workers may make judgements about whether clients keep house well, or about the environment in which they live based on aesthetic judgements. I have often seen aesthetic comments like 'drab decorations', 'unkempt hair', 'unmatched, ill-fitting clothing' or 'a dismal housing estate' in formal reports.

So, moral values are not the only relevant ones to social work. In many social work judgements, social values deriving from economy, politics, logic, epistemology and aesthetics have a major impact on how we describe and evaluate the practice, purpose and nature of social work. Yet these are almost wholly absent from texts about social work values.

Wider social principles
Social work operates within the general system of social provision in any country. Accounts exist of some conflicting principles which underlie such social provision. These offer some comparisons with social work ethics.

Accounts of the 'welfare state' and of 'welfare' are helpful since social work is historically a product of the development of social services provided by states. Social workers are bound up in a system of welfare services which are primarily managed or enabled by state organisational structures. Voluntary and private services developed in reaction to state provision or the absence of it. Meanings of welfare enable us to examine different ways of looking at objectives and not just the possible content of them. Two examples of accounts of the welfare state and welfare are as follows.

Spicker (1988) identifies seven aspects of the welfare state:

- *Democracy* assumes that people govern themselves, through a voted majority or consensus, and minorities are protected by being given rights. Self-determination is the main underlying principle, and this has led to an emphasis on participation by the governed. Taking this sort of social objective, ethical social work would promote participation by people in society and in making decisions which affect them.

- *Power* is distributed or retained by welfare, and all, institutions. They therefore control clients of services, but they also offer opportunities for transferring power, through participation. This is a central tension in social work, which is considered further in Chapters 5 and 6.

- *Inequality* - Welfare often comes from control over resources, but this is distributed unequally. Social improvement implies redistributing resources and therefore reducing inequality. Increasing everyone's resources improves the position of people with fewer resources, but does not give them greater control over the total of resources in a society. Ethical social work would reduce inequalities by its actions.

- *Equality* - Promoting equality as opposed to reducing inequality of treatment, of opportunity or of outcomes seeks to put people in the same position as others. This might apply to individuals or to groups Ethical social work would enhance equality.

- *Social justice* - Welfare should be distributed proportionately to accepted criteria, such as needs, deserts, work and so on. We may not agree about the criteria or what should be distributed (eg should it be money or or should it be rights to apply for a service even though one may not know about it). Even so, ethical social work would try to respond to clients fairly according to various criteria.

- *Structural change* - Social welfare services might seek to change society. But how should the changes be chosen? This might be based on some ideal model of what a society should be like, by making changes which seem positive at the time and adding them togethe (incremental change) or by following some ethical principles.

We cannot define our social objectives simply by referring to some of these general concepts. Sometimes, we can identify practical consequences of accepting such purposes. For example, participation might enhance democracy. However, this is a distant connection. It requires us to assume that, by participating, people actually become more self-governing. But inequalities, injustices and power relations might interfere with using participation in this way. Alternatively, we might argue that participation in social work and the social services offers experience which will enable and enthuse people for greater democratic participation elsewhere. Debates about such issues allow us to consider how practice might contribute to ethical objectives.

These objectives are themselves in dispute. There are many different criteria and ideas about appropriate objectives for empowerment, or promoting equality and justice. A well-known analysis of types of welfare by George and Wilding (1984, 1994) provides an alternative approach concerned with different political positions about welfare rather than different objectives of a welfare state:

- *Anti-collectivist or the 'New Right' approaches* emphasise individual freedom within a philosophy of liberal individualism. People should be free with minimal coercion to pursue their economic and social well being as they think fit, with minimal state interference.

- *Reluctant collectivists or the 'Middle Way' approaches* want to maximise individual freedom, but insist that this should be regulated to reduce disadvantages arising from inequalities.

- *Fabian or democratic socialist or 'reformist' approaches* emphasise the value of state welfare services developed through democratic activity by working class or oppressed groups as a response to the inequalities of capitalist societies.

- *Marxist approaches* emphasise the struggle to replace capitalism by a democratic, industrialised society. The State would be allied to popular control of the means of production through such systems as co-operatives, national planning and widely distributed ownership of industry. This would reduce inequality and the concentration of wealth in a few hands.

● *Feminist approaches* emphasise that welfare is about women's positions in society, but we have neglected this because we design services from a men's perspective. Welfare should recognise obstacles to meeting women's important needs and reconstruct gender relationships so that services respond differently but equally and appropriately to the needs of both men and women.

● *Green approaches*, contrary particularly to New Right and Marxist approaches, propose that societies should not continue to seek greater consumption and economic growth. They should replace this with a wider definition of appropriate activity using ecological resources more carefully, living closer to Nature and fragmenting centralised states into more co-operative forms of living. Welfare would provide a basic level of support as part of a contract for active involvement in maintaining a more balanced form of economy.

The welfare state is a discourse among these different views. Nearly all these accounts of the welfare state and of welfare are concerned with freedom, inequality, injustice and power. It seems, then, that social work debates about what constitutes social improvement must circle around the extent to which and the ways in which social work promotes or does not promote these aspects of social life. However, Parton (1994b, p108) suggests that modern societies raise the question of control over choice and decision-making as an important social principle. In modern social work there appears to be a movement away from choice and consent towards a more authoritarian and controlling practice (Thomas and Forbes, 1989). Siporin (1989) also criticises rights-based social work approaches. He argues that most interpersonal social work is concerned with helping people with moral dilemmas, such as those discussed at the beginning of this Chapter. In this context moral or virtuous person ideas are more useful than consideration of rights or political objectives. Such analyses of social work as being concerned with the beautiful, the true and the good (Howe, 1994, Parton 1994a) are also typical of post-modern views, and the dominant reflexive-therapeutic approach of much personal and interpersonal social work. Rights-based and political ideas such as these form their objectives within which the different ethical stances identified above can operate. Concerned as they are with social objectives, they are more characteristic of socialist-collectivist approaches to social work.

Ethics in related occupations

Our next approach to evaluating social work's ethical discourse involves examining comparatives for social work values outside social work. I look here at four related occupational groups: medicine, nursing, counselling, and teaching. I have chosen these for the following reasons. Medicine is considered almost the archetype of professions. Nursing, counselling and teaching are perhaps occupational groups aspiring to professional status, but without the achieved acceptance of this status that medicine enjoys. All these groups work closely with social work, and might therefore be expected to have standards which are relevant enough to provide sensible comparatives. There are a variety of statements of medical ethics and many analyses. I examine three well-established formal statements with an international credibility and then two texts, one American and one British, which have been recently published, but have gained acceptance through many previous editions. I look at nursing and counselling more briefly, based on the codes published recently by the United Kingdom Central Council on Nursing, Midwifery and Health Visiting (UKCC) and the British Association for Counselling (BAC). These are up-to-date examples which reflect trends throughout these occupations and would be recognisable in other countries where these occupational groups exist. Colleagues in teacher education were only able to identify for me an elderly code of ethics produced by a British trade union, and I also examined an American Code produced by the National Education Association (NEA, 1975). This perhaps expresses the importance given in this occupational group to the purposes of education, on which there is an extensive literature, and the pragmatics of pedagogy, rather than values in practice. From this, it would be possible to argue that it is conceivable to pursue a recognisably professional activity without necessarily focusing on moral values in the way that social work does.

The Hippocratic Oath for doctors is often mentioned as a basis for medical ethics. This comprises six elements.

- *Respect for the traditions and membership of the profession:* 'to consider dear to me . . . him who taught me this art . . . to impart to . . . the disciples who have enrolled themselves and have agreed to the rules of the profession, but to these alone, the precepts and the instruction.'

- *Acting for the good of patients and doing no harm:* 'I will prescribe the regimen for the good of my patients according to my ability and my judgement and never do any harm to anyone.'

- *Refusing to do the 'immoral' whatever the incentive*: 'To please no one will I prescribe a deadly drug, nor give advice which may cause his death. Nor will I . . . procure abortion.'

- *Maintaining high standards of general conduct* : '. . . I will preserve the purity of my life and my art . . . In every house where I come I will enter only for the good of my patients, keeping myself far from all intentional ill-doing and all seduction, and especially from the pleasures of love with women or with men.'

- *Not acting outside competence*: 'I will not cut for stone, even for patients in whom the disease is manifest; I will leave this operation to be performed by practitioners (specialist in this art).'

- *Maintaining confidentiality and discretion*: 'All that may come to my knowledge in the exercise of my profession or outside of my profession or in daily commerce with men, which ought not to be spread abroad, I will keep secret and never reveal.' (Mason and McCall Smith, 1994, App. A).

A noticeable thing about this formulation of an ethical code is that it requires generally high standards of behaviour throughout life. With the status of profession goes general probity, not only good behaviour in professional activities. Another crucial point is the requirement both to do good and not to do harm to patients; allied to this is the requirement to keep within one's competence, and to act according to one's ability and judgement. This recognises that not all professionals are the same, or are equally competent: the requirement is, however, to recognise one's limitations and restrict oneself accordingly. Another comment is that some acts are identified as improper (abortion, murder) and must be avoided. I take this to be an example of an injunction which requires the professional to respect widely-held moral limits.

Quaint though it is in presentation and language, this code is not too distant from modern formulations of medical ethics. The Declaration of Geneva, amended last in 1968, (Mason and McCall Smith, 1994, App. B), requires the doctor '. . . to consecrate my life to the service of humanity . . . give my teachers the respect and gratitude which is their due . . . practise . . . with conscience and dignity . . . maintain . . . the honour and the noble traditions of the medical profession. My colleagues will be my brothers.' 'The health of the patient will be my first consideration; I will respect the secrets which are confided in me . . . I will not permit considerations of religion, nationality, race, party politics or social standing to intervene between my duty and my patient; I will maintain the utmost respect for human life . . . I will not use my medical knowledge contrary to the laws of human-ity.' The International Code of Medical Ethics (Mason and McCall Smith, 1994, App. C) divides responsibilities into three: duties of doctors in general (ie.'always maintain the highest standards of professional conduct . . . testify only to that which he has personally verified'), to the sick (eg 'bear in mind the obligation of preserv-ing human life . . . a doctor owes to his patient complete loyalty and all the resources of his science. Whenever an examination or treatment is beyond his capacity he should summon another doctor who has the necessary ability') and to each other (eg 'behave to his colleagues as he would have them behave to him').

Beauchamp and Childress (1994) explore the principles which lie behind 'bio-medical ethics' as follows:

- *Nonmaleficence* - not doing harm. Among the issues that doctors face are deciding which treatments are optional and which are required; making a distinction between killing someone and letting them die and how far they should make decisions for patients who are unable to make them for themselves.

- *Beneficence* - doing good. Among the issues that doctors face are deciding how much good they must do. Is it 'everything possible' or 'just enough'? They must decide whether doing good interferes with patients' rights to autonomy and deciding for themselves . This is an issue in mental health legislation for compulsorily admitting people to hospital contrary to their freedom but possibly for their good since they can receive treatment. Benefits must be balanced against costs and risks and considering the quality of life obtained after some action.

- *Justice* - being fair. Among the issues for doctors here are giving people opportunities to use medical help against rationing its availability so they can give enough to be effective and enough people can receive it. Problems of rationing scarce or expensive treatments arise from this.

- *Maintaining professional relationships with patients.* Among the principles which seem relevant are veracity (being honest and open), privacy (not interfering unnecessarily), confidentiality, and fidelity (maintaining 'good faith' in keeping promises, responsibilities and relationships even when there are difficulties).

- *Maintaining ideals and virtues.* Four important virtues are: *Compassion* - '. . . combining an attitude of active regard for another's

- welfare with an imaginative awareness and emotional response of deep sympathy, tenderness and discomfort at the other person's . . . misfortune or suffering' (Beauchamp and Childress, 1994, p466).

- *Discernment* - '. . . sensitive insight involving acute judgement and understanding...decisive action' (Beauchamp and Childress, 1994, p 468). This involves making judgements without being affected by irrelevant factors, such as fears or emotional attachments.

- *Trustworthiness* - '. . .a confident belief in a reliance upon the ability and moral character of another person . . . that another will act with the right motives in accord with moral norms' (Beauchamp and Childress, 1994, p469).

- *Integrity* - '. . . a coherent integration of aspects of the self - emotions, aspirations, knowledge etc. - so that each complements and does not frustrate the others . . . the character trait of being faithful to moral values and standing up in their defense. . .' (Beauchamp and Childress, 1994, p471).

Many of these ideas are present in social work, as principles of practice. For example, many ideas within the ideals and virtues just considered relate to the principles of effective relationships such as congruence, genuineness, acceptance and empathy. However, here they are considered morally valuable behaviour, not simply effective or useful behaviour. Some of them appear in the over-arching social work ideal of respect for others. Beauchamp and Childress's (1994) account is impressively clear about difficult concepts of moral behaviour.

We can sum up this account of some aspects of medical ethics by identifying the emphasis given to general moral behaviour and integrity, and also to appropriate behaviour within professional activity. This approach seeks generally good standards of behaviour, of virtues and ideals, in life, which would extend also to professional life. Some of these formulations require virtuous behaviour. The worker must consider in each instance what this might mean, rather than the rule-bound behaviour implied by some social work codes. This accepts the importance of using codes as a map of disputed territory where one should stop and consider rather than as rules for behaviour.

Another point which is absent from some (but not all) social work codes, is identifying and accepting the worker's own limitations, calling in others if one cannot act. An interesting feature is the acknowledgement that not everyone can be equally good with every problem. Such a suggestion raises questions for the intent, apparent in some approaches to organising social work education, to achieve basic levels of competence for all practitioners. It may be more useful to seek to specify kinds of competence and establish an agency system for working together to achieve a service. This is a possible outcome of promoting teamwork rather than individualistic practice.

Medical codes also require professionals both to 'do good' and 'not to do harm'. Sometimes these are defined as scientific knowledge or accepted professional practice. Such general injunctions do not exist so clearly in social work codes. However, professional control of knowledge has implications for the power of an occupational group. A characteristic of the doctors' codes is the requirement to respect the profession and colleagues. Some analyses of professional power would argue that these injunctions exist to maintain professional power to the detriment of those who are served. Professional control of knowledge is itself a basis for excessive power.

Turning now to nursing, the UKCC (1992a) sets a code of professional conduct. There are various specific adjuncts and additions to give greater detail and explanation, for example codes on advertising (UKCC, 1985) and confidentiality (UKCC, 1987) which expand on the main Code. Additions for specialists are published, for example midwives (1991a&b) or for specific tasks, for example, on record-keeping (UKCC, 1993) and administering medicines (UKCC, 1992b). The fact that such additional explanation of the guidance is needed suggests the areas which this profession has in debate at present. Some of these contentious issues, such as confidentiality and record keeping, are shared with social work. Others, such as advertising, are not, because the organisation of the occupations is different. No doubt if social work in Britain were to develop a substantial private practice, conventions about appropriate advertising would develop, as they have in the USA.

The main Code (UKCC, 1992a) gives four basic principles of behaviour:

- Safeguarding and promoting the interests of individual patients and clients (beneficence and non-maleficence).
- Serving the interests of society.
- Justifying public trust and confidence.
- Upholding and enhancing the good standing and reputation of the professions.

There are sixteen prescriptions which include not acting outside your competence, avoiding abuse of privileged access to patients' 'person, property, residence or workplace' and confidentiality. Specific requirements are included to report to a person in authority circumstances where standards of practice are jeopardised. There is a co-operative ethic including patients, carers and families, other professions and colleagues. Respect for uniqueness and dignity of patients and clients and avoiding prejudice on any factors is enjoined upon nurses. They must seek to improve their professional knowledge and competence.

Compared with social work codes, this code focuses on interpersonal work rather than wider social responsibilities. The duty to report risks or inappropriate environments for services appears to bring to an end the nurse's wider responsibility to take action on social inadequacies. Accepting 'the interests of society' avoids questions about differences of view about what those interests are, but suggests that nurses need to be aware of the issue, by drawing attention to it. However, equal weighting is given to the interests of society and to public trust as to individual patients' interests, which suggests an acceptance of compromise of patients interests.

The British Code for Counsellors (BAC, 1993) defines the nature of counselling, and relies heavily on the importance of 'relationship' as the basis for counselling, as opposed to the use of counselling skills. The Code of Ethics focuses on clients' safety, entitlement to a clear contract with a counsellor and the importance of counsellors monitoring and improving their own competence, especially by having supervision.

The Code of Practice identifies responsibilities to clients as the primary responsibility so the balance of priority seems to differ from that in the nursing Code. Responsibility also exists to former clients, to themselves, to other counsellors, to colleagues and other related professions and to the wider community, including law and responding to clients' 'social contexts'. Rules are presented about ensuring the availability of supervision, confidentiality, advertising and public statements, in research and in resolving conflicts between ethical priorities. There are additional codes on the use of counselling skills where counselling as such does not take place, in supervision and in training.

The National Union of Teachers published a code of ethics for teachers (NUT Executive, 1975). There are fourteen points. Confidentiality is enjoined about 'any discussion with individual teachers about their professional problems and difficulties'. This may be a statement about not disclosing other teachers' problems which are revealed because subsequent clauses require confidential discussion with a colleague if a teacher is dissatisfied with colleagues practice. There is also guidance on not denigrating others publicly, consulting each other in an atmosphere of mutual respect and, if you are a manager, making clear to others what their responsibilities are and consulting with them about changes and complaints made by parents about them. Confidentiality about information on pupils is required in another paragraph, and discussion with pupils about their problems is allowed, provided it does not involve discussing other teachers' conduct. Various abuses of relationships with pupils are prohibited. Teachers may not canvass for a job, allow unqualified teachers to do teaching work and bring the profession into disrepute.

The American Code of the same period (NEA, 1975) presents two principles: commitment to the student and to the profession. 'The educator strives to help each student realize his or her potential as a worthy and effective member of society' reflects the social work general principle of respect for persons. Specific follow-up statements include allowing independent learning activity, not distorting or suppressing subject matter, not disparaging students and not using relationships with students for personal advantage. The second principle leads to very similar statements in the British Code. Strike and Soltis (1992) identify several issues in teaching which might have implications for social work values:

- *Punishment and due process* concerns the importance of procedures to make sure that decisions about them are not arbitrary or capricious, particularly if they involve punishment. People should also have the right to a say. Social workers could well remember this in the decision-making structures they use, which are often private and do not involve clients appropriately. Decisions are often explained and clients are persuaded to accept them, rather than being involved.

- *Intellectual freedom* is similar to social work values about autonomy and self-determination, although for different purposes.

- *Equal treatment of students*. Social workers are sometimes concerned when making a decision about precedent, which implies a concern for equal treatment. However, the discretionary nature of much social work decision-making and social work's individualistic approach does leave open the possibility that people would be treated unequally. In many agencies, they would have difficulty in finding this out, so social workers are protected from worry about this issue. However, in residential care, where residents can compare notes, it is much more obvious. It might be the case that social workers should more broadly be concerned about equal treatment of their clients.

These Codes represent a range of issues which are not apparent in the other professions' codes that we have been examining, but which are present in the RCA Code for residential workers, discussed above. This seems to stem from the group nature of much teaching and the reliance on the school as a system. So they are less individualistic in their requirements and concerns. Social work values would benefit from exploration of some of these concerns in relation to teamwork and group and intergroup activities that they undertake, in due process and equal treatment. These concerns might also be relevant to many community and residential work tasks, because they address issues of confidentiality where professional behaviour takes place in groups of 'clients' (in this case pupils) and where various interests, such as those of parents and pupils, might be in opposition. It is easy to see that these issues might be of strong concern to teachers, but it is hard to understand why related issues have not arisen so strongly in codes for social workers.

Social work's values and social work's position
I have sought in this chapter to present texts and codifications of social work value positions, while also evaluating and criticising their adequacy. I have argued, first, that social work's values come from codification of experience in practice. Since practice is largely personal and interpersonal, the issues raised have been therapeutic and individualistic in character. Therefore, they neglect important potential issues which have not as yet led to issues in practice or which are available in alternative perspectives on human nature, society and welfare or from discussion within other professional value systems. Moreover, the political and socialisation purposes of presentations of codifications and texts lead to the neglect of the dualities inherent in value debates. We can see this process at work in other professional codifications of values, which supports my contention that this is what happens in social work. Moreover, we can see particular features of the social work value system which stand out. In spite of its individualistic character, it does contain a wider concern with social objectives than many related approaches to ethics, and socialist-collectivist perspectives offer an alternative system of ethics based upon rights and social change objectives which are available and to some extent incorporated into social work's value system.

These distinctive professional objectives are worked out as we turn away from the interpersonal focus of the previous chapters. This is also characteristic of the experience of social workers. They begin, as I began, with a focus on interpersonal activities as the meat of social work. However, the ambience of the restaurant, the cooking process, the vegetables and the whole menu has a crucial influence on how we need to see the nature of social work if we are to explore the full range of its complexities.

Chapter 5
Social Work and the Agency

Getting into trouble

When I was an area social services officer, the budget for street wardens to visit elderly people in their homes to check that they were safe was reduced. I had to cut the number of people who received this service. A staff member prepared a priority list, and we arranged to notify them all of this decision. We also wrote to them and said that if they or their relatives were concerned about their safety, we were prepared to reconsider the situation. Finally, almost as an afterthought, I wrote to the two local councillors in the area, letting them know what we had done, and saying that if they had any particular representations, I should be happy to reconsider particular cases. I finished off the letter to this effect: 'I am sorry that this budget cut may mean that some of your constituents will be more at risk than previously.' Satisfied by a difficult job sensitively carried out, I went off on holiday.

A week or so after I returned, I found a paragraph in the social services committee reports saying: 'It was resolved that Mr Payne be reprimanded.' Not having had this mentioned to me, I rang my boss and pointed out the paragraph, which contained no clue to my crime. He harumphed. 'I was going to mention that to you, although I don't think I'd go as far as a reprimand'.

Apparently, a councillor had mentioned my helpful letter at some committee and this had led to an impassioned discussion. During this, an inexperienced councillor had proposed a motion that 'no action should ever be taken by the social services department that placed anybody at risk'. Explanations had ensued. The chair and the director of social services tried to persuade anxious members of the committee that social work always involved taking risks. Another councillor pointed out that this was not about social work, but concerned a service which the agency was providing, and the budget cut had placed people at risk. Another discussion about the practical consequences of broad political budget decisions followed. Finally, the motion was put to the meeting. It only failed by one vote. The chair, irritated by the closeness of political disaster and the embarrassment of the discussion, complained that I should never have written the letter in the first place.

Another situation in which I got into trouble arose when I was responsible for a voluntary organisation which co-ordinated the work of others. A series of public disturbances in the area by people mainly from minority ethnic groups led to great public concern and a secretary of state, a senior government minister, visited the area to investigate. He agreed to meet voluntary organisations. Following our agency's role, we organised a meeting for the organisations to plan what they were going to say to most effect.

Some organisations were conventional service-providing charities. They wanted to use the opportunity to press upon the minister the value of their services in developing community involvement. Several black groups representing various minority groups were also present. They argued that we should boycott the meeting to make clear to the minister the seriousness of the problems. We took a vote, and agreed the policy of boycott, but several traditional charities refused to walk out of the meeting with the minister. They thought it would damage their reputation for 'professional' responsibility. In the event, having organised the representative meeting and taken part in the vote, I felt we had no alternative but to leave the meeting with the black groups.

This led to a great deal of criticism of my action at our management meeting. Many charities regarded us as having abandoned our responsibility to speak for all of them. They thought we might have damaged their relationship with an important source of finance and an important decision-maker. I had associated them with radical causes instead of getting on the right side of him.

These two anecdotes illustrate some reasons why, in practice, the fact that their work always takes place within agencies constrains social workers in their activities. Various points emerge:

- Social work is not the only activity in a social services agency as the councillor made clear in the visiting wardens' case. Services are also provided, and these are subject to budgetary and political decisions rather than professional ones.

- Also in the visiting wardens' case I was, as a social worker, using social work skills to make judgements about need and risk, and using social work communication skills to convey the decisions effectively. In this way, social work is often indivisible from decisions about services and budgets. But the judgements made did not arise from the presentation of a need by a client, which is how we usually describe social work activities. It came from the agency's needs. Increasingly, social workers feel they are using their skills to effect political or budgetary decisions rather than acting on behalf of clients.

- Agencies' needs often differ from clients' needs or wishes. In my second anecdote, the representatives of minority ethnic groups were the people whose needs everyone in the situation was supposed to be attending to. None the less, some agencies wanted to do something which the minority ethnic groups felt was contrary to what would achieve the best results for them.

- As a result, social workers get involved in organisational politics. In the first case, both I and my superior were fairly relaxed about matters. We also managed to ignore a formal reprimand resolution from the committee. This does not fit with the formal picture that we have of big organisations. How did this happen? In sorting out the second problem, I went through two or three weeks of serious conflict. It damaged my credibility with my management committee to some extent for ever, and certainly for a while in a difficult period. After a conflict like that, you inevitably take care about other actions, when taking a risk might be the best thing. So dealing with internal conflicts can take away from good practice.

Taming the agency

Would social work be 'pure' if it did not take place in an agency? We can explore this by looking at two situations. Can workers ever make decisions freely in an agency? Are they freer in private practice?

At times, social workers make professional decisions which apparently have no budgetary or political implications. They only involve the worker's time and efforts. Nevertheless, this still reflects the agency's or more distant political decisions to provide, for example, social work rather than other services and to let workers make priority decisions about their time over certain things but not over others. Also, workers, making priority decisions, still choose to use resources in one way rather than another. For example rather than doing the work, they could refer it elsewhere. So workers are never free of the political and budgetary decisions of an agency context.

The same applies even if the worker is in personal private practice. This context limits the worker's freedom to choose clients. To make an income, the worker has to limit clients who do not generate income, and find clients who can pay or be paid for and who can subsidise those who cannot. Because they are practising outside an agency, the range of services they can offer is limited. Even where there is a private agency, it will still be constrained. For example, there are the legal constraints of the companies acts, regulation if official registration of the service is required and political pressure from media comment. Commercial pressures also arise if there is complaint or dissatisfaction among clients or customers.

Here, too, although we conventionally do not talk about a private practitioner being in an agency, similar pressures affect them.

So, a characteristic of social work is that it is practised in agencies. This has been controversial. One reason for the controversy is the reflexive-therapeutic perspective which, we have seen, dominates the narrative of value-based personal and interpersonal social work. This assumes a personal responsibility to and for the client on the part of the social worker. Practice of this kind seems less possible if the agency intervenes in the personal relationship and process. Rife managerialism damages personal discretion and autonomy. As a result, some have argued, as we shall see, that social work cannot be a profession because its professional autonomy is interfered with by agency power. The debate on this issue is what makes considering the agency and its interaction with social work practice an important matter to explore when trying to understand the nature of social work.

I take a different view. My argument here is that the role of the agency injects an individualist-reformist requirement into social work practice, because it requires acknowledgement of political and social influences on the nature of social work. This must be rejected if you take a purely reflexive-therapeutic view of social work. However, individualism is not wholly inimical to a therapeutic perspective of social work. Such views are individualist because they concentrate on personal growth. Also, they largely ignore social objectives, and so do not conflict with a reformist perspective on social change. Indeed, in some respects reflexive-therapeutic views are themselves reformist, since they assume that change comes from the self-fulfilment of individuals.

Including an individualist-reformist perspective into the reflexive-therapeutic perspective on social work requires us to recognise the political and social pressures within it, in a way which individualist professions find it less easy to analyse. In social work, the analysis is easier, although this does not make it any easier to do something about social and agency pressures as we work. It is possible to identify and analyse the processes by which the agency operates to control and intervene in social work practice. This chapter attempts some such analysis. I go further. I argue that because the individualist-reformist perspective is not inimical to the reflexive-therapeutic core of social work, both become entwined in the agency. In this way social work tames the agency and learns to live with it. The agency becomes adapted to the needs of semi-autonomous social work, as social work adapts to the power of the agency.

The question to ask about this symbiosis is whether, in accepting the agency's power, and taming it a little, therapeutic social work becomes so allied with reformism it denies social work's other social objectives. The socialist-collec-tivist view would say that, in being seduced by and seducing, the agency's power it abandons its potential alliance with the oppressed people who are the clientele and the justification for social work's existence. We shall explore this further in Chapters 6 and 9.

Social workers and agencies

I have argued, then, that there is no idealised 'pure' social work practised on its own terms with its own ideals or dirty or degraded forms of social work practised in agencies. All social work is affected by the organisational instrument through which it is provided. The agency is a proxy for social, political and economic pressures which in part create social work and the services with which it is often associated. The process also works the other way round. By being part of an agency, social work gives it special characteristics which we would not see in other, similar agencies.

My view of the relationships between social workers and agencies can be sum-marised as follows:

- Agencies are organisations. Organisations are '. . . large association[s] of people run on impersonal lines, set up to achieve specific objectives' (Giddens, 1993, p 286). As a result, organisations are structures for achieving control of people in compliance with the objectives.

- Agencies form a negotiated order in which different groups contend for influence over the purposes and methods of the agencies' work.

- Social work has an influence on the order, depending on its success in the negotiation. Agencies respond to the characteristics of the professions operating within them. Social work agencies, therefore, adapt to the requirements of social work in the way they exercise control and achieve compliance with their objectives.

- Control and compliance mechanisms in social work agencies tend to lead to relative autonomy of action for social workers.

Agencies and how they are organised express something about the nature of social work because they have developed characteristics which reflect its needs. Social work as a profession and as a form of activity at the personal and interpersonal level discussed in previous chapters is in constant negotiation within agencies. At least three other aspects of the agency are relevant:

● Powerful élites which construct the social welfare system within which we work with particular political, social and economic assumptions about the sort of society which a welfare system should support.

● Social developments and movements demonstrating and representing the social and personal needs of clients and groups of people in society, who are potential and actual clients of the welfare system.

● Internal organisational politics and organisational inertia come from imperatives for organisational survival, maintenance and development which we find in all organisations.

These three aspects of organisations and their negotiated interaction with social workers are explored below.

Occasionally, as social workers, we are brought up against individual manifestations of this negotiation. More frequently, this negotiation goes on within and through our agency. Sometimes, we see limitations upon us as deriving from organisational sociology and psychology, and the failings of political decision-making and social systems of provision. I argue that ideas from social work are in constant tension and dialogue with ideas representing other interests and priorities. This tension and dialogue occur within and through agencies so we come to see agencies rather than the social ideas they represent as limiting social work practice.

Groups with power to construct social agencies
Agencies are formal organisations. This notion excludes informal face-to-face groups, where the emphasis is on personal relationships among the participants. Some social agencies, based on small community groups or self-help groups and perhaps employing a few workers, are less formal organisations. By employing workers and having social purposes, though, they acquire many features and problems of formal organisations. They plan their activities, organise finance and budgets and relationships among the people involved in formal ways uncharacteristic of completely informal groups. The same applies to a small private practice run by an individual or by a small group of social workers.

Because they are formal organisations, agencies have specific objectives. The organisation is set up to achieve these purposes, but does not necessarily make it. Other objectives are usually present and pursued. There is usually a formal statement of aims, but there are hidden informal purposes. One is usually to maintain the existence of the organisation and to provide employment. We can imagine others: for example, to promote the use of social work. Individuals within the organisation may also have their own objectives. These might include having an interesting job, gaining experience suitable for promotion or further training, improving their social life, giving a time structure to what would otherwise be empty lives and so on. These might or might not support the organisation's stated objectives, and they might conflict among themselves. The agency's stated objectives might also be inconsistent.

Organisations are 'associations', that is, collections of people who have connections among them. Both the connections, and also the fact that organisations are made up of people, are important. We sometimes think of organisations as though they were entirely impersonal, and treat them as a thing rather than as collections of people.

People also construct organisations, in the sociological sense. That is, the kinds of people involved and the things that they do in the organisation create the nature and direction of the organisation. Social work agencies are constructed by both internal and external factors. These factors derive from people - very often in groups. Having sufficient power to make a major impact on the construction of a social agency is rare for individuals, and influence accumulates in groups. Patterns of influence create patterns of accountability and sanctions. As a group influences all or part of an organisation, it often demands accountability, formal or informal, for the actions of others in the organisation over matters which concern it. In turn, there are sanctions that the group can apply which force others to comply with their wishes. Let us look at two examples of this. The first is a fairly formal and conventional system of influence, accountability and sanction. The second is a real situation in which informal systems of influence created unhelpful accountabilities and sanctions, leading eventually to disaster.

The first situation is a typical national voluntary organisation providing residential and other services for a particular client group. The director is a well-known figure in the field who is concerned mainly with policy, finance and overall direction. Although the director is responsible to a board of management, they perform mainly a fund-raising role and act as a sounding-board for the director. There is a group of assistant directors, each responsible for a division: residential care services, day care, development and policy, administration and training. One of these acts as deputy for the director and exercises considerable directorial powers over the daily management of the organisation. Each assistant director has a group of middle managers responsible to him or her and each of these has a group of staff carrying out their work. In turn the various services provided by the organisation have their own groups of staff with a team leader responsible through the hierarchy. Of these, the younger staff meet regularly for training, and through their group cohesion have a good opportunity to raise issues of concern to them. The team leaders of the separate services also meet regularly and have immense influence as a group because of their importance in keeping services running smoothly. The assistant director for development and policy has little to do with the service-providing arms of the organisation. However, the policy work, and the fact that development work involves raising capital monies, particularly creates influence and involvement with the director. So, there is a formally established hierarchical system, with logically designed responsibilities. Overlaying this are informal networks of relationships and accountabilities which create influences and sanctions beyond and perhaps in conflict with the formal system.

Now, the second situation. In 1987, an old people's home was closed amid allegations of neglect and abuse of the residents (Gibbs, *et al.*, 1987). A group of untrained but experienced care assistants were accused of various malpractices and of running the home to suit their personal arrangements, rather than for the benefit of the residents. They had gained this position by various means. Sometimes, middle management staff had felt threatened and intimidated by aggressive behaviour and a longstanding culture of leaving the care assistants alone. One factor in this was that one of the assistants was an official of the trade union. This in turn had had considerable influence with the left-wing local government council which was responsible for the home. The manager of the home was respected and competent, but had lost some of her abilities through excessive drinking. A factor in this was the residents' bar, which had been used by various local people, including councillors, for parties. To some extent the independent authority of the managers and the council was vitiated by these and other occurrences. The most senior staff of the council had tried several times to take action but felt that the council's inability to take decisive action against the wishes of the trade union limited their room for manœuvre. A complex of personal relationships outside the formal structures prevented people from being clear about the responsibilities and roles of the various people involved. Various informal influences and sanctions prevented problems being dealt with. In other situations, informal relationships often help to sort out limitations within the formal structure of the organisation.

Any groups involved in an organisation *may* influence its construction by their interactions. Even quite informal groups or those without formally defined power can do so by the relationships they construct. However, writers have tried to specify the sorts of groups which do have influence in the construction of agencies. James (1994, p76), for example, relates the influence to accountability to meet certain kinds of objectives. She identifies:

- *Politicians*, who seek accountability for having policies carried out.

- *Funders*, who seek accountability for having resources used efficiently.

- *Professionals*, who want practice standards met.

- *Managers and practitioners*, who want organisational objectives achieved.

- *Users and the community*, who want their needs met.

Johnson (1992 pp205-6), more comprehensively, identifies the following extrinsic groups, and I have added examples and some discussion to her bare list:

- *National, regional or local government*, which might regulate, manage and finance the agency.

- *Professional organisations* to which workers belong, which might also regulate the occupations. In countries other than the USA (where Johnson's analysis originates) it would be conventional to mention trade unions.

- *Colleges, universities and other agencies* that educate or train people for the occupational groups involved, and bodies which validate or accredit the qualifications awarded. Their students and tutors, through contacts with the agency, research and by mutual influence in various organisations have influence on how agencies do their work.

- *Organisations that the agency belongs to.* There are associations of local authorities, of directors of agencies, and of groups of agencies with shared interests or in particular sectors.

- *Local, national and international funding bodies.* Examples are charitable trusts or foundations, central government departments, agencies and quangos (quasi non-governmental organisations) and international agencies, such as in Europe the European Union.

- *Other social agencies in the local and national networks* with which the agency tries to interrelate. Their referral patterns and policy will influence how an agency organises its work.

- *Local community organisations and volunteer bodies*, including religious and secular organisations.

- *The community or communities* from which clients come, and organised and unorganised groups in those communities. For example, the growth of a group of young drug abusers is likely to have a major impact on social agencies in the area.

- *Individuals, families and groups* who receive the agency's services, or who request them for others.

This last category is particularly important. They may be powerless to have an explicit influence on policy development. Still, the issues they present to workers form the basic construction of the tasks which have to be undertaken by the agency. Moreover, on the route to the agency, personal experiences, community perceptions and the views of other referring agencies will have influenced them to form a view of the agency and its likely response to them. This in turn will affect the problems they think it right to present, and the way in which they present them. Thus indirectly, clients' and community views can significantly affect agency practice and priorities (Payne, 1993b).

Besides these external groups, we might identify the following internal ones:

- *Management committee*, board of directors or elected representatives of the community such as Members of Parliament or local council

- The Director or *chief executive* of the agency and the associated senior management team.

- Other *managers*, both individually and in groups, since they usually meet in some representative process.

- *Informal groups* which grow up in any organisation.

- *Staff* providing direct services to the public, often divided into several groups according to professional qualification, role or geographical division. They often form working parties or specialist groups which may be influential at particular times or with particular matters.

- *Trade union, staff association or professional association* officers and members.

- *Support staff*, such as caretakers, drivers and manual workers.

- *Groups of clients* might form advisory groups, or be influential through making complaints. Alternatively, they have impact because they are dealt with in groups, of a therapeutic kind, or in residential or day care institutions

So far, we have identified many groups which have an influence on the construction of social work through agencies. Internal groups form the basis for mediating such constructions, taking them into the agency and beginning to make changes which implement the constructions in actual practice. Pithouse (1990) shows that commitment is to the local team in social work agencies rather than to wider professional and managerial structures. As a result, the local team and its interpretations of the world construct how social work is for the people within it. The next section looks at the kind of social movements which might lead to changing constructions. The following section examines how the ideas from social movements interact through the groups we have been examining to create the construction of social work in agencies.

Social developments and movements

Social agencies are not only influenced by the people involved with them. They also respond to social developments, movements and trends, applying pressure to the organisation. We might identify the following:

- *Political ideologies and policies.* We noted in Chapter 4 how political philosophies affected values.

For example, social services work in Britain and the USA was affected by Thatcherite and Reaganomic policies of the 'New Right' during the 1980s.

- *Government policies.* While these may be related to political movements, how government does its business changes.

A tendency to centralisation or decentralisation, for example, or to be universalist or selective subsists in the government system whatever party is in power.

- *Community needs.* New issues arising cause movements which affect the responses of social agencies.

Concern about AIDS and HIV-related illnesses in the 1980s, for example, created a new range of agencies grafted onto the social service system, but with their own characteristic ways of working. Some of these, such as the 'buddies' system of volunteer support, are attractive and may be borrowed by other services.

- *Management policies.* These may derive from government policy, but they may also reflect changing and developing approaches to management ideas more generally.

One approach which has come from government in the UK is the 'purchaser-provider' split in a 'mixed economy of care' within community care policy.

Agencies or parts of them providing services to service users contract with purchasers or commissioners of services, who assess the needs of clients for a package of services. They then put together the package from services offered by various contractors. This leads to an emphasis on needs-led assessment, supposedly a new approach to social work assessment. Management ideas such as concern for the culture of the agency or for quality assurance and enhancement may also lead to differences in approach to providing services and doing social work within the services. Challis (1990) discusses various ideas which cause tensions in the organisation of public social services in Britain. Examples are the tension between specialism and genericism, between residential and community care, between centralisation and decentralisation and between provision and acting as brokers and regulators of others' provision. Obviously, views within and influencing an agency about each of these tensions will affect how the work in the agency is constructed.

- *Ethnic and other diversities in the population.* Related to community needs is the issue of the diversity of the populations with which social workers deal. Particular concern has been paid to ethnic diversity. One consequence of global movements in population in recent centuries is that few countries have a unitary or homogeneous culture and ethnic origin.

Different countries face this issue in different ways. South Africa, for example, has a small white population which has been politically dominant over a majority black population until recently. Services to the different groups have been divided. The social services system has to deal with wide disparities in wealth and welfare between the groups, feelings and attitudes deriving from previous dominance and conflict, and the nature of the divided services themselves. The USA has a longstanding division between African American people, whose ancestors were originally imported as slaves, a white population which emigrated from many European countries and newer waves of migrants from Latin American countries. Britain has a majority white population from four nations (England, Ireland, Scotland and Wales) and two major religious groups (Roman Catholicism and various kinds of Protestantism), a longstanding minority black population and migrants from many different countries in the nineteenth and twentieth centuries.

- *Economic change.* Major economic changes affect countries from time to time.

Eastern European countries and states of the former Soviet Union have experienced major social changes related to economic change. Different employment patterns which are leading, worldwide, to loss of unskilled work in manufacturing and to significant levels of unemployment require different forms of social provision.

● *Social movements* such as consumerism and feminism have affected our understanding and public acceptance of the relations between social services and the population.

Clients are less deferential in the 1990s than in the 1960s. They are more inclined to demand their rights rather than remain silent if they are unhappy with services. There is a more-aware concern for the needs of carers who may be exploited by social assumptions that women have a duty to accept caring responsibilities. Changes like this in perception might alter how social work and social services respond to needs that they perceive. They also affect how needs are perceived and what responses are considered appropriate.

Historically, changes such as these have affected the social services since they have existed. Services, including social work, have changed as there have been waves of children being born, and the population of elderly people has grown or as wars have led to special needs in dealing with refugees or evacuated children. Inevitably, therefore, the nature of social work changes as it responds to new perceptions of need, social justice and social provision. Some of these pressures affect the agency through political pressures on its decision-making structure. Others affect social workers directly as they become aware of needs and interests among clients, to which they have failed to respond. Yet others enter the world view of social work through theoretical developments which affect training.

Many developments and movements affect all groups which influence the construction of social work and social agencies and have an impact on social work through different routes. Ideas about responding to ethnic diversity, for example, have come from political pressures to deal with obvious groups among the constituency of politicians. Community pressures led to new agencies offering specialised services and to social workers wanting to respond to new needs. Agency management also had to respond to demands or problems which arose. Eventually, such pressures came out in theoretical perspectives and practice concepts in social work courses, and in the organisation of the courses themselves.

Developments and movements will lead to interactions within agencies about the nature of social work. Such interactions partly construct how social work will evolve. This is the subject of the next section.

Internal politics in social agencies

We saw above that both formal and informal group relationships affect the construction of agencies. Interpersonal and intergroup relationships form an internal politics of organisations. Internal politics is concerned with the power relations between groups within an organisation as they attempt to affect the processes and outcomes of the association which forms the organisation. Obviously, these are interpersonal and variable according to the individuals concerned. There are, however, several fundamental issues in agencies:

- *Control and influence.* How do different groups within the agency seek to gain control of or influence the work done?

Systems of control are often represented as hierarchical, so that authority descends from the instructions of the most senior in the organisation through a chain or line of command to the most junior. However, different workers through teams, professional groupings or trade unions, seek to control their work. Also, clients seek to control what is done for them, through trying to influence workers, by giving or withholding information or avoiding an agency altogether. External groups, such as members of other agencies, will also try to influence what work is done and how. James (1994, p80) identifies central control of ideology as associated with setting a culture for the organisation. Other forms of control related to this are of staff (by appraisals, through supervision or by negotiating conditions with trade unions), standards (by quality systems and inspection) outputs (by performance indicators), information, tasks (by funding, contracting management arrangements), policy and procedure (by mission statements, guidelines, manuals of procedures) and funding (by systems of budgeting and delegation).

- *Communication systems.* These are important in identifying relationships between groups within and outside the agency.

Officially, communication in agencies follows the hierarchy. As people form groups, however, communication within the groups becomes more important than communication from outside. It is useful to see communications relationships as a network. Individuals are part of many different sets of relationships, some close with many complex interacting links, some looser and relying on just one or two links.

- *Gender relations.* Relationships between a variety of groups are likely to be important, but we must pay special attention to gender relations in social work.

This is because it is a predominantly female profession, and it most often works with the female members of families rather than male members (Hallett, 1989). In spite of this, there is evidence of male management models being dominant in many agencies (Eley, 1989), which are uncongenial or disabling to women managers. Also, men acquire most powerful positions in agencies (Hallett, 1989). Thus, patriarchy, a system of relations based on ideologies which value the dominance of men, has influence on a variety of relations within social work agencies. It is expressed particularly in the structure of power relations in the management of agencies (Dressel, 1992).

- *Stratification.* Partly because they are hierarchical, but also because they reflect social class relations, organisations are stratified.

A group in the highest stratum is called 'senior management'. Their work includes responsibility collectively for the strategic direction of the organisation. Middle management directs work on a day-to-day basis and mediates between workers and senior management. Professional staff have relative autonomy in their work, but non-professional staff are more subject to work schedules or detailed direction of their activities. Some staff within each of these groups can be regarded as aspirant. They seek to achieve a status in a higher group. As a result, they may become involved in more important or testing activities or have greater influence because they are seen as being capable of, or wishing to be, promoted to higher statuses.

Bamford (1989) argues that the latter part of the twentieth century has seen a movement away from professional power towards managerialism. This arises, he says, because of the increase in the number and range of staff in various social services agencies. Yet professional discretion for social workers has been little changed, although they have been more strongly aware of their vulnerability to criticism if mistakes occur. This comes from the greater size and political importance and media visibility of the social services. Following this argument, managerialism has grown up because of the size and importance of the social services, and this has also given importance to the social work role. However, managerialism increasingly limits that role, because social workers seek protection of decision-making structures. The reality of their range of discretion has been little changed, however. I would argue, therefore, that social work has used agency and managerial structures to conceal and defend their discretion. This comes about through the various mechanisms by which interpersonal relations are pursued in social work agencies. Scott (1975) found similar processes at work in American agencies in the 1970s.

Among the important mechanisms used for interpersonal relations in social work agencies are:

- *Supervision*, a technique peculiar to social work and related occupations.

Workers receive from a supervisor who is usually but not always their manager a form of oversight which includes elements of management control and direction, personal support and education. This leaves to workers a high degree of discretion about actual actions undertaken by them. The process of supervision is indistinct. Pithouse (1987) studied some specialist child-care teams and found a pattern where workers conveyed in supervision sessions a caring involvement through close understanding of the families with which they worked. The supervisor listened to oral accounts of workers' relationships with families, to adjudge their conformity with the service ideals of caring. If this is generally typical, and it fits with my experience, it does not mean close checking on what the worker actually does, or compliance with specific agency objectives or practices but is concerned with attitude and approach. A variety of surveys show that it is sometimes minimal after early induction into agencies (Payne, 1994a).

- *Teamwork* involves social workers both in work groups with other social workers and with non-social workers, and in multi-disciplinary teams with other professions. This might take place either within the agency or outside it.

Teamwork is an aspirational term implying a wish for co-operation and collaboration. Working through teams implies a wish to create shared objectives. Workers can develop personal commitment to and identification with the objectives of the agency. A shared ideology develops about the purposes of social work, which can become strong, as in the views about child care of the intake and long-term teams described in Chapter 2. This is important because what social workers do is not observable, and, as we saw when discussing Pithouse's (1987) research into supervision, above, commitment to caring objectives is the major form of ensuring responsiveness to organisational aims. However, teamwork may be perceived managerially as a tool for promoting agency aims. Simultaneously team members see it conversely as personal support against the stresses of the work and the agency's pressure to conform.

Teamwork's importance in social work derives from a significant role of social work in promoting co-ordination and creating linkages between agencies and other professionals. It might be better to describe the relations between social workers and others as participation in a network of relations both inside and outside the agency. The vision of teamwork allows this network to be perceived by those involved as fulfilling the interpersonal ideologies of social work agencies. It also, as we have seen, helps to protect and defend their ideologies against political and managerial pressure.

- *Social work skills* are particularly important in the construction of social work organisations.

Social workers are interested in interpersonal relations, and have a role in creating networks for co-ordination among agencies. So, there is particular concern with interpersonal relationships for therapeutic, advocacy, linking, negotiating and broking purposes. Because of the importance of interpersonal relationships, unusual attention is also given to the effects of interpersonal stress and the need for personal support within supervision, teamwork and in the organisation of the agency. Coulshed (1990), for example, gives great importance to this aspect of management in a recent text, arguing that it reflects the female aspect of managerial skills which is neglected in male-dominated organisations. The gendered nature of relations in social work organisations, discussed above, suggests that social agencies might be inadequate in meeting the needs of all staff in this respect.

- *Communication of directions and standards.* One tension which exists in social work agencies is the need to respond to the political and bureaucratic requirements of organisations which must reflect public policy and social expectations.

In contrast to the general reliance on interpersonal skills and personal commitment as management devices, activities are often specified in detail through practice manuals and guidelines. This helps the organisation deal with the potential difficulties deriving from the high degree of professional discretion available to most workers. It can say it has enforced political and social requirements to be equitable between clients and social expectations of practice, without inhibiting workers discretion. It also helps the social worker deal with the stress of personal isolation in making complex decisions based on interpersonal relations. Thus, practice guidance is both resisted as oppressive and embraced as a source of relief from stress, and is used selectively to support decisions already made. On other occasions, it is avoided or rationalised away when interpersonal relations suggest the importance of an alternative response.

● *Systems for review of decisions.* This process of resistance to and acceptance of managerial guidance in its tension with autonomy in interpersonal relations may also be found in systems for the review of decisions.

These are important in social agencies, since detailed planning must be made for individuals. Individuals are not usually amenable to outsiders planning their lives, but still the agency must present their activities as consistent with policy, good practice and the needs of other agencies and the social services system generally. So, there are several models for interpersonal planning, such as case conferences, independent programme plans, care or case management and care programming. In these, agencies, users of services and others involved come together to look at events in the past, make shared and agreed judgements about them and plan future action. These processes are particularly strong where clients are in expensive long-term care or where legal requirements might impose authoritative action, such as removing a child from the care of its parents. These allow agencies to justify publicly that the use of resources is carefully considered, involving managers as well as individual workers. However, frequently decisions are not made in these conferences, since they merely reaffirm what has previously been agreed (Payne, 1994a). For workers they are another way to relieve stress in their interpersonal work by providing support and affirmation rather than genuine critical review. In numerous child care scandals, social workers have been criticised for failing to react to signs of adult physical or sexual abuse of children or for over-reacting. Case conferences in these situations rely on the interpersonal skills and on-the-spot decision-making by social workers and other professionals. So, while they provide the image of shared review and decision-making, and relieve the stress that workers may feel about it, they have often been wanting as forums where accountability and stress-reduction can be genuinely achieved.

Endword: social work and social work agencies
There is an apparent tangle which we have begun to unravel. On the one hand, social work appears, in the reflexive-therapeutic perspective, to be a relatively autonomous, interpersonal activity with a strong ethical value base. This is how we have been seeing it in previous chapters. However, one of its characteristics as an occupation is that it is carried out in agencies which limit its autonomy. In the individualist-reformist perspective it cannot respond only or mainly to the needs of clients rather than political and social objectives mediated through the structures of agencies. This factor has led some writers to argue that social work cannot be a true profession, and we shall look at this issue further in Chapter 7.

I have argued here that many groups, social factors and social movements that contribute to the social construction of social work agencies take part in creating a negotiated order which responds to some of the needs of social workers to create a form of autonomy for their interpersonal work. It also seeks to limit the stress of the political and social requirements which makes the interpersonal work difficult. Moreover, the management of social work within agencies is usually in the hands of promoted social workers. They operate special professional forms of management and control which also reduce the impact of political, bureaucratic and social controls on professional autonomy. Thus I argue that the fact that social work is practised in agencies is one of its special features and it has created agencies to accommodate rather than inhibit its other characteristics.

An important feature of this analysis has been power relations in the agency, and I have suggested that power relations tend to support professional autonomy. The next chapter looks more closely at a wider variety of power relations relevant to social work, while also taking into account the importance of the agency as a source of power and a place in which power relations are negotiated.

Chapter 6
Social Work, Power and Society

Using power in practice

I first met Sylvia when I was a probation officer, standing in for the colleague who supervised her because of a series of theft offences. She was a lively teenage woman who had just started in employment. She had failed several days to turn up for work and had been sacked. On behalf of my colleague and her distraught mother (a lone parent), I summoned her to the office to remonstrate about her lack of commitment. She giggled through the interview and probably ignored everything I said.

Sometime later, I took over a new caseload in the social services department, and Sylvia's was a name on it. She was not present, having absconded from a residential school for delinquent and maladjusted teenagers, after throwing a senior member of staff across the room (she was a big woman). I renewed my acquaintance with her mother, and waited until she reappeared. This happened in due course, when a police officer saw her shopping near home. I talked to her in the police cells. She had been living at home for about six months, had found a new boy-friend and had not got into trouble.

I wondered what to do. The conventional course was to arrange for her to return to her school for delinquent youngsters to finish her programme. I thought this was inappropriate. For one thing, I knew that she had already been out at work, and I thought putting her in a school was a backward step in her personal development. Unfortunately, we did not have any facilities for providing her with employment or workshop experience. Anyway, I thought, obviously relationships had broken down at the school and sending her back was likely to lead to another outburst. Also, although she had a history of committing thefts, she had remained at home for six months without being picked up by the police at all. Another factor in my mind was the positive relationship with the boy-friend.

On the other hand, I (representing the public through the social services) could not condone the violence, the absconsion and the record of offending. So I did a deal with her. I said I would have to place her in a residential school: she understood this and why it was necessary. But, I said, I would send her to a different one. If she behaved impeccably, just as she had done all those months while she was 'on the run' at home, I would do my best to persuade senior officials to allow her home after two weeks. So she would get her punishment, she would have to prove she could contain herself, but there was a realistic target, she would soon be back with the boy-friend, and she would not have to face the place from which she had run away. I kept my side of the bargain. She was a totally acceptable resident in the school. After dire warnings and threats of blame from my superiors if anything went wrong, I was allowed to follow this course of action. A year later, I was able to discharge her supervision, since she had settled down very successfully.

Later still, Sylvia's mother died, leaving her youngest child an orphan. I knew nothing of this until Sylvia arrived at the office to see a colleague, with her husband, the former boy-friend. Could we do anything to help her look after her sister, since their incomes as teenagers were not enough to maintain her? We arranged a guardianship allowance and other support, and found that Sylvia acted as a very competent substitute parent. Her preparedness to come to the agency at all was, she told my colleague, a result of respect I had shown her in her own difficulties a few years previously.

With Sylvia, I used official powers on several occasions. As a probation officer, I carried out the form of the responsibilities which came from those powers, by berating her for her behaviour. This was an oppressive use of power, without any worthwhile outcome, because it did not involve her participation or commitment. The best that could be said for it was that justice was done. When probation orders are made, the courts and the public expect probation officers to be clear about the requirements set by the order and to ensure that people on probation are picked up on their responsibilities. We saw in Chapter 5 that agency expectations represent a negotiation between various interests in society. Going through the form of the use of official powers when their use is in itself pointless is one compromise which arises from that negotiation. It allows at another point useful social work to go on, and allows others in society to feel that justice is done. Form is very important in matters of justice: it must be seen to be done.

As a social worker, I used the powers given me by the court to incarcerate Sylvia in residential school. This also made clear to Sylvia her responsibilities, as the courts and the public required that I did. Therefore, it had the same worth in meeting that public responsibility as berating her for not being committed to her work. But it was a much more valuable use of professional power, although it was potentially even more oppressive. Power was properly used here because it was used with understanding and participation, if not consent, and used with a purpose which might (and in the event did) achieve valuable results for Sylvia and for the general public. I also used my professional powers in a different way: to work out and argue for a beneficial course of action within the agency. Here I used my thinking and analytical powers and powers of persuasion in getting managers to go along with my ideas. So personal power can be used against clients and not for their benefit, with them, perhaps to their benefit, and with others, to their benefit or perhaps not. In gaining a guardianship allowance, we used our knowledge and skills to obtain a right for Sylvia and her sister.

In social work, then, we can identify different powers:

- Legal powers.

- The capacity for personal influence which we saw in Chapter 3 is so important in social work seen as a personal activity

- 'Professional' knowledge and skills.

- Used with clients, to their benefit or disadvantage.

- Used with others, for clients' benefit or disadvantage.

In another case, I was called to see an elderly lady who had residual problems from very severe schizophrenia. She now managed a relatively normal life, with only occasional relapses. However, her life was chaotic, and her small flat was stacked with years of accumulated newspapers and magazines. I found more than twenty layers of dirty plates and half-eaten food interleaved with sheets of newspaper used as table cloths on her table. Her bed was covered with various items obtained from dustbins. Some of her symptoms probably came from tiredness, since she was unable to sleep properly because her bed was unavailable for this purpose. I persuaded her to accept, somewhat reluctantly, help in tidying and cleaning the flat. A team of home helps sorted the place out. Unfortunately, when I returned a week later nearly all the property had returned, retrieved from the dustbins as soon as the home helps had left.

In this case, I used no statutory powers, but she would have known that I had these in reserve, since many social workers in the past had been responsible for her compulsory admission to mental hospital. This factor may have persuaded her to accept my pressure to tidy up her life, although obviously, with hindsight, the removal of her unhealthy accumulations was distressing and uncomfortable for her. More likely, her befuddled mind accepted the arguments of this bright young man, knowing that if it all went too far she could get her own way in the end. The power of my speech and mental strength, my enthusiasm to help, and perhaps my middle-class assumptions and official role just bowled her along. She agreed to something that she did not really want and she frustrated my aims because I did not take the trouble to get real consent from her. On the other hand, she retained her own power and control over the situation.

These case examples make the point that we can have all kinds of formal and informal powers. We often use them legally to ensure compliance or informally to achieve results. But our efforts can be frustrated unless we genuinely achieve agreement and participation. This is something that senior politicians in democracies learn at the highest levels of political activity: that you cannot in the end govern without consent or oppression. In the sense that social work is about social governance, this is also true of social work activity.

However, that 'consent' may be achieved in all sorts of ways, many of which are overtly or covertly oppressive. Concern about these issues has surfaced at two different levels in social work debate:

- The role of the occupational group and social services agencies within the system of social governance or control. This level concerns social work as a profession.

- The use of various powers during the practice of social work to achieve clients' compliance with social or agency policies or the worker's wishes. This level concerns personal and interpersonal social work.

These levels of debate, while they are separable, are connected, since the use of powers within practice at least partly achieves the social control sought in systems of social governance. The different levels also relate to the distinction drawn in Chapter 1 between professional and interpersonal aspects of understanding social work. Both these areas of analysis need to be considered to gain a rounded view of how power in social work relates to power structures in society.

Social work debates centre upon this distinction. The *individualist-reformist* view is that social work at the personal and interpersonal levels necessarily involves the exercise of authority and power, to the benefit of clients who gain from having an ordered society. The *socialist-collectivist* position is that social work as a profession often sides with powerful groups in society to the client's disadvantage and this must be resisted. This view argues that the individualist position accepts and carries out the present order rather than seeking change for clients benefits. The individualist position, because it sees social work as primarily or only personal and interpersonal, regards the achievement of significant social change as impossible for social workers operating at this level. It would be relevant only to political action, which is seen as outside the role of social work. The *reflexive-therapeutic* view argues that attaining personal power over one's own life and development enables people to exert power more generally, or at least not to be oppressed by external power.

Some ideas about power and authority

Some consideration of ideas about the nature of power and authority is helpful, to inform our understanding of the debates within social work. Power is a capacity to influence and achieve others' compliance with our wishes, which comes from a variety of sources, including personal qualities and the resources to apply coercion in various ways (Lukes, 1974). Its existence is distributed among groups and organisations in patterns which reflect people's ability to control agendas and expectations - so its exercise may be hidden. People and groups exercise power in pursuit of their interests. Patterns of power within societies and organisations persist, even when the ability to apply coercion is not exercised regularly.

Morriss (1987) argues that power must involve intending or wishing to achieve something when we act. It is not power, in his view, unless there is the wish to achieve something with the changes we bring about, with the control we exercise over the agenda for action and with our ability to construct a social situation which avoids people being aware of our control. Just affecting the circumstances we are involved in is not necessarily powerful. We all affect situations merely by being present in them, and that cannot be considered the exercise of power. For us to be considered powerful, we have to want to get some results out of the changes that we effect.

Morriss (1987) also makes a useful distinction between power and the exercise or vehicle of it. So, the elderly woman probably perceived my power to have her compulsorily admitted to hospital and that I might do so simply because she knew of my official position and saw the aura about me of a young man in a hurry. I did not have to exercise any actual powers to put her in the position of agreeing to what I wanted. Similarly, my official position, my skills and my manner were the vehicles of my power, they are not in themselves powerful. Morriss would argue, I think, that they only become so because of my purposes in being involved with her at all; that is, my attempt to help her live a more satisfactory life and my wish to avoid the neighbours being troubled by her behaviour.

Therefore, social workers must always be powerful in relationship with their clients, because of the professional nature of that relationship. A professional is not in a relationship merely for mutual interest, as in a friendship. Workers are always in the situation for particular purposes. If they have the capacity and are disposed to use power, the fact of having professional purposes will construct many of their acts as powerful. People will see them as powerful and they will in fact use power a great deal. The corollary of this analysis is that if social workers are not disposed to use their power, or if they are pursuing the relationship for confused or uncertain objectives, they will dissipate their power and make it less influential were they to use it.

Another set of distinctions are made by Bachrach and Baratz in formulating a typology of different types of power, which Lukes (1974) adapts:

- *Force* where A gets B to do what A wants by removing or reducing the viability of any alternatives.

- *Manipulation* is force where B is not aware of its use.

- *Coercion* where A gets B to do what A wants by threatening deprivation in some way in a situation where there is a conflict between them.

- *Influence* where A gets B to change in some way without any actual or implied threat.

- *Authority* where A gets B to do what A wants because of a recognition that what A wants is legitimate and reasonable.

A well-known psychological analysis of power comes from the work of French and Raven (1959), who distinguish five types of power:

- *Reward power* where A has power over B because B thinks A offers rewards or advantages.

- *Coercive power* where A has power because B thinks A can apply punishments or disadvantages.

- *Expert power* where A has power because B considers that A has greater skills or knowledge than B.

- *Referent power* where A has power because B identifies with and respects A.

- *Legitimate power* where A has power because B accepts a general view of society that A has the right to control or influence B.

Is social work practice consistent with exercising power?
Debates about using power in social work for the purposes of social governance reflect a debate between the reflexive-therapeutic concern with personal fulfilment for clients and the individualist-reformist acknowledgement of the role of social control. Views which see social work mainly or solely as personal or interpersonal helping for altruistic purposes assert the incompatibility of its objectives with the exercise of power. Since, however, power is obviously exercised and is only partly damaging to the overall project of social work, individualist-reformist accounts of social work assert the need to contain within social work a tension between social change and social control objectives. Day (1981), for example, studied people on probation, who recognised power differences between them and their officers (who in Britain were at the time social workers), but accepted the usefulness of the helping and directive aspects of the worker's role. Rooney (1992) argues that voluntary psychotherapy has been the most prestigious form of social work (in the USA). Therefore, theoretical concepts for working with 'involuntary clients' have not developed. Value and ethical systems confirm the importance of individual help rather than the community role of the worker and agency. Also, authority is seen as coercion and ideas such as rehabilitation have been replaced by justice and fair treatment philosophies in work with offenders or 'rights' approaches for others who might have been seen as the objects of therapeutic rehabilitation work.

Davies (1994) presents a coherent account of the individualist-reformist position. He has no doubt about the power of a social worker's role and the responsibility that goes with it:

> ... *the social worker, caught up in the affairs of the State, is necessarily a party to the State's programme of policies and practice* ... *Social work not only has to operate within that framework, it has to ensure that its practitioners fulfil statutory and agency responsibilities to the highest achievable standards of professionalism* ... *The crucial role of social work is to influence* the way in which *welfare policies are put into action,* the way in which *power is wielded* ... (Davies, 1994, p116, original emphasis).

He includes in his analysis of social workers' powers, responsibilities for oversight and containment of clients, involvement in making critical decisions about them (in courts for example), allocating resources (for example, through the British community care legislation which delegates decisions about making care plans) and 'gatekeeping' (that is, deciding who should have access to services). His argument, here, is that professionalism requires the acceptance of the status quo in daily practice on behalf of agencies and within the present legal system. He argues that it also requires involvement in associated campaigning and political movements for change in the system which would permit better practice. However, he sees this as part of the professional role of social workers, but not as part of their job responsibilities when doing social work.

The individualist-reformist position on social work's use of power derives from denial of the voluntary, therapeutic and non-directive nature of social work. Many agencies have legal powers and social workers exercise various forms of authority, and there was concern that this was inconsistent with voluntary social work. The central debate has been described as follows:

> *Does the use of authority in social work practice conflict with basic values and principles of social work? What conflicts and limitations arise when social workers carrying some form of authority are called upon to help their clients?* (Yelaja, 1971, p170).

This debate was also allied to concern about professionalisation. Unless social workers were autonomous and therefore independent of the need to carry out agency and other social requirements, they could not, it was argued, be or become 'professional'. Thus one concern about the use of power and authority within practice was that it might take away from the possibility of becoming a recognised profession (see, for example, Ohlin, *et al.* 1956, on probation and related work).

Analysis of situations in which authority was used in social work practice leads individualist-reformist texts to contain the tension between helping and authority as follows:

- Clients needing non-directive, therapeutic casework are distinguished from those for whom '[a]ssertive methods, more controlling techniques, may be more effective in helping. . .'(Foren and Bailey, 1968, p24) and '. . . which enforces and controls in the interests of the client.' (p29, emphasis original). This is particularly so in probation, prison welfare and parole work (Hunt, 1964; Ohlin *et al.*, 1956; Fink, 1961).

- Using controlling techniques occurs in many different settings, even those where the agency is voluntary or not-for-profit (that is, it is not only associated with statutory functions) or even where the purpose is not particularly controlling, such as in social work in hospitals (Foren and Bailey, 1968, pp114-32 & 196-225).

- Controlling is related in many instances to caring activities. Parents (or workers dealing with child care and welfare) set boundaries of acceptable behaviour as part of the educative and socialising role which adults undertake. Depressed people might commit suicide, and control might prevent loss of life, and allow them the opportunity to build a more satisfactory life afterwards. Satyamurti (1979, p95) argues that, in Britain, the 'repressive and consensual functions' became merged as the Poor Law disappeared and the traditions of social work which came from the pre-second world war voluntary sector began to interact more closely with the Poor Law tradition in the new local authority welfare and children's departments of the 1950s.

- Control is justified by public policy. We all have an interest in preventing people from assaulting their spouses, or abusing their children and a general social duty to act to prevent such things happening (de Schweinitz and de Schweinitz, 1964; Yelaja, 1965). We also provide social services and other agencies to take on these responsibilities more widely.

- Other professions, such as medicine and the priesthood, have powers because of their occupation and social status. Sometimes they also have legal powers (to make medical recommendations for compulsory admission of mentally ill people to hospitals, to marry people). These factors do not prevent them from having recognised status as a profession.

- Authority and power could enhance the activity and make the social worker more effective, '. . . to support and educate his client' (Studt, 1954, p122).

The consensual nature of these approaches to the use of power and authority in social work is, as Day (1981) notes, a fundamental problem. They assume that we all have an interest in an ordered society, and so, therefore, both those who are coerced are helped and those who use authority and power can benefit society by what they do. Use of power to achieve compliance is valued because it leads to effective organisations and well-ordered society. However, a well-ordered society is of benefit mainly to those who are advantaged by present arrangements.

The use of power continues to disadvantage those who do not have it, since they might achieve more from society if they were not so compliant. These views also focus on personal and interpersonal aspects of social work. They ignore the problems caused by the social work profession's position using power on behalf of the already powerful.

Radical and empowerment views

Radical (socialist-collectivist) and empowerment views take up the alternative, conflict, conception of society and the consequences for authority and control in social work. They focus on the role of the profession rather than the interpersonal aspect of social work. Among the origins of this approach are:

- Consumer research showing that clients were confused by neutral, non-directive approaches, disliked the lack of advice and opinion in tradtion al non-directive casework and expected a degree of direction (Mayer and Timms, 1970; Rees, 1975). This pointed up the extent to which submission to authority was an accepted part of welfare practice.

- Experience of larger state agencies set up in many countries as part of the development of the welfare states of the late twentieth century.

In Britain, the Seebohm reorganisation of welfare services and local government reorganisation which created larger units of service. Garrett's (1980) account of the experience of the use of authority starts from various experiences of workers who, in responding to their clients' needs and wishes, aroused the opposition of managers in the organisation. Satyamurti (1979, p97) reported from an interview study of local authority social workers that they all disliked exercising authority. Various writers argued that large bureaucratic, authoritarian organisations were a hostile environment for social work (Glastonbury et al., 1980). These agencies made more apparent social work's controlling activities were on behalf of people with power.

A fundamental feature of socialist-collectivist approaches to social work has been a continuing critique of controlling functions exercised by social workers (Fook, 1990). This relies upon a Marxist class analysis of power. That is, power is held primarily (in industrialised societies) by a class of capitalists who own the means of production, and society is organised so that working class people are available to fulfil the needs of industrial production. The State, including social workers, is part of the system which maintains capitalist power, and in some cases there is a considerable commitment to the status quo, emphasised by statutory responsibilities and professional power. This leads to a separation between social workers and clients (Statham, 1978, p33).   The welfare state is a result of struggle by working class people to achieve collective benefits within this system, and is accepted by capitalists because it maintains the system which strengthens their wealth more or less intact.   Social workers are thus put in a contradictory position as representatives of the welfare state.   They help working class people but while doing so maintain the power of the owners of capital.

The socialist-collectivist critique of the use of power by social workers asks, in essence, 'whose side are you on?' and presumes that you must be on the side of clients.   If you are not, then you must be against them.   Individualist-reformist views of the issue argue that it is much more complex.   Power may be helpful or inevitable.   Its problems must be set against the advantages of making available to disadvantaged people the role of social work.

An important aspect of the socialist-collectivist critique is the idea of 'hierarchy'. We can see this in systems within which people with power can get others in lower-status positions in society to comply with their wishes.   This is also true in families.   There is a hierarchy of power with, usually, a male 'head of household' figure, and female 'mother' and children in lower positions in the hierarchy. Grandparents in many Western societies, who would have had leading positions in the hierarchy of their own 'nuclear' family, lose this when they retire from active work and family leadership, especially if they join the household of one of their adult children.   However, in some Eastern cultures, they would retain their position of respect and 'headship'.   The fact that this is so illustrates how significant hierarchy may be in families, although there are other bases of interaction within the relationships involved.   Hierarchy is also important in many organisations and in the development of professional careers, from learner to junior to senior positions (Hugman, 1991, pp53-81).   An important aspect of many radical, and especially feminist, views of social work is to reject hierarchical functioning in agencies and families and seek a more participative style (see, for example, Harrison, 1990).

The failing of the individualist-reformist position is most starkly apparent when important issues of the 1980s and '90s are considered.   During this period, social workers have faced significant social consequences of wide-scale inequalities which render the practice of interpersonal social work impossible without con-comitant wide-scale action about inequality.   Underlying this development of ideas is the 'oppression' thesis that significant parts of society are oppressed by social relations which act always to oppress people within those parts of society. It is well presented by Dominelli (1988, pp158-9):

Oppression can occur along any number of dimensions. Oppression on the basis of class, race, gender, disability, age and sexual orientation is central to our present society which is permeated by relations of domination and subordination. Individuals experiencing oppression through a number of these dimensions experience them simultaneously, not one by one.

Here, oppression is concerned with domination and subordination. Thus, the exercise of power by social workers is an issue in all types of inequality, because it is part of the social relations which lead to oppression.

The radical, class-based analysis was still important in the 1980s because of the attack by Thatcherite and Reaganomic dogmas on welfare state ideologies. However, other important social movements dominated the oppression thesis:

- *Feminist analysis* argues that a system of 'patriarchal' relationships exists in which men as a class dominate and have power over women. We saw that this was an issue within organisations in general and social work agencies in particular in Chapter 5. There are different kinds of feminist analysis, not all of which take similar stances about every issue. Dale and Foster (1986) focusing on state welfare describe some areas at issue:

. . . the distinctive contribution of radical feminism has been in areas where women are clearly oppressed as a sex: in particular in their critique of male violence, and their demand for the right to a self-defined sexuality. . . (Dale and Foster, 1986, p52).

- *Anti-racism and anti-discriminatory practice perspectives* argue that inequalities deriving from 'race' or assumed ethnic differences can not be understood as deriving from individual prejudice against minorities (Husband, 1991, p50). Instead, they derive from a system of social relations which depend on prejudice and discrimination against ethnic minorities, in what Kwhali (1991, p41) describes as:

. . . a complex international and historical context. . . Issues of control, containment, inequality and oppression are central not simply to the social worker's daily tasks, responsibilities and dilemmas but to the wider organizational and societal context within which social work is located.

These perspectives go beyond the socialist-collectivist thesis that social work uses power to control oppressed groups in the interests of dominant élites through social work activities. While social workers' power is not denied, and its use is necessary, the oppression thesis would require social workers to see where it is being used to support wider oppressive social systems. Clearly this is inadequate as a prescription for social workers' use of power, since it offers mainly an injunc-tion to 'be careful'. Anti-discriminatory practice, however, goes further and argues that social work should actively organise its work to oppose and compen-sate for these oppressions. We saw in Chapter 4 that this is a feature of relevant Codes of Ethics in social work. A theoretical perspective and technical vocabu-lary have become available for this: the idea of empowerment. This approach draws together interpersonal and social action perspectives on social work (Furlong, 1987).

Several perspectives are available. One, represented by the work of Rose and Black (1985), draws on the work of Freire (1972), a radical Latin American edu-cationist who seeks to make people the 'subject' rather than the 'object' (that is, active rather than having things done to them) in their lives. The worker engages people in 'critical debate' through a dialogical process (see Chapter 3) for con-sciousness-raising.

An important feature of Rose and Black's work is advocacy. This can be seen as a professional task as in welfare rights work (Bull, 1982), or workers seeking resources within the social services system for their clients. However, a substan-tial movement towards citizen advocacy and self-advocacy has grown up (Brandon *et al.*, 1995). It emphasises enabling service users to develop their own skills in seeking their rights and in building services relevant to them. Service user involvement in managing and developing services is an important feature of such approaches (Beresford and Croft, 1993; Beresford and Harding, 1993).

Ideas have also developed which seek to shape the perceptions which social work-ers and others have of the services they are providing. For example, normalisa-tion requires workers to seek socially valued environments and methods of prac-tice to develop patterns of life for people receiving care services which are as close as possible to the lives of ordinary people (Brown and Smith, 1992). Disabled living approaches to care focus on enabling people with disabilities to manage and control services to develop patterns of life that they value (Morris, 1993). Social models of disability (Oliver, 1990, 1991) and political economy models of ageing (Laczko and Phillipson, 1991) seek to show that these are not conditions which result in inferior or disadvantaged lives for those affected. Rather it is the way we organise society to exclude people affected by disability and ageing which leads to their social isolation and many of their 'problems'. These ideas relate to anti-discriminatory work. This seeks practice where workers actively approach people and services organise their activities in ways which do not fall in with social assumptions which exclude people from good-quality lives.

In some continental European conceptualisation of social work there is an important element of informal social education. Dutch 'agology' offers a methodology for active learning among adults, assisted through groupwork and community support. French *animation* offers similar learning of skills in interaction and participation through involvement in artistic work of various kinds (Lewis, 1973; Lorenz, 1994, pp98-104; Cannan *et al.*, 1992, pp111-2). This intends to stimulate skill-development and community participation throughout society. Mullender and Ward (1991) describe a form of groupwork specifically directed towards empowerment. User-led groups develop ideas from participants on areas of their lives which are significant to them. This is both for personal development and to affect the ways in which the community around them respond to problems. In this way, people learn about how power structures in society affect their lives. They also learn methodologies for transforming power structures so that they might use them too.

Empowerment theories of practice relate to all these ideas. They argue that oppressed groups suffer from barriers or blocks (Solomon, 1976) in the attitudes of the majority, the organisation of society and the provision of services which render them powerless. This prevents them from expressing their emotions and hopes and achieving what they are capable of. Rees (1991) argues that five main features of practice define empowerment theory:

- *Biography* - people's experiences in life prevent them from gaining power over their surroundings.

- *Power* - we must understand influences which affect how we can participate in social situations.

- *Politics* - power involves access to and use of resources to gain independence of action and thought.

- *Skills* - helping people to gain skills such as negotiation and self-advocacy which will give them power over their surroundings.

- *Interdependence of policy and practice* - we must work directly on changing the environment within which we practise as an essential part of interpersonal work.

Empowerment implies seeking change in the capacity of clients to deal with many aspects of their lives and in the capacity of societies to recognise and respond to a wide range of needs among their citizens. Friedmann (1992) argues, referring to social development approaches, that three forms of empowerment must be attempted. Psychological empowerment is required to enable people to believe in their own capacities for change. Social empowerment is required to help social structures to alter to accommodate the personal empowerment achieved by individuals, and if necessary changes wrought by political and social movements. Political empowerment is required to facilitate change in the fundamental power structures in society. More broadly, worldwide, social movements for change involve communities in seeking political change (Costa, 1988; Wignaraja, 1993), and social workers need to be aware of these and consider their alliance or failure to ally with such groups.

*The implication of empowerment and related strategies is of a greater
degree of 'self-help' among clients and a devolution of power and control
from the worker to clients* (Adams, 1990).

How is this possible in a professional role? Surely, the power which I have argued above always goes with a professional position, will always be present, and will continue to oppress clients. Does this mean, in turn, that the individualists might criticise empowerment approaches for their failure to acknowledge the essential tasks involving protection and social governance? Also, is empowerment practice practicable in a situation in which social workers carry considerable authority on behalf of society?

In answer to these points, empowerment theory has a more sophisticated analysis than radical views of the use of power. Power is not simply rejected as oppressive. The fact of oppressions and the use and existence of power within societies are acknowledged and accepted. Anti-discriminatory perspectives argue, instead, that the consequences of the patterns of power and oppression which exist in society must be recognised. Something must be done *at the same time* about individual consequences and the general social patterns which produce oppression. If workers themselves avoid discrimination and the inappropriate use of power, they will make some contribution to righting long-existing patterns of oppression. If, further, services are organised and developed to avoid perpetuating existing patterns of power, greater progress may be made. If these new patterns of provision become established as the appropriate pattern there will be further shifts in the structures of power which are currently oppressive.

Furthermore, these approaches seek to transform power through the model of practice proposed. By assisting people to take control of aspects of service, by recognising and responding to the barriers which prevent them from having greater control over their lives and by promoting control of things that they can take power for, social work acts therapeutically, in the sense that people are helped with the issues they need help with. It also acts socially by extending and expanding capacity and perception, both of the people helped and of the community and society which respond to them. Thus, a professional helping role is accepted.

By making this argument, however, empowerment theory merely takes on a more sophisticated form of individualism. It is presenting the view that empowering people is beneficial for the order of society and for the people themselves. This suggests that the radical and empowerment theses can incorporate within themselves an individualist approach to the use of power and control as benign influences. But this is not the original project of radical, oppression and empowerment theses, which seek to change the pattern of power and influence in the lives of oppressed peoples.

So, a final question about empowerment as an approach to social work: is it necessary? Is it not merely possible, as the individualist-reformists argue, for a social worker to carry out the tasks of interpersonal social work without taking up *within social work* the task of social change? This would avoid the need for the constant tension between radical and individualist writings and the need to incorporate these objectives together pragmatically.

Trying to merge individualist and socialist-collectivist views of social workers uses of power for the purposes of control in their work is, however, unacceptable to both positions. Jordan (1990, pp106-8), for example, argues that individualist-reformist and social-collectivist views cannot be linked together. Seeking a co-operative, shared, committed way of life and responding to individuals' needs and wishes are each in themselves part of the 'positive potential' (Jordan's words - p106) of social work, but lead to ways of practice which if taken up fully would lead to inconsistencies. We cannot pursue a wholly co-operative, sharing position when children need to be protected from their parents and mentally ill people may need compulsory treatment. However, we should not ignore the fact that a more just distribution of resources and opportunities would often take away the need to act individualistically and controllingly. He argues, therefore, that we need a form of rights- and value-based work for small-scale social relations. This must be combined with a concept of citizenship conferring rights to resources and opportunities at the level of society as a whole. This would reduce the need for impositions of power simply because resources or opportunity were lacking.

This is another statement of the socialist-collectivist view of social work as about collective empowerment in order to seek social betterment. However, Jordan links these two areas compellingly by drawing attention to the way in which the lack of human rights at the wide scale leads to impositions upon individuals at the scale of interpersonal social work. Individualist-reformist views on the use of power fail to develop a project which integrates action upon injustice at the wide scale - they treat this as *voluntary* and outside the activity of social work - with the acceptance of the uses of power which they insist upon as a *requirement* of the activity of social work. I have not focused on the third view of social work here, the reflexive-therapeutic. But a view exists, expressed, for example, by Rogers (1977), that one of the main purposes of counselling activities is to increase the personal power of individuals to understand and use their personal capacities. This has links with Freire's (1972) objectives in popular education as seeking to make individuals actors rather than being acted upon by others. There are also connections to Jordan's view here. As at other points when we have considered the reflexive-therapeutic view, it seeks radical social objectives through personal growth, so it has alliances with the social objectives of socialist-collectivist views and links with the non-oppressive aspects of the individualist position.

The history of social work offers some reason why the tension between socialist-collectivist and individualist-reformist views of social work's use of power is always present and needs always to be there. Experience of Fascism in Germany during the 1930s and '40s led to the incorporation of social work activity within the National Socialist (Nazi) state. It proved very difficult to distinguish legitimate social work activity from the requirements of an outrageously oppressive state (Lorenz, 1993). The existence of a tension within the objectives of social work will help to illuminate the conflicts for social workers presented with such situations. As social work is part of social governance and must use several varieties of power, it is as well that this activity raises tensions and conflicts for the people who must act in this way

Another answer to this question lies in the ever-present experience of the diversity of human kind. In many aspects of life our assumptions about the appropriate way to behave and to provide services are not absolute, but derive from cultural assumptions. Thus, the role of family members may be assumed to be fully interdependent in some Eastern cultures, but in Western individualistic cultures we tend to assume a nuclear family that prepares children for independence. The same applies to services. For example, Britain has been described as having a very legalistic approach to child abuse, concerned with regulation and securing evidence for criminal conviction of parents. The Netherlands, on the other hand, has a confidential, multi-disciplinary teamwork approach to dealing with child abuse which avoids legal procedures almost entirely (Armstrong and Hollows, 1991). Social assumptions about the family and its role in society, or social and legal systems which define certain welfare activities in certain ways are constantly needy of questioning.

The sharp point of any questioning that we need to do is when we come to exercise our personal, professional and socially defined power. This is so in the same way as we noted in Chapter 4 that disagreement about values most often arises when we are in conflict with others about them. We have seen in this chapter, when considering the use of power within social work, that it is inevitable and contained within the nature of social work. This has been constantly reasserted. We also need the constant reassertion into our ideology and practice of the empowerment thesis, because this equally strongly points out the need to exercise that power within clear moral restrictions. The empowerment thesis presents a methodology and also an ideology for doing so.

Chapter 7
Social Work as a Profession

Is professional action common sense?

I was called out one evening to investigate whether a woman should be compulsorily admitted to mental hospital. The somewhat inexperienced doctor thought she was manic. She was pacing round her house picking things up and putting them down, unable to concentrate and muttering to herself about her life. I began to walk around with her, joining in the conversation. It eventually came out that her husband had earlier declared his homosexuality and left to start a new life with a man. This had disturbed her, and she was trying to work out its implications for her life and her view of herself. I spent much of the evening talking this through with her as she calmed down.

In another case, a colleague and I worked with a Pakistani family whose parents had returned to Pakistan to resolve some family problems. They left two young people - one a sixteen-year-old, the other seventeen - in charge of three younger children. We did not immediately intervene, but standards of care began to slip and we feared for the safety of the younger children. We arranged for local foster care, which would also involve the older family members. When the time came to carry out the arrangements, they hid the younger children. Again, we did not immediately react. Instead, talking through the arrangements, they came to see that they could not continue the care that they had been trying to give. Eventually, the arrangements worked out well until the parents returned.

Both these cases involved the possible use of the sort of powers discussed in Chapter 6. In neither case, however, were the powers used precipitately or excessively. They came from an official role, but they were used in a human way. We reacted with an awareness of human response to distress in the first case, and, in the second, anxiety at the inability to fulfil responsibilities that the young people were entrusted with and wanted to fulfil. There was some technical knowledge involved - of the law, medicine and child care standards. Reading these accounts, however, you could easily argue that the social work response was only a common-sense human reaction. Did they require someone special, given particular official powers and educated in an activity called 'social work'?

These questions bear on the nature of social work as an occupation, rather than as an activity. In this chapter we ask: is social work, or in what ways is it, a profession? There are some common-sense understandings of 'profession' to consider:

● *As paid rather than unpaid activity.* We sometimes say that someone is a professional because they are paid and employed to do a job, rather than being unpaid and an amateur (for example, the 'professional footballer' as opposed to the participant in a Sunday league). Social work is such a job, but some people also do voluntary work, or work at social services tasks without being a social worker. What distinguishes paid social workers from them? Is it only the pay?

● *As implying a recognised type of job.* We sometimes use 'profession' as a polite way of asking what someone's job is, at parties or on forms. Sometimes other occupational groups such as police officers or teachers complain that they are having to do social work as part of their tasks. Thus, they simultaneously recognise it as something different from their occupation, but also imply that doing it would be possible for them if they did not have other important priorities in their work.

● *As implying that someone has turned in a creditable performance in some task.* We sometimes say that someone did 'a very professional job' or that she is a 'real professional'.

● *As a description of a special category of occupation.* We talk about the medical and legal professions, but we would not generally refer to the 'plumbing' or bricklaying' profession: these are crafts or trades.

The critique of expertise

These four meanings of profession are related. Being paid rather than unpaid, being in a recognised job, and carrying out a task well are related to the idea of a special occupation. Professionals *profess*: that is, they claim that expertise makes their occupation special. They seek to define an area of specialisation which is theirs alone (Wilensky and Lebeax, 1965, p285). We saw in Chapter 1 that seeking control of knowledge or expertise implies seeking power over a territory. Wilding (1982) identifies a critique of professional power which argues that seeking power through such claims disadvantages people whom professionals seek to help. There are seven points of criticism, and I give some examples which might apply to social work:

● *Excessive claims and limited achievements.*

Chapter 2 noted criticism of claims that casework in the 1950s could deal with a wide range of human problems, and evidence in the 1960s that it was ineffective.

Not all such claims are created from within the profession itself. Unrealistic expectations are laid upon the profession from outside. Government and the public, for example, have laid upon social work in many countries the expectation that social workers can protect children at risk of being abused in their own homes, while being able to avoid excessively punitive action against parents. Evidence of effectiveness of social work is at the small scale, rather than presenting achievements of wide social significance.

- *Failures of responsibility.*

Scandals about failure to act have affected social work. There have also been problems with heavy-handedness where social workers have official or bureaucratic roles, the frequently poor quality of residential care, and the inadequacy of services. Social workers say that these are exceptions rather than the rule, and that many failures stem from poor resources for services rather than professional inadequacy. Organisations and professions often make such points when protecting themselves from criticism. While much social work may be helpful, it is still often experienced as oppressive.

- *The claim for neutrality.*

Expertise and a 'scientific' knowledge base are claimed to give professionals independence from political pressures. Therefore, they should be able to make decisions altruistically in the best interests of the people they serve, rather than pursuing their own or other sectional interests.

The knowledge base of social work is criticised as inadequate to support claims for effectiveness. Social work decisions often reflect fashionable or organisational, political or social objectives rather than concern for the individual needs of clients. The second criticism of 'neutrality' is that social work is always on the side of those governing, those with power, against the governed, those without power. It might be argued that social work is more aware of this issue than many professions, and thus less liable to be unconditionally oppressive. It is also, as we saw in Chapter 6, more inclined to do something positive about it. A third criticism is that professions are inherently about enhancing their own power, and oppression of clients inevitably derives from that objective.

- *Neglect of rights.*

This criticism is also about the powers that social workers exercise on behalf of society in pursuit of social governance. There are systems for complaint and occasionally appeal, but much decision-making goes unobserved, is practised on shaky evidence and a poor knowledge-base. Frequent scandals about particular cases have led to concern about social work's tendency to ignore rights in its everyday work, contrary to the rhetoric of its value system.

- *The service ideal.*

Professions are supposed to give priority to their clients needs, and act from altruism in their work. However, use of industrial action to pursue salary payments, influence and conditions of service and evidence of incompetence or failures of service raise questions about the service ideal.

Altruism is, in any case, a controversial issue. It has been seen as natural (most human beings will help another) and as exceptional (most humans are egoistical). We often associate altruism with individualist-reformist views in which one individual is prepared to help another and societies are assumed to provide such help in an organised way in order to contribute to the social order. However, Schwartz (1993) argues that market societies which assume individualism and autonomy for individuals are the least likely to encourage altruism among their citizens. Committing oneself to helping may also bring social work into conflict with justice and equality according to some views, because it involves responding to people's needs whether this is fair to others or not. It marks the difference between a strict points system for allocating a service and an interpersonal assessment using discretion. Wakefield (1993) argues that one of social work's roles in society is to form the altruistic side of a range of services with alternative objectives, such as justice and equality. There is a collective interest in the availability of altruistic services which becomes apparent only when a market-based society evades the social responsibility to offer them. Thus, social as opposed to individual altruism may be a characteristic of socialist-collectivist views of social work.

- *Disabling effects.*

The argument here is a personal and social one. At the personal level, individualists argue that professions actively take away responsibility and impose control on people so that they are forced to act in ways which are alien to their culture and preferences. This might have been so in the Pakistani family with child care problems, for instance. At the social level, collectivists argue that people come or are sent to social workers for help, but eventually become dependent on that help. Then, personal and social capacities to deal with problems are gradually reduced. These criticisms come from the political left, in its concern for the empowerment of oppressed groups in societies, and from the New Right in its concern for the way in which dependence on the welfare state is created.

- *Lack of accountability.*

If professionals are independent, who are they are accountable to? Clients may not have power or knowledge to make them accountable, and professional associations may be more interested in mutual protection rather than abuses of power or incompetence. It is impossible to turn to complaints systems, courts or tribunals for rulings on every occasion. Many discretionary decisions are made in private and are not observable. It is difficult to explain to outsiders the complexity of social work decisions and issues.

Moral approval and the profession

Professionalism implies more than claiming expertise. It also implies an element of altruism and a basis which allows the occupation moral approval if it is done well. We saw in Chapter 3 that social workers influence clients with a 'genuine' and 'empathetic' relationship. Yet the relationship is not like any friendship or volunteer-helper relationship. It is, instead, a special kind of relationship. It implies altruism, but uses that impression to conceal the fact that the worker is motivated by the fact that the tasks are carried out for pay, and on behalf of agencies and public policies. As Davies (1994) writes:

> . . . the **true professional** is not someone who is cool, detached, career-minded and disinterested, but is the worker who can display friendliness. . ., understanding and warmth of a manner which convinces the client of her active interest in and concern for the client's plight. And clients are remarkably sophisticated in being able to recognise that such professionalism is part and parcel of a social worker's formal occupation. . . There is clearly an element of acting in this, but the performance emerges as crucial to good social work in the eyes of the client. Professionalism is the projection of a concerned interest in the client's welfare (Davies, 1994, pp51-2 emphasis original).

However, altruism and moral approval are constantly negotiated. We saw in Chapter 6 that social work often seeks compliance with social expectations and conventions. Using power to achieve compliance can hardly be seen as altruistic. We saw when looking at values in Chapter 4 that the moral values are complex and dualistic. Sometimes the worker acts on behalf of agencies, sometimes on behalf of clients and sometimes for carers or other interested parties. The value base of any action may be unclear, or it may vary among many different interests.

Moral approval for social work relies not only on the display of altruism but also on meeting public and social expectations. Defining these expectations is a matter for negotiation. Strictly, there is a hierarchy of responsibility from the law and the statement of objectives of a voluntary organisation or company, through the organisational hierarchy outlined in Chapter 5. There are also pressures from clients and their representatives. An advocacy, complaints or welfare and legal rights scheme might ensure that these are strongly pressed. External pressures from the Press and other ways of presenting public perceptions will also be influential. None of these stands alone: each influences the other. By negotiation, a position about any particular matter is arrived at.

A factor in the moral value attributed to an agency or a profession will be its perceived competence. This, again, might be arrived at in various ways: by influential research evidence, by the accumulation of people's experiences, by publicity about scandals or by assiduous public relations activities. Particular people may be influential in arriving at a view about a profession: community leaders, politicians and the complaints they receive, press and other media and the matters that they hear about and take up.

A special kind of occupation
I have argued that a profession is a special and valued kind of occupation, associated with expertise, altruism, moral value, meeting social expectations and competence. If this is so, what gives it that special value? Has social work achieved it? We have seen that being given or obtaining that special value has been criticised. Is that criticism reasonable, or should social work still seek to professionalise?

The nature of professions has been of interest to sociologists for many years, and social work has been one of the occupations studied in relation to this sociological concern. There are three approaches to understanding the nature of professions:

● The *trait* view. This suggests that an occupation which is a profession has particular characteristics or traits which identify it as a profession.

A statement of the traits which have been important in social work is that of Greenwood (1957) who lists systematic theory, authority, community sanction, ethical codes and a culture as the main attributes of all professions. Some professions have limitations by their nature which make it impossible for them to acquire all the necessary characteristics. These can then be seen as occupations in a different category like 'semi-professions' (Etzioni, 1969) in the middle of a continuum from established to would-be professions (Carr-Saunders, 1955; Toren, 1969). Social work is sometimes classified in this way because its practitioners' authority is not independent of the managerial control of agencies. The social worker is also a bureaucrat and this lies uneasily with the aspirations to autonomy and allegiance to clients, rather than organisational needs (Toren, 1972). Also, its knowledge base draws on and overlaps with knowledge which is more centrally within the control of other areas of study or other professions. As a result, the public is less willing to grant autonomy and authority to semi-professions. Bureaucratisation leads to frequent staff turnover and slowness in developing a professional culture. All these features may be exacerbated by the fact that many semi-professions are peopled primarily by women, who find it less easy to be accorded high status in organisations and society more generally (Simpson and Simpson, 1969).

One attribute that is sometimes identified is the aspect of class. Occupations described as professions are knowledge-based, rely on higher education and involve a great deal of desk-work and a high degree of literacy, rather than being mainly practical. They are, therefore, often strongly associated with middle-class people. This class distinction is often one which distinguishes social workers from care assistants.

Jones and Joss (1995) identify the trait view with a structural-functional view of the professions. This argues that they are useful in organising knowledge and skill to meet society's needs. They may also be helpful in promoting a moral order. This view, as with a trait view, relies on an assumption of social order within society, with professions and professionalisation both contributing to that order (Turner, 1987). Both views are individualist-reformist in failing to acknowledge the potential disadvantages of and conflicts within and between professionals in societies, discussed above.

- The *process* view. This view proposes that the significance of professions is the process by which they become professions: professionalisation.

Wilensky (1963) proposed that all occupational groups were professionalising. However, some have argued that de-professionalisation is taking place. This occurs as jobs are split up into less-skilled elements, workplaces are controlled by higher authority, and workers are paid salaries negotiated through membership of trade unions in the market rather than individualised fees (Oppenheimer, 1973). All occupations are always changing within themselves and in relation to others. It is often unclear whether an occupational group has become a profession.

This view would say that we do not need to examine whether social work has 'arrived' as a profession. Instead, we should explore its features as an occupation, compared with other occupations. This helps us to understand the different ways in which these occupations manage their separateness from other occupations and their relations with the political system, public opinion and their clients. Social work is clearly separate and independent from other groups, such as doctors, nurses or priests, although it has some connection with counselling. It is recognised as an occupation in legislation and in the organisation of agencies in many countries. In many countries it also has its own education and is part of high-status universities. Clients come to it, or are referred by others recognising it as an area of expertise.

Brewer and Lait (1980, pp117-25), however, argue that because the public will not pay for social work, it cannot be said to be an accepted profession. They argue that what social workers sell in the USA through private practice is a form of mainly psychodynamic psychotherapy, and that this is an entirely different activity from social work. However, against this view, I would argue that social work should not only be compared with established 'private practice' professions such as medicine and the law. Other occupations such as engineering or accountancy are equally well accepted, but more distant from social work. They are much more likely to have some of the features that social work has. Some architects and accountants, for example, work for public authorities and have as little (or as much) autonomy as social workers in that role. Because in many countries social work is a form of state employment, it appears to have little autonomy. However, it is little observable, largely unmanaged and is supervised and educated for mainly by social workers. Similarly, although it borrows and interprets knowledge from related areas, much of this is adapted to social work use and is researched and developed in a specifically social work way. A good deal of autonomy in organisation, education and in the use of knowledge therefore exists in social work. We looked at such an analysis in Chapter 5.

By studying a variety of characteristics of an occupation, and how they are changing, we can see the extent to which and the ways in which it is professionalising. Some characteristics might be shared with related professions. For example, Lorentzon (1990) argues that both nursing and social work derive from a 'feminine service ideology' in which these professions offer women's work, seen as an altruistic caring contribution to society. Sometimes, related professions overlap and intertwine. For example, Brearley (1995) discusses the relationship of counselling and social work in Britain. Counselling may be used to describe particular aspects of social work, as the Barclay Report (1982) distinguishes between the social care planning and counselling roles of social work. In this sense, it is akin to describing the modern role of casework or what in the USA is called clinical social work. However, counselling is also a separate professionalising group. Individuals pass backwards and forwards between social work and counselling. There is also a permeable and changing boundary between the two occupational groups. Both these points relate to the account of occupational relationships given in Chapter 1. However, Brearley points out that counselling as a set of skills has a role in social work. It underpins a range of other social work tasks. It is involved in care management in community care, for example, and advising parents at risk of abusing their children. It may be a component of work which uses a range of approaches. In a few cases it may be an explicit part of the job description, where for example a counsellor is employed to assist children in a residential centre.

- The *occupational control* view. This view is based on the work of Freidson (1970). He argues that the nature of professions can be explained by their wish or need to seek autonomous control over the organisation of their work, their knowledge and their education. Similarly, Larson (1980) argues that a profession's status depends on its capacity to create and control a market for a service that people want.

The crucial element is achieving the recognition that only the occupational group can understand the specialist, expert knowledge sufficiently to judge the appropriateness of any practitioner's work and the validity of the education required for entry to the profession. Ultimately, professions will be subject to the power of the State through legal process. However, their success as professions can be evaluated by the extent to which they have relatively autonomous systems to control knowledge of their activity and access to it - the idea of occupational closure. This is usually done by establishing systems of qualification through higher education and credentials for practice through registration. In Chapter 1 and above, we noted the importance of control of knowledge as an aspect of power. Lowe (1987) argues that early social workers in the USA confused the need to attain occupational control with achieving occupational status. Thus, they discredited the project of professionalisation within social work in the eyes of radical critics by seeking status, which is a corollary and not a prerequisite of occupational control.

Social work has relatively little autonomy in control, since most people would consider that they are able to judge the actions of social workers. Indeed, a study of Australian social work (Martin, 1992) argues that its inability to control a domain in the face of demand from social and political pressures is a crucial aspect of its lack of political influence. The lack of power may also be related to social attitudes towards women's participation in the labour market, since social work has been predominantly a women's occupation. Martin's analysis of Australian professionalisation would be shared in many countries.

Outsiders regularly take on the power of judging social work through the court system and enquiries into scandals. However, in many countries, education is controlled largely if not completely by members of the profession. Also, in most countries it is accepted that management and supervision of social work need to be by those qualified and experienced in its practice. We saw in Chapter 6 that social work's specific methods of supervision and management may defend it in relation to bureaucratisation. General managers and accountants may have influence in the overall management of service-providing agencies, but the control of practice is largely left to social workers themselves. Howe (1980) distinguishes between 'private practice models' of professionalism, such as medicine and the law, and 'public models', such as that experienced by many social workers, where there is a greater degree of control by the public.

All occupational groups are increasingly subject to external influence, through complaints systems, consumer movements and other systems of accountability. People are much less deferential in the 1990s than they were in the 1950s. Governments and public bodies insist on much greater control, often in search of financial controls, than they did in the mid-twentieth century. All occupations, even medicine and the law, find that autonomy is circumscribed by these movements in public consciousness. The kind of distinctions made in studies of professions may, as a result, have less importance than once they did.

Alternative models of occupational control

An important issue for social work as a profession is whether and how it achieves power through the control of a specific area of knowledge. Four models of occupational control may be identified within social work:

- *Professionalisation.* This view proposes that social work is developing or should develop a professional identity similar to that of other professions.

- *Managerial control.* This view proposes that social work is inherently part of an agency and concerned with developing a form of social governance. It should, therefore, be managed and sanctioned according to the objectives of politically defined social policies. Managerial and bureaucratic control through agencies would be the main way of carrying this out. Workers' interests would be protected through trade unions.

These are both aspects of an individualist-reformist view.

- *The socialist-collectivist view.* This view proposes that professionalisation and managerial control lead to dominance of social work activity by powerful élites in society. Social work should develop mechanisms to permit users of its services to be empowered to control its aims and activities.

- *The reflexive-therapeutic view.* This view proposes that social workers should use their knowledge reflexively to empower clients to develop their own skills and knowledge. Social work's professional base then becomes the skills of empowerment and reflexivity.

Professionalisation

The professionalisation view argues that the trend towards professionalisation is a characteristic of modern society, and social work is necessarily forced into this pattern. Professionalising allows it to compete effectively for resources and support against other occupations and views of the world. At the general level of social comment, a significant strain of writing suggests that Western societies have become professionalised over the last century or so replacing class interests and conflicts with relationships and conflict between professional interests.

Perkin (1989), for example, argues that English society before the nineteenth century had allied wealth first with ownership of land and then ownership of capital. Class interests created horizontal relationships among interests: landlords and capitalists forming a small élite, a small middle class of professionals in the law, medicine and the church and a large working class. Growing professionalisation created vertical hierarchies based on specialised training and expertise. These did not reach the heights of wealth and power, but stretched down through the middle classes into the working class. Such changes permit progression through social hierarchies by people with skills, abilities and motivation. To Perkin, professionalisation also creates a social ideal - the view that merit, training and ability should determine social relations. Bell (1974) argues that these developments are integral to a post-industrial society where knowledge-based service occupations are more important than labour in manufacturing.

For many years, professionalisation in social work was eagerly sought. Partly, this was to gain influence in institutions such as hospitals and courts where other recognised professions were dominant. Social work also sought to distinguish its paid workers from its volunteer roots.

In many countries, including the UK, from the middle of the twentieth century, increasing numbers of social workers were employed in state services. Sometimes these were newly created. Elsewhere, they were developments of existing provision, such as, in Britain, the Poor Law. These formed a more bureaucratised group. In Britain, child care officers joined the public service professions along with probation officers and were later joined by mental welfare and welfare officers. In Scotland, these groups were reorganised to form the new social work departments in 1970; England followed suit in 1971, but left the probation service as a separate entity. At around the same time, a unified British Association of Social Workers was created, although the probation officers decided not to join. A similar unification had taken place in the USA in 1955, and other countries have experienced similar developments at different periods.

All these reorganisations derived from a feeling that social work was generic: that is, one activity rather than a collection of specialisms with some overlap. We have met some issues about this idea in previous chapters. We saw in Chapter 2 how these changes led to activity in trying to define the profession as a whole.

These developments, then, the creation of one conception of social work and the development of codes of ethics were intended to create a profession with many of the attributes discussed above. In this 'struggle' for professionalisation, as Hugman (1991) describes it, were the seeds of its own destruction, since it immediately raises alternative views of organisation and development of an occupational group. Sibeon (1990) argues that the construction of a professional position removed the indeterminacy with which psychotherapeutic mystique shrouded social work. As a result, greater technicality in the work permitted more powerful interventions from other interest groups such as politicians and managers. In turn, this led to greater managerial control of social work and a deprofessionalisation of its activities and the occupational group.

Managerial control

The managerial control view of professionalisation sees occupational groupings as a way of organising relationships within work organisations. Giddens (1993, pp296-7), for example, points to the importance of knowledge, expertise and the transmission of information in modern organisations. Professionals have a long period of training and socialisation which gives them allegiance to national and perhaps international conceptions of what they do and should do. Their expertise, the fact that it gives professionals the power to control public access to services or qualifications and the availability of external standards and expectations to which professionals look, gives them more autonomy than other equivalent functionaries in work organisations, all of whose authority comes from the organisational hierarchy. In any organisation, therefore, professionals and their professionally defined roles are likely to be in tension with the organisation. The professional works with people who are mainly functionaries of the organisation, but who contain within themselves elements of the functionary and of the professional.

In this view, social work is a professional kind of occupation group in tension with managerial and bureaucratic aspects of the organisations of which it is a part. Bamford (1989) argues that this form of managerialism has grown more important in the social services of the late twentieth century. This is supported by research such as Howe's (1986), which shows how much professional practice is restricted by welfare bureaucracies. Britton (1983) and Rojek (1989) show how this may become alienating and destructive for professional workers. However, Freidson (1986) notes that people in different positions within professionalised bureaucracies hold power of different kinds and over different issues. Thus, social work teachers may have influence over knowledge, the practitioner over practice and the manager over resources. Moreover, as Britton describes, workers may gain fulfilment through commitment to a form of organisation of their work which involves allegiance and participation with clients and supportive team structures. Alienation of professionals is, therefore, not a necessary concomitant of managerialism.

Responsibilities to agencies and clients conflict. They are not and cannot be adequately defined in a professionalised occupation, since professionalisation inherently relies on discretion and altruism among the profession (Payne, 1989). The managerial view argues for explicit systems of management through agencies. Stakeholders' interests can thus be dealt with in formal systems of decision-making. Examples are democratic representation, complaints systems and managerial control of decision-making according to defined and sanctioned criteria.

Halmos (1965) argues that 'counselling' has to some extent replaced the traditional advice-giving professions of the law, medicine and the Church with a more secularised and accessible form of response to the more complex social difficulties of industrialised societies. These counselling occupations have shared views of human nature and of appropriate social responses, that have come to influence the organisation of many social institutions, including business organisations (Halmos, 1970). Halmos was writing when it appeared that there was consensus about social responsibility. Following the period of the 1980s when New Right political influence reduced the social consensus that Halmos observed, the importance of these trends may be doubted. However, Halmos's analysis draws a parallel between the group of 'counselling' occupations of which social work is one and the more general historical and social trends which Perkin and Giddens identified. Social work is developing alongside the same professionalising social trends and, at least at some times and in some quarters, its ideals have had recognition and even influence.

Socialist-collectivist models of professionalisation

Many would criticise that participation in the trend towards professionalisation, because it moves away from an immediate response to the needs expressed by clients and potential clients. Critics of the professionalisation of social work have argued that it would lead to less commitment to activism on behalf of and with clients. Reeser and Epstein (1990) carried out a study in the USA to see if commitment to professionalisation reduced social workers' commitment to social action. They found that, as a group, social workers in the 1980s were more aware of social-structural (that is, radical) explanations of poverty and more likely to approve of conflict strategies than their equivalents in the 1960s. They were also more likely to be politically active in conventional channels of protest. They did not, however, work with radical movements alongside poor people. There was incomplete development of a 'professional community', one of Greenwood's (1957) attributes of a profession, but where there was participation in professional activities, workers were more politically active.

The socialist-collectivist model argues that social workers should primarily respond to the interests and wishes of their clients. At a personal and interpersonal level, they should use methods such as task-centred work which are transparent and involve clients in decision-making. They should also use methods which are explicitly on the side of clients, such as those discussed in Chapter 5. At the level of profession and agency, there should be participative systems of planning for services. Workers should empower self-help and self-advocacy groups so that clients are more able to take action themselves.

Reflexive-therapeutic views of professionalisation

One response to these issues is to approach social work knowledge and expertise in different ways from those of professions schooled in more positivistic sciences. This approach can be seen in the work of Schön (1983). Reviewing the criticisms of professions, he argues that rather than basing their action on 'technical rationality', effective professionals in different occupations have common techniques for improvising according to informally learned guidelines. They react to a variety of situations using these guidelines in a spontaneous, intuitive way. However, the variety and complexity of the situations that they deal with often present 'surprises' which their intuitive guidelines do not help them to deal with. They then reflect on the situation and adjust their ways of working to deal with it. In turn, this alters their guidelines for intuitive action.

One attraction of this formulation of professional epistemology (ways of knowing), especially for social work, is that it recognises the interaction between client and worker. Schön puts this at the centre of professional activity, and shows how social work and other professions may be reflexive. They adjust their practice in response to the stimuli coming from the people they serve. This respects and makes a role for clients in the formulation of social work, rather than seeing it as constructed in theory or research by the profession and in higher education. As with other professions (Eddy, 1984), social work is inherently about the use of discretion, since it is often used in social service systems to deal with complex problems which are not amenable to merely administrative actions.

Social workers are, therefore, always conscious of the uncertain, debated and provisional nature of knowledge. They may be better able to recognise and reflect on the uncertainties of their knowledge base than more-positivistically-trained professions. Social work is in a contradictory position. On one hand, it is a relatively low-status profession, so clients might not be so oppressed by it as by others with more status. Its awareness of the issue prevents an unreasonable concern with professional status. On the other hand, a concern with what Hugman (1991) calls a 'struggle' for professionalisation might lead social workers to be more rather than less status-conscious.

Education and professional standards in social work
An important aspect of professional power and occupational control is the way in which access to and standards of an occupation are controlled. This takes place at various stages in social work. People have to gain access to a job in social work to practise and to education to obtain a qualification. Often, qualification is one indicator of standards in practice.

In the twentieth century, education in social work has been regarded as appropriate to higher education. That is, it builds on the standard of education normal for someone completing school in any particular country. It is organised either in universities, in higher education institutions which specialise in advanced professional and vocational training or in higher education institutions specialising in social work training. Sometimes, there is a mixture of two or three of these. There may also be some more basic level of qualification for less skilled care work at lower-level institutions, or provided by employers.

Social work education also involves practice experience. How this is organised varies, but most countries provide for placements or work experience, integrated into the higher education experience. These two aspects of education inform each other, either by direct teaching about the integration of 'theory' and 'practice', or by students performing that integration themselves.

Validation of courses refers to the process of deciding whether a course is suitable to lead to the qualification it offers. Universities are generally independent validators of their own courses. In some countries, including Britain and the USA, a professional qualification in social work is also validated by a specialised validator. In the UK, this is a quasi-government body, CCETSW. In the USA, it is an association of schools of social work, CSWE. These bodies prescribe an official curriculum. The government sets this in other countries, such as Denmark and Russia. Elsewhere, as in Germany, colleges' validation has no professional oversight.

The title 'social worker' is not reserved to qualified people in most countries, but recognition to practise is often restricted to registered or accredited workers. The government authority for the area where the social worker practises may undertake such accreditation, the state in the USA and the equivalent, the *länder*, in Germany. Professional organisations have sought similar arrangements in the UK in a prolonged campaign for a general social work or general social services council. This terminology reflects an analogy with the General Medical Council and the United Kingdom Council for Nursing, Midwifery and Health Visiting.

Views on education and accreditation reflect the different views identified above about professionalisation. The professionalisation view argues that attaining the attributes of a traditional profession is the best way of maintaining standards for the benefit of clients. This neglects the disadvantages that occupational closure brings, as professional power might advantage the occupation rather than its clients. The managerial control view argues that education and accreditation should be in the hands of employers, who can implement controls on workers in pursuit of agreed policy objectives and standards of practice. However, this approach allows no independent recourse in the interests of clients. Clients interests might well be very different from the social élite's who define and impose social policy on the social groups which mainly form the clientele of social work. The socialist-collectivist view argues that control of education and accreditation should be developed in alliance with representatives of client groups, rather than in the interests of employers. They should pursue advocacy and empowerment strategies rather than therapeutic or social control strategies as the focus of social work. This neglects the legitimate interests of stakeholders in society who finance and control social services. To meet their needs requires therapeutic and social control objectives. Service users interests need to be negotiated and developed alongside the interests of other stakeholders. The reflexive-therapeutic approach would argue for the development of relevant skills within social work, but neglects the need for more-explicit and organised forms of accountability.

Many of these views can be seen in the British debate about a social work or social services general council and in debate about the role of social work education. Attempts by professional bodies to develop a social work council have been frustrated by both managerial control arguments and radical criticisms. For example, Malherbe (1982) argued that managerial control was the most important way of ensuring clients needs were met and that accreditation had not worked well in the interests of clients in other countries. Parker (1990), reviewing this debate, emphasised how, in the 1990s, changes in the organisation of social services by fragmentation due to privatisation of services, made managerial control less possible. Instead, greater inspection and regulation of non-state services had grown up, but this did not provide for the supervision of standards of work.

In the 1970s, attempts were made to develop a critique of social work education which would make it more responsive to clients' interests (Cannan, 1972). Among the arguments of citizen participation and advocacy movements in the 1980s was the value of involving service users in training for social workers. Attempts during the late 1970s and early 1980s to increase agencies and employers involvements in the management of social work education through partnerships in providing social work education reflected a struggle for control of education (Payne, 1994b). Here, managerial control became dominant. In the mid 1980s, an attempt was made to develop a three-year professional qualification, enabling a wider range of professional knowledge to be taught with greater flexibility. If it had been successful, this might have strengthened the professionalising aspect of social work courses. This move failed when the Government refused to finance it. Several attempts have been made to develop post-qualification studies for people with some years of experience after their qualification, but this has never taken off. Much post-qualification training is under managerial control, being provided on a relatively small scale by employers themselves to meet their managerial needs.

In the reform of social work education at the end of the 1980s, a radical and reflexive demand for extensive commitments to anti-discriminatory practice was included in the objectives of social work education in Britain. However, a backlash against this attempt to strengthen service users' interests against the interests of other stakeholders led, in the 1995 reform of social work education, to a further reimposition of explicitly managerial control objectives. In this instance, more explicit competencies were defined to restrict the reflexivity and flexibility of social work roles. Also, the anti-discriminatory perspective was reduced in favour of a more managerial interest in pursuing equal opportunities.

The UK thus has relatively strong central control of the validation of qualifications, but no way of ensuring that workers update their knowledge or develop their expertise through post-qualification education. There is evidence of codes of practice, but many of these are issued by government in pursuit of political and service objectives, rather than being autonomous statements of practice. Compliance with the code of ethics depends on membership of BASW, which is limited. The absence of a social work or social services professional council limits the possibility of regulating practice after qualification, except through the responsibilities of employers and government, who may have interests (such as cost control or compliance with politically motivated policies) distant from achieving good practice.

The focus of British social work education is largely on managerial control, and efforts to achieve professionalisation and radical or reflexive approaches have been relatively unsuccessful, although all have influenced some developments within the overall managerial control perspective. From this example of the position of British social work, we can see that the form and nature of education for an occupation and the means of regulating them are being constantly renegotiated among the interested stakeholders.

Endword: social work as a profession

In summary, then, we can see that social work is a profession, in the following senses.

- It is a widely recognised job, which people distinguish from related jobs.

- It is recognised to require training at a higher education level and a degree of expertise.

- It is part of a general movement in society to create occupational groupings with their own hierarchies. These have a degree of autonomy in defining tasks and standards, but are part of large-scale organisations, dominated by the State.

- It has a recognised position in many societies as part of public provision in competition with other related agencies and professions. In competing for resources as an occupational group and as the dominant profession in a set of definable social agencies, it also has an accepted social role.

- It receives a degree of moral approval and recognition of altruism among its practitioners. They are not generally regarded as doing it for their own benefit, even if they derive benefits from doing it as all people who work do. Its value system (see Chapter 5) shows acceptance of moral responsibilities.

- It meets social expectations and carries out recognised social functions.

- It is generally regarded as competent and effective.

Not all of these comments would be regarded as 'true', in the sense that people could argue with justification against each of them, and the balance of their accuracy would vary in different countries. There is no final answer about whether social work is a profession. There is no 'truth' about this matter. A debate takes place. In many countries, the involvement of social work in widely recognised social trends in the development of occupations, in discourses about training, moral approval, effectiveness and in negotiations for resources and recognition among its sister occupational groups marks it out as in the category of a profession.

Part of the discourse about the nature of social work is the different views of professionalisation identified here and the criticisms of social work as becoming professionalised. One crucial area is debate about the nature of knowledge and power in social work. Socialist-collectivist views of social work professionalisation argue that the control of knowledge which is implicit in professionalisation or managerial models of the occupation of social work operates against the interests of clients. Instead, this view proposes, social work must take the side of the client, and this involves the rejection of managerial or professional models of control within the occupation. The individualist-reformist view of this argument is that such a rejection is impossible. If we accept this view, managerial and professional models of occupational control offer different but perhaps practical ways of respecting the interests of clients.

However, the reflexive view of social work takes a different perspective on this debate. By their understanding of the ambiguous nature of social knowledge and its reflexive methodologies, social workers necessarily become entwined in the value systems and objectives of their clients. Together, they explore the territory of personal and social progress, using the professional resources of the worker and the structure of the agency. In this view, professionalisation and managerial control are the servant of the client's aims through the skilled involvement of the worker. Such a view returns the debate about the social aims of professionalisation to the personal and interpersonal role of social work. It defines social work as a profession as made up of the myriad actions of its constituents. In doing so, it rejects the distinction made in Chapter 1 between social work as an activity and as an occupational group. The occupational group is the sum of the activities of its constituents and how they are known by the participants. In the sense that knowledge derived from reflection about participation is the only way of ultimately knowing a social activity, this is a truism.

But if we are to understand the social nature of social work, we cannot neglect the preceding discussion of its characteristics as it professionalises, and views about that process. We can 'know' that social work is a profession, in the ways outlined above. Also, we must reflect and criticise that knowledge constantly, balancing it with our perceptions of actuality. In our practice, we must recognise the problems, contradictions and criticisms that the social process of professionalisation brings for interpersonal and personal work.

Chapter 8
The Globalisation of Social Work

The social worker abroad

I visited Peru in 1990 and saw what was said to be the only old people's home in the country in the capital, Lima. It was a modern building, quite like a similar home in Britain. Later, I talked with a middle-aged man in another city, and he told me about his arrangements for caring for his parents. He had a job in the city, but his parents had been peasant farmers and had a small plot of land. As they reached middle age, they transferred this to my informant and his brother, on condition that they farmed it and provided the parents with food and clothing when they eventually became unable to provide for themselves. The parents were now quite elderly and incapacitated. My informant and his wife produced food for several members of the family. Every month, they visited his parents with food and other goods that they needed. His wife provided help around the home. They did this in return for the benefit of having the food from the land. I told him a little about community care services such as home helps, meals on wheels delivered to an elderly person's own home, and the possibility of being admitted to a residential care home. The existence of such arrangements appalled him. Not taking responsibility for his parents was unacceptable socially for him. Of course, he was advantaged in doing so, compared with many people from his country, because their land allowed them to make a contract with their children. They had benefits to barter for their care.

In a poor country, few had such advantages. Women organised soup kitchens on a communal basis. International and local charities supported these to promote community development through co-operation, the development of women's rights and involvement in society. They provided food for people without any resources in shanty towns around the capital and other cities.

In Peru, many of the small number of people employed as what were explicitly called 'social workers' worked in the court system, dealing with adoption, and in hospitals. There was a problem of children without care because in parts of Peru guerilla action and army and police responses had killed so many people that there were insufficient relatives to provide for the remaining children. Whole families lived on the city streets, selling things or begging. A crime problem existed because of gaps in wealth between rich and poorer people. People moved to cities from jungle and mountain areas where they were self-sufficient, to obtain the benefits of civilisation. Schemes to resettle people away from the cities or to develop rural areas to reduce the demand on public services that this migration produced were relatively unsuccessful.

Peru is not by any means the poorest country in the world, and since my visit has made considerable economic, political and social progress. The needs in this country, however, and in many poorer countries around the world, suggest that the social work typical of Western societies may be irrelevant. In many countries there are few welfare services and social provision is concerned with social and economic development rather than welfare needs.

One characteristic of present-day society is the effect of globalisation, ' . . . the compression of the world and the intensification of consciousness of the world as a whole' (Robertson, 1992, p8). Peru experienced this through people from the jungle and mountains wanting the benefits of urban society. They were aware of this possibility through television and through greater contact with city people. Communication media such as television, the information superhighway and speedy travel have made contacts between different cultures more frequent. As a result, inequalities, conflicts and strains between different cultures are more evident.

This is important in all aspects of society. Cultures are more likely to clash because of greater contact. Change is speeding up. Knowledge is so extensive that we cannot know it, so specialisation grows apace. Changes in employment, social structure and social expectations affect us all.

Globalisation is also important in understanding social work. First, it provides the opportunity for a critique of ideas about social work. If it is a universally relevant body of ideas and discourses, it must also be relevant outside the societies of its formation. Since it is supposed to be about helping people attain social better-ment, seeing if it offers something to poor nations is a test of its universality and general relevance. Worldwide inequalities and problems raise questions about practising social work with a restricted focus on the problems of Western soci-eties, serious though they may be. Since social work is supposed to be anti-dis-criminatory, valuing and respecting human beings, it is a test of its values to see if its construction is relevant to the differing needs of non-Western countries. So, social work ought to have things to offer poorer countries in the world.

Second, globalisation inevitably faces social work in Western countries with the inadequacies of models claimed to be universal. There are also demands for attention from models of practice meeting alternative cultural perspectives and social needs. So, the discourse of social work should gain from poorer countries in the world.

Third, globalisation is at the same time both an opportunity for progress and growth and a risk to culture and individuality. Global culture attacks national or regional culture; it homogenises the individuality of the world. It takes away specificity and replaces it with generality. There are gains and opportunities, but there are also losses. On the other hand, culture is powerful and it never was unchanging. Worthwhile specific perspectives on life are likely to maintain their strength and to be valued for their contribution to the global whole. We must never see a culture as unchanging. Neither must we see the global culture dominated by American values as impossibly powerful. Many countries and cultures reject it, or are selective in their choice from it and many are able to contribute to it.

So it is with social work. I argue in this chapter that 'Western' social work is available to the world, and can be used elsewhere, or rejected. It must also be adapted by learning from the myriad kinds of knowledge in the world.

But we must not try to homogenise what is incompatible, and we must avoid controlling the media of knowing to make them inaccessible. That is an oppression of many cultures by the few.

Strategies for global knowledge
Three possible strategies exist for dealing with the problems presented by globalisation:

- *Holistic strategies* - These involve trying to understand the conflicts, and make our own conceptions of the world, and the world of social work, more complex. Eventually, we should be able to encompass the whole, or create conceptions which, if not all-encompassing, are at least widely acceptable.

Such an approach is potentially oppressive of particular cultures, or imperialistic, since the attempt of overall conceptualisation inevitably comes from one set of cultural preconceptions. On the other hand, seeking a common conception may make it possible to give greater power to conceptions other than those of the West. It is not clear that all conceptions can be incorporated into one overall perspective.

- *Partialising and comparative strategies* - Here we try to limit conceptions of social work so that they apply only to particular countries or to particular cultures.

Once we accept that we cannot conceptualise different forms of social work as a whole, we can develop a related strategy of trying to compare different conceptions. Brown (1994), for example, argues that we can only learn about alternative approaches by confronting the differences between them, rather than asserting their wholeness. The problem with this approach is that it denies the possibility of wholeness and implies that there is no social work. In fact, however, there seems to be a collection of 'social works'. At least, we can see connections between related ideas.

- *Discursive formation strategies* - These extend the approach I have taken throughout this book. We see the nature of social work as a collection of competing and interacting sets of ideas, presented as actions and concepts. The discourse about them forms social work.

In this approach, we do not seek wholeness through one perspective. Instead, we value the discourse between perspectives as constructing a whole while exploring and valuing difference.

The argument of this chapter, then, is that social work's universality does not come from the dominance of one conception of it. Rather, it comes from its engagement in a worldwide discourse about modes of social action in response to fundamental value objectives. The next section argues that social work varies even within Western societies. After this, I review the argument that Western models of social work are irrelevant to needs elsewhere. The following section explores the shared values and objectives which lead to a shared discourse between social work and related modes of social action. At the end, I argue that the opportunities offered by globalisation broaden the discourse of social work. However, we must acknowledge the power of Western forms of knowledge and construct ways of ensuring that other forms of knowledge about social work can have stronger influence in the discourse.

Variations in understandings of social work

In different countries, the boundaries of what might be described as social work vary. We explored the relationship between counselling and social work in the last chapter, for example. In the UK, to give another example, there is a distinction between social workers and youth and community workers, which would not be recognised or which would be implemented differently in other countries. Each occupational group has different qualification-awarding bodies (CCETSW and the National Youth Agency, at the time of writing) and there are different career paths. Traditionally, youth and community workers regard themselves as informal educators and work in education departments of local authorities, or in the allied voluntary sector. Social workers, on the other hand, have careers in social services departments and their allied voluntary sector. Overlaps exist. Sometimes settings overlap, and one is employed within the traditional setting of the other. Methods also overlap. Social workers focus on individual counselling work, but youth and community workers might do some such work. Youth and community work focuses on groupwork and community work methods, but social workers also often take these up.

Such divisions might be recognised differently in other countries. In the USA and Nordic countries, there would be no distinction. Youth and community work would be regarded as part of social work, carried out in agencies specific to the purpose of groupwork with young people and community development. In Britain, on the contrary, youth and community workers sometimes regard social work as alien to their central informal education purpose. Danish social peda-gogues, on the other hand, would accept the group and community work focus with young people in a variety of settings and be committed to informal social education as a central concept of what they do (Davies Jones, 1994). They would see themselves as separate from social work, but would accept a therapeutic pur-pose more readily than British youth and community workers. In Germany, youth work and child welfare work would go together in the same agency in many regions and might include social pedagogy, which there, unlike Denmark, is more strongly focused on children rather than informal education for all. Other social work would be carried out in other agencies and would be separate from children's work, although recognisably social work. In Norway, social work (meaning case work in local authority social welfare and social security services), child welfare work and social pedagogy were until recently separate occupational groups, only recently united into one association, which retains separate divisions and loyalties.

Even in these broadly similar countries with related traditions, we can see varying definitions of social work and social welfare, different theoretical understandings and priorities. Almost any concept within social work could be subjected to the same sort of analysis, given sufficiently broad knowledge of different systems.

Western and other social work models
There has been a substantial critique that Western models have dominated the development and understanding of social work in countries of quite different cul-ture and with differing needs (Midgley, 1981; Nagpaul, 1993). This is the product of colonial organisation in the first instance. Subsequently imperialist and racist attitudes have led to the rejection of alternative values. This is evident in the title of this section: treating all alternatives to 'Western' models as 'other' and inca-pable or unnecessary of definition in their own terms. It acknowledges the truth that Western models have been dominant and more fully defined, at least in the materials available to this Western writer.

There are three points of concern. The first is that Western social work may be culturally inappropriate or alien, based on values which are irrelevant to or in con-flict with dominant values in other societies. The second is that the needs of many other societies are different, and require different modes of action. Because of imperial and colonial dominance, these differences are ignored and inappropriate models invested with greater importance than is justified. The third is that the dominance of Western economic power, Western languages and academic and professional modes of communication prevents the emergence and validation of alternative models. Thus, Western power over knowledge prevents the empowerment of alternative knowledge.

Cultural conflicts

Some examples of different social and cultural assumptions and how we might deal with them will illustrate some difficulties with these various approaches. Chinese social assumptions would reject the individualist assumptions of much Western social work thought (Chow, 1987). Instead, Chinese culture (and other Eastern cultures) would assert the value of interdependence and group reliance within families and communities. Similarly, it would reject the Western concept of absolute truth. Instead, it takes the view that each should present the world as they understand it, leaving the wise person (and social worker) to sift alternative conceptions and arrive at a judgement about appropriate action (Chau, 1980).

We can take ideas such as this into Western ideas to enrich our approaches. Confucian welfare philosophy might have much to teach Western social work (Chung and Haynes, 1993; Chu and Carew, 1990). Hu (1993) explores links between Confucianism and psychoanalysis; Pearson shows how different attitudes to leadership, change, self-disclosure and conflict affect groupwork with Chinese people; and Young (1983) relates Chinese philosophy to Western ideas of crisis. We can, perhaps, acknowledge and value for young people the idea of creating warmth and mutual reliance within a family, rather than making them feel that the objective of becoming independent from the family is essential to achieving adulthood. Equally, we can understand the responsibility to assess in a different way if our view about evidence is not so absolute. But adaptation in this way allows us to ignore the fundamental critique of our individualist social expectations which Chinese cultural assumptions imply.

Silavwe's (1995) discussion of social work in an African society presents similar issues. He argues that in many cultures, resolving family problems requires involvement by the community rather than privatised help from a professional. Social workers would invoke community support in working with family problems. On the other hand, Ejaz (1990), discussing similar problems in India, found that using Western approaches to interaction allowed family members to see how to manage the problems caused by traditional values in a new way. Nartsupha's (1991) analysis of the social development implications of Thai conceptions of 'community' makes it clear that some service ideologies derive from a philosophy independent of Western ideas.

These contributions suggest that cultural differences may allow workers to interrogate cultural tradition with new methods and judge and select from methods according to the demands of culture. In some cases, however, the conflict is so significant that compromise is unjustifiable. Fattahipoor (1991), for example, compares Muslim fundamentalism in Malaysia and its social expectations with Western social assumptions. Evidently, there is a fundamental criticism and rejection of Western social values. We can learn from this, but we cannot adequately assimilate part of these ideas for therapeutic purposes or to achieve social change, neither can we attempt to incorporate them holistically. We either accept or reject these views, in the same way that they reject Western views.

Different needs and structures
Different societies have significantly different social needs and structures for taking social actions. These often derive from economic power. For example, a country able to afford fairly comprehensive social security provisions in unemployment, disability and old age can approach these social issues differently from one where substantial numbers of the population are without shelter, water or food. None the less, in most countries some Western-style social provision is available. This was true in Peru, for example.

In India, as another example, a study on psychiatric social work shows that in Western-style hospitals attempts are being made to introduce social workers and gain acceptance for their role in a traditional, medically oriented service (Verma, 1991). This is, however, an insignificant aspect of total provision for people with mental illnesses in India. Bose and Gangrade's (1988) review of problems of ageing in India focuses on stimulating neighbourhood and family help rather than social service provision, except for older people who are sick or disabled. There is a focus on helping older people continue to work and earn their living. Ejaz's (1989) study of social workers in Bombay shows that there is limited provision for conventional social work, and that the focus of social action is elsewhere, in social development. Osei-Hwedie (1993) argues that the need for focus on development is also true in Africa. Attempts might be made to use culturally appropriate agencies such as local community organisations and co-operatives, rather than conventional agencies (Tesfaye, 1987).

Dominant and excluding Western knowledge
Western social work appears to exclude from consideration important ideas which can be used in other societies. Two important developments are:

- *Latin American conscientisation, reconceptualisation and liberation theolgy.* Ballon (1992) argues that Latin America is characterised by popular social movements through which organised groups of the population struggled against dominant conservative political ideas and oppressive social structures to create their own responses to social needs. Such movements have had influence on ideas for social action (Comacho, 1993; Costa, 1988) and indirectly on social work.

Freire's (1972, 1974) work on popular education led to the idea of conscientisation entering social work. The idea of dialogical debate also emerged as a radical methodology for empowering people to be able to act for themselves rather than being acted upon by others. The reconceptualisation movement incorporated the idea of alliance with popular social movements as a crucial part of social work in contexts of severe poverty and political oppression. Liberation theology (Gutiérrez, 1992; Evans, 1992), important in predominantly Catholic countries, focused similarly on concrete work with poor people and commitment to them.

- *Social development.* The dominant model of professional and official social action in Third World countries is social development, often allied to wider development of the economy, industry and urbanisation.

Midgley (1993) distinguishes between individualist strategies where the aim is to improve individuals' capacities to improve their lives (eg Sinha and Kao, 1988); collectivist strategies which seek the development of organisations (eg Khandwalla, 1988) and state provision to encourage development (eg Jones and Pandey, 1981); and populist strategies which advocate small-scale local development to create social movements (eg Jones and Yogo, 1994). Individualist strategies also include the idea of human development, which emphasises developing individuals' rights and choices within underdeveloped societies (David, 1993).

These perspectives on appropriate social work respond to the different cultural expectations and social needs of the societies that have developed them. Moreover, the methodology of social development is relevant to all societies, although it developed and is mainly used in poorer societies at present. It could be a part of social work more widely in combating social inequalities at a 'macro' level. Personal social services and the kind of social work we have been discussing so far may still have their relevance to Western societies, but they may need the addition of theory, expertise and methods of poorer societies (Elliott, 1993). Growing equality between nations, if it can be achieved - there is little evidence of substantial progress - might make personal social services a relevant provision more widely in poorer countries. In the same way, continuing inequality within Western nations makes social development a valid contribution to social work in richer countries.

Many such ideas of practice are related, although they come from different origins. For example, the United Nations Centre for Regional Development promotes 'local social development' for use in development contexts in Third World countries (Jones and Yogo, 1994). This has many conceptual links with ideas of 'community social work' promoted in the UK for broadly similar purposes. Both are concerned to see that action is decentralised and localised, arising from locally determined requirements. Local social development envisages four intervention strategies (Jones and Yogo, 1994, p42). Similar methodologies exist in Western social work, from which techniques might be borrowed, and which might learn from those approaches developed in Third World countries:

- *Resource approaches* - like Western welfare rights and advocacy approaches, these seek to increase resources for families and communities.

- *Organisational approaches* - like Western community development and self-help approaches, these seek to strengthen organisations in the community and capacity for self-organisation by people facing shared problems.

- *Normative approaches* - like Western consciousness-raising or conscientisation, these seek to create or heighten people's awareness so that they can take action on their own behalf.

- *Integrated approaches* - like Western social action, these try to combine or bring together different aspects of the other approaches.

Significantly, these approaches do not focus on individualised therapeutic work discussed in the first few chapters of this book. It is in their focus on social action perspectives that they deviate from the conventional model of Western social work. However, the dominance of this socialist-collectivist approach in poorer countries raises questions about the individualist-reformist assumption that collectivist strategies are not possible in government provision in the West. It seems that the dominance of individualist approaches in the West is a matter of cultural or political preference.

Shared values and objectives
To claim that all Western social work is irrelevant to non-Western societies, then, goes too far. It ignores, first, that there is a continuum of societies and values which change over time. There is not one set of Western values and one other

opposing set. Links and commonalities exist as well as differences. Second, adaptation may be possible, in both directions. Third, while approaches and understandings may be different, the issues faced by different societies are similar. So, connections and alliances across countries may be available. Fourth, in principle, there is no reason why we should acknowledge national boundaries as the limitations of action on human need. However, we must acknowledge the importance of valuing difference as well as seeking co-operation. Finally, the reality of globalisation means that there will be influences. The task is rather to plot the interaction of ideas and concepts. To avoid inappropriate colonisation by the power of knowledge, we must understand how ideas interact among cultures. We come back to exploring and understanding the discourse. If we engage in discourse together, we are inevitably sharing some areas of action and notion.

Continua of culture and need

Midgley's (1981) conception that Western social work models can be contrasted with non-Western models which are in some way more appropriate for other cultures sets up a dichotomy between two different types of social work model. Estes (1992, pp23-34) presents these models alongside a third. He describes them as:

- *social welfare models* - these are individualist-reformist constructions which presume policy, psychological and sociological analyses which enable us to understand different welfare systems. By also appreciating cultural differences, we can respond to the needs and preferences of different ethnic groups and communities.

- *social development models* - these are socialist-collectivist in character and focus on empowerment through developing collective action among powerless peoples in search of social justice, equality and education.

- *new world order models* - these reflexive models focus on the inter-relatedness of peoples, in which rich countries exploit poor countries, thus maintaining the divisions and inequalities between them. By doing so, the ecological system is placed under strain by the assumptions that economic development in poor countries must follow that of the industrialised Western countries. Responding to these issues requires us to see the world in a new way. Social developments need to interlock with actions to develop more shared responses to wider human problems.

In equating these approaches with the three viewpoints to be found in social work discourse in its other aspects, I am suggesting that the discourse about social development is related to the social work discourse. Debates about appropriate social work responses to widely differing cultural and social environments present the same discourse about values that occupied us when looking at social work in more narrow confines.

Interpretation and adaptation

We have seen above that non-Western models of social work are and perhaps should be adaptable to Western societies. Also, some countries have used conventional Western social work. Others see the worth in adapting it. Indigenisation (altering important ideas to make them relevant to local needs) and authentisation (developing local ideas with imported concepts to create a new structure of ideas) can use Western models in ways which can benefit different cultures (Walton and el Nasr, 1988). It might potentially allow them to be reimported and permit other cultures to have influence on Western ideas. This has happened at least once in the impact of the work of Freire on Western radical social work (Payne, 1991, pp206-7).

Denying that this might happen implies that Western ideas can never be influenced by alternatives. There is a modernist argument that this will not happen because Western ideas are built on 'scientific knowledge'. So, the reason for the success of this culture is that this 'epistemology' (way of knowing about and exploring the world) produces evidence of reality, which can therefore be used to create ways of controlling nature successfully. Other ways of knowing are less successful. Even if this were true, this does not necessarily mean that Western social relations, which are based on human preferences and culturally learned interactions, are irrefutably correct. Indeed we have already seen that Muslim fundamentalism has severe criticisms of our approach to social order. Social critics in the West from a variety of political persuasions would share these doubts. Clearly it cannot be true that Western social (and so social work) ideas are always going to be dominant.

Shared issues and objectives

There are many shared conceptions about modes of action and the focus of action is often strikingly similar in different parts of the world.

For example, conceptions of participation and empowerment are just as important in social development work as in Western social work. Burkey (1993) in writing a guide to Third World rural development, for example, argues that self-reliance cannot be developed without significant efforts to achieve participation in planning and action. This has political consequences. As we saw in Chapter 6, participation is integral to the successful achievement of influence in social relationships. Similarly, Friedmann (1992) argues that economic and consequently social development cannot be successful unless local populations can be empowered to decide and take their own action in pursuit of their own definitions of development. Very similar ideas about empowerment arose from a survey of social action organisations in the USA (Mondros and Wilson, 1994) and from Solomon's (1976) analysis of empowerment practice with oppressed black communities in the USA.

The focus of concerns is similarly relevant. Coleridge (1993) argues that a reconceptualisation of disability is needed in Third World countries as in the West. Seipel (1994) regards it as a global challenge. Promoting a social model in which all accept the responsibility for providing a social environment which enables people with disabilities to live positively and take control of their own lives is necessary to fight against prejudice and fear. The same point is applied to the British situation by writers such as Morris (1990), who argues that integrated living models of service to people with disabilities should leave them in control of decisions about managing their lives, and Oliver (1993), who argues that a social model of disability is necessary to overcome stigmatising medical models.

Chan's (1993) study of neighbourhood helping networks in the People's Republic of China, shows that the government-inspired view that mutual informal help is available in local communities is just as much a myth as it is in Conservative Britain. Studies in the UK have shown that neighbourhood help arises from shared adversity, and is a political ideal of a rosy past that never existed. Social trends make it difficult to realise in practice (Abrams, *et al.*, 1989; Bulmer, 1987, 1988).

Equally, the role of women is a crucial aspect of social development (see Fisher, 1993; Harcourt, 1994b; Yasas and Mehta, 1990). Conventionally, women become objects of Third World development work because they occupy a crucial position in the management of resources, in farming and in education of young people. Influencing and helping them can assist in other development objectives. Harcourt (1994a) argues, contrary to this, that they must be seen, because of their position, as a powerful resource which can be mobilised to achieve sustainable development objectives on their own account. This is similar to the argument of Hanmer and Statham (1988) and Dominelli and McCleod (1989) in relation to the UK social services. In their view, instead of being seen as the objects of welfare services and the victims of discrimination in the welfare system, women must be enabled to identify and pursue their own issues through shared experience and personal development.

National and cultural boundaries and globalisation
Related concerns and conceptualisations, therefore, represent another aspect of globalisation. Theory and ideas also flow around the world just as quickly as

globalised communications make possible. The nation cannot limit the interaction of ideas and in many nations there is no cultural homogeneity which can restrict the influence of particular ideas and modes of action. But the 'nation' here is really a summary for the five contexts (see Chapter 1) of legal, organisational, educational, professional, and theoretical systems which provide the basis for social work. Inevitably, individuals, groups and cultures seek control over action and concepts which affect them. Social work is about working with people, groups and communities affected by social change. It will, therefore, be working with the consequences of globalisation in its practice as well as in itself as a profession.

Although the possibility of mutual influence exists, however, control of it is still largely in the hands of Western societies. Western publications and other media can have a far greater impact on Third World ideas than the reverse. What is seen as important derives from Western concerns. They are reported, rather than concerns which are as important, or more so, but do not raise the same concern. For example, an account of the lives of several families in India (Baker, 1991) shows explicitly the feeling of oppression experienced by many women in their daily relations with men, due to social and cultural expectations. However, sometimes a struggle for mere survival, a sense of wider injustices because of caste and a feeling of anxiety because of inadequate welfare services are also present in these accounts. Western concerns about gender and class oppression condition what is reported. None the less, real injustices and oppressions exist, and are genuinely felt by those who are suffering, even if culturally accepted means of expression of these feelings of oppression are not available. While we must be concerned not to misinterpret conventions by raising concerns which arise because of Western cultural expectations, injustice and oppression which is perceived by people but whose perception is repressed by tradition must be acknowledged and worked with.

Moreover, some issues are genuinely international. Globalisation leads to rapid spread of diseases such as HIV-AIDS and social issues such as drug misuse encouraged through international criminal activities. At a smaller scale, missing people move from country to country, children are abducted from one parent by the other in disputes over custody and adoptions take place across national and ethnic barriers. Leisure trends for young people and technological change for everyone may mean substantial social changes in the nature and experience of work and unemployment. Different countries respond in different ways. Each of these issues has a particular pattern in each country that it affects and raises varying concerns depending on its local manifestations. None the less, international co-operation is necessary to respond effectively to many such issues.

Understanding and information need to be widely shared to develop awareness of problems and global links in problems which are faced locally.

Endword: discourse and opportunities

The argument of this chapter, then, recognises major differences, oppositions and conflicts in purposes and understandings of social work. However, there is also a shared discourse round the world. This discourse derives from a shared conception that organised social action and intervention are worthwhile, for related social purposes. The purposes are those we found in Chapters 2 and 4 on definition and values. Thus I argue that a shared discourse about *social work* exists.

Arising from this, there are many aspects of an organised occupational group which suggest that social work is not only a profession in Western countries, as I argued in the previous chapter, but that it also has features of a profession globally. So the organisational structure of a profession in its agencies and power relations, discussed in Chapters 5 and 6, is also relevant. However, I argue that we need a changed conception of social work which represents effectively the whole range of its knowledge and skills throughout the world. Western social work discourses only include the international discourse in pale reflection.

One aspect of the global communication of concerns, practice methods and dominant ideologies in a common discourse is the availability of international structures for these various forms of communication. These provide the mechanism for the global social work discourse. While social work is in each place a response to local social and political expectations and pressures, there are also some aspects of international organisations. These fall into four types of organisation:

- *International social work organisations.* Three organisations have had a continuing existence since the 1920s. These are the International Association of Schools of Social Work (on social work education), the International Council on Social Welfare (representing agencies and primarily voluntary or non-governmental agencies) and the International Federation of Social Workers (a grouping of national professional associations of social workers). Although of varying strength and size, and having different purposes, these provide a means of communication through publications, conferences and joint projects of various kinds.

- *International non-governmental organisations (INGOs).* Examples are international charities and welfare groups like the International

Red Cross or Crescent, Save the Children, Caritas, and *Médicin Sans Frontiéres*. These provide welfare services for people who are crossing borders, such as refugees, and development activities or welfare services in emergencies. Although these are not conventional 'social work' as it is known in Western countries, these organisations represent international commitments to welfare in various ways.

- *Governmental and intergovernmental activities.* Examples are the provision of aid and joint projects such as the many European programmes which encourage shared training, research and other transfer of expertise across the European Union and, more widely, with the eastern European countries and the states of the former USSR. Similar schemes exist more widely, for example between the USA and Latin American and Pacific nations.

- *International organisations.* Examples are the various United Nations agencies. In this context, we should not forget shared policies represented in various UN conventions, such as that on children. Many nations become signatories to these. They represent policy and ideological objectives and markers against which local policies might be measured.

These different forms of organisations allow for international interchange of ideas and to some extent of personnel. They lead to the suggestion that in many parts of the world, social work and welfare activities are well established, though in different ways. However, this has not always been so. In many formerly and present communist countries, there was an ideological resistance to social work activity. It was seen as inconsistent with the dominant ideology, although social work activities were undertaken in association with related occupations. These countries have become interested in taking up social work professions and methodologies, and eventually may come to interpret them in preferred ways.

These developments suggest, as in the work by Chan (1993) in China, discussed briefly above, that expectations that welfare help would be unnecessary in such regimes were unfulfilled in reality. An alternative interpretation is that, in taking up Western democratic forms of government and economy, these countries may have been forced also into the concomitant ways of easing the social consequences of capitalist social organisation. Moreover, the fact that such developments have taken place might be more a testament to the activities of ideological colonialism. The 'social work' ideas of the West have been 'sold' alongside other economic and social ideas.

None the less, we can see various pieces of evidence which might suggest that social work as an activity and as a profession has a character independent of national and political environments. In several countries, social work was reintroduced during the communist period, as different views of welfare gained influence and declined. Moreover it is evidence of a degree of international organisation that Western social workers sought to influence the former communist countries to take up social work during the early 1990s. Recognition by government and intergovernmental funding agencies supported this, but also commitment and belief existed in the value of social work among Western nations. It was this that led them to 'sell' the idea in countries where social work was relatively underdeveloped.

National, legal and cultural specificity means that social work must be specific to the environment in which it is practised. Shared characteristics of its practice and the issues it tries to deal with also exist. International structures enable communication among social workers of different nations. There are also services and international organisations which appear to value it and use it. This may be at least partly because globalisation increases the degree of shared perceptions about problems and issues which societies face. It may also hasten the transmission of social, health and welfare problems which are the main focus of social work activity.

International social work thus represents a tension between pressures towards cultural and national specificity and pressures to generalise features of social work. Important aspects of the pressure to generalise social work derive from the dominance of Western and particularly American media and information sources. These forces have contradictory effects. On the one hand, their dominance leads to resistance from alternative cultures; on the other, it prevents the emergence and influence of alternative ideas and methodologies.

The project of social work on the global stage, therefore, should be to hold in place the tension between specificity and generality. In looking for and acknowledging aspects of shared experience and generality, we should nurture and foster specificities which enrich other specific approaches. While doing so, we must identify and resist trends which merely incorporate specificities into a generality, since this denies difference. Using ideological power which seeks to impose the generality on the specificity of other conceptions of social work denies the cultural and social needs of different peoples. The continuing discourse of social work enforces activity and conceptualisation in pursuit of the complex of ideas about social work. It makes available for incorporation a range of actions and ideas. What it must not do is permit cultural dominance for one part of the discourse.

Chapter 9
Social Work: Personal, Political and Professional?

Public and private humiliation

One day, the social security office rang up. They had had a call from a neighbour complaining about social security being paid to the O'Gradys, when Sam was such a fit and healthy man. He spent all his money on drink. Yesterday, he had been so drunk that he had fallen in the gutter. They should withdraw his social security at once and make him go to work. She had told him so in the street there and then. And he had terrible drunken rages. Neighbours often heard him shouting at his poor, uncomplaining wife. The officer asked for my opinion. I said I would go round and check what had happened.

Sam very definitely headed the O'Grady family. He was strong in physique and personality, a skilled, hard worker in a local factory and dominant but much loved by his wife and two daughters. They had been on their way up, having just bought a new house. Then, there was an industrial accident. Sam was brain-damaged, lost his job and ended up at home all the time. The accident changed his dominant personality into aggression and violence. Money was tight, they lost their home because they could not pay the mortgage and had to move to a rented house. The loss of a good lifestyle and the change of Sam's personality placed strains on the family. They limited the teenaged daughters' social lives and transferred the work of financial support and family management and leadership to Mrs O'Grady. I got involved because of the mental health problems, but also supported the family in a variety of ways, including helping to sort out their finances. It was not only Sam's personality that changed. Mrs O'Grady also suffered from depression arising from their change in lifestyle and the pressures of unaccustomed family responsibility in a very stressful situation.

I visited to find Mrs O'Grady in tears. She had received some nasty comments from two or three neighbours at the local shop. Apparently, Sam had been coming home from somewhere and had had a blackout. He fell over in the street, recovering to find himself being berated by two neighbours, but unable to reply because his speech was slurred and would not work properly. He felt totally humiliated. He had not been drinking, and rarely did. Although he often shouted at her and behaved aggressively, he never hit her or the girls. But he was not the man she had married. She did not want to tell the neighbours about their business or difficulties because Sam would feel even worse. I explained the position and agreed that I would let the social security office know enough to maintain their benefit.

This had taken place during one of the Government's periodic campaigns about social security scroungers, so no doubt people in the neighbourhood were particularly aware of the issue. The 'community' was not helpful to this family, but part of the reason for this was their wish for and right to privacy. Because of this, the ethical rule of confidentiality limited me from disclosing to others information which might help them deal with the family in a way which reflected more accurately their situation. This is an example of a duality in values like those mentioned in Chapter 4. Independence and respect for persons and their ethical consequences came up against a need to act in the community in more open ways.

This account draws attention to some important issues about the public and private nature of social work:

- It is about personal and interpersonal experiences in people's private domains. The O'Grady family were anxious to keep their problems within the private domain. Social workers, entering private domains, bring private material into the public domain. This happens because they are from outside the private domain but have the right and privilege to intervene within it (see Chapter 3). Also, they are part of an agency or a private practice arrangement which gives a formal and public existence to their activity within clients' private domains (see Chapter 5).

- Social work's access to private domains and the fact that it brings private issues into a public domain almost define it as a professional activity. Because of their public position, we accept that social workers have access to private issues. Thus, the social security office felt it right to ask me to investigate and enquire into the situation. Also, the family were prepared to allow me to be involved in their private concerns. However, this is a negotiated involvement: people have to agree to it and social workers have to behave in ways which are acceptable. We codify conventions about these acceptable forms of behaviour into conventions of practice, such as those we examined in Chapter 3 and of values (Chapter 4). These form the professional character of social work.

- Social work becomes a political activity in two ways. First, because it is in the public domain and often serves the purposes of the State alongside the private concerns of its clients, its nature as a professional activity is a public concern as well as a professional one. Thus, the public and the State have interests in and influence on how social work is conceived and carried out. Second, it is concerned with issues which are often political, in two ways. For example, party political views on social security affected the O'Gradys. Power relations in their community also affected them and their family. At the human level, politics is concerned with the processes by which people and groups gain power over others. In their case, we might look at the importance of work, the sick role, gender relationships and expectations, and community power.

As with the O'Gradys, all of these factors interact. The distinction made in the first chapter, between social work as a personal and interpersonal activity and as a profession, may be helpful in explaining and analysing. It cannot, though, be sustained in the complexities of human life. Similarly, the distinction made in Chapter 2 between the social improvement or betterment purposes of social work and its personal and interpersonal character is also helpful in analysing and explaining. In the end, though, in this last chapter, we must understand all three aspects, the personal and interpersonal, the political, and the professional together.

These three aspects of social work come together in two different ways. In one way, they represent broader or narrower conceptions of what social workers work on. They provide *contexts* for each other. So, dealing with an interpersonal problem, such as Mrs O'Grady's depression and Sam's humiliation, I could look up and see a broader political perspective of social security campaigns. This helps to understand why they faced this aspect of the problem. Campaigning for better understanding of head injuries, I could look down during that work and realise the personal and interpersonal consequences of my work through that experience. The fact that I did both comes from my conception of my profession which includes both social improvement and interpersonal work.

In the other way, these factors constantly *intervene* one with the other. So it was impossible to do interpersonal work with Mr and Mrs O'Grady without responding to the party political context of social security campaigns affecting them. I had also to be concerned with the interpersonal politics of expectations of what a wife does and how a husband is within family relationships. I also needed to use and decide upon professional values in deciding on issues about privacy, confidentiality and openness. A head injuries campaign would constantly face me with the participation of the people with head injuries and with their carers. This in turn constantly confronts me with the appropriate role for a professional in political action. I have to think what it would be right to do and what it would be better for service users and carers to do. However, I cannot just avoid doing something if I am to assist in social betterment through service development. I must help and support users and carers to make the progress in services and in social thought that they would wish.

Political, personal and interpersonal, and professional aspects of social work constantly involve each other. They are also external to and comment upon each other. The purpose of this chapter is to consider accounts of how we understand and characterise these relationships within social work.

Different kinds of political conceptions

Three kinds of political conceptions about social work are:

- *Interpersonal politics at the human level.* This type of politics concerns how social groups and human beings gain power and influence over one another. Social work as an activity plays a part in interpersonal politics between itself and other occupational groups and its clientele and communities from which its clientele is drawn.

- The role of social work within the *politics of social welfare.* This type of politics concerns how social work as an occupational group or profession has, or fails to have, an impact on social welfare systems and social reform.

- The role of social work within the *politics of democracy and equality.* This type of politics concerns the role of social work in a democratic system.

These three types of political involvement weave together to form a requirement for social workers to see political activity as central to social work. In Chapter 1, we saw that social work was part of a network of related activities. The boundaries between them could not be unambiguously drawn for all time. A constant negotiation takes place among different systems of education, occupational and professional groups, theories and legal and organisational structures of services. This reflects the reality of the myriad social and political influences on human welfare. We may approach welfare from different positions and with different focuses. Social work must find a role within those different approaches in playing its part in the system, social workers must find and establish roles to play their part. This is necessary if social work is to have influence for its own approach to human welfare and for its clients' needs.

Major aspects of human welfare, considered in its broadest sense, form central aspects of political debate, but are very distant from the politics of the personal social services. As examples, I choose the areas of peace and the environment. Whether a country is at peace or war and the extent of pollution in the environment have effects on individual welfare, personal risk, health and life opportunities. The impact of social work on these issues, or on people affected by war or environmental problems, is minimal. We need political action to affect such matters. However, the need for help to deal with the consequences of wider problems of human welfare implicates the personal social services in trying to prevent problems arising or being worsened by damaging events. Need for expenditure on such issues affects the priority that can be given to personal social services spending. We could do more to meet social requirements if we did not need to spend money on war or pollution.

Social movements in society may seem distant from social work but inevitably have influence on social work developments. Experiences in social work may also influence them. Thus, development and influence from feminist ideas have had a major impact on social work practice and social policies during the latter part of the twentieth century. Some effects are direct, as feminist theories have changed social work theories and practice. Others are less direct, as general ideas about appropriate behaviour and ways of living have changed. Different views of gender relations would cause social workers to react differently to a problem between husband and wife now, compared with their reaction in the 1950s. Change in interpersonal politics of this kind, therefore, affects the objectives and methods of social work practice. Experiences in social work can also influence how ideas develop within society.

One aspect of politics is about democracy and its maintenance or rejection. Influence in decision-making affects our lives. At the personal and interpersonal level, social work contributes to democratic participation. It does so through its concern with self-determination, with user participation and consumer power and with empowerment techniques (Beresford and Croft, 1993; Beresford and Harding, 1993; Mupedziswa, 1988). Promoting anti-discriminatory or anti-racist work seeks to change how social work and social work agencies deal with oppressed groups. It also seeks to have a wider impact on how other related services work by taking a special concern in relationships with other agencies for anti-discrimination.

Welfare is not very important in political activity. The main feature of political life is economic concerns: development and decline, management of the economy and related matters. This has a major impact on social services at any time and in any country. We noted, in Chapter 4, that economic values have become more important than we once might have thought in political life and debate. Economics is not just a technical servant of governments. Views about it have major effects on how welfare is seen in any society. This is as relevant to people in Western Europe worrying about whether their welfare states are to be residual or maintain some semblance of universality as it is to people in Africa wrestling with the social consequences of the World Bank's structural adjustment policies. As a consequence, social work practices such as anti-discrimination may not have wide scale effects on political and social change. Also, political and economic changes may have major and uncontrollable effects on social work. Social work needs to have involvement in political activity to gain appropriate influence on its own nature and development and to influence relevant social changes. Its insignificance as a political force suggests that this might most helpfully be achieved through co-operation and alliance with other groups in society.

Social work is integrally concerned with other major aspects of the State. It is involved with the court system, with the police, with education, with health provision, with social security and with housing. Many social workers have a role as part of the staff of these social institutions, more so in some countries than others. This permits social workers involvement in developments and changes in these services which might benefit or disadvantage social work clients. It also allows others to influence changes in the personal social services.

There are two types of reasons for social workers' concern about wider political issues: the instrumental and the congruent. The first type of reasoning argues that to make social work more effective, we should consider, understand and have impact on policies which will affect services and clients. The second type of reasoning argues that to be congruent and genuine in the pursuit of interpersonal social work, we must have wider concerns than just the welfare system. You cannot genuinely argue for the needs of the young person living on the street in London and dismiss the plight of the street children of Latin America.

Personal, political and professional conceptions of social work
Throughout this book, I have drawn attention to individualist-reformist, socialist-collective and reflexive-therapeutic perspectives on social work. Each of these positions implies a particular point of view about the relationship between personal, political and professional aspects of it. Each position implies a view about the causes of social problems and appropriate responses to social issues. In essence, though, each position reflects a view of the problem of social order and the role of social work in creating, maintaining or changing it.

The individualist - reformist position accepts an existing social order and focuses on helping individuals to adjust to it, and promoting social change within it.

Social problems and issues arise from individuals' difficulties in adjusting to social change and the inadequacies in social provision which might be available to help individuals to cope with change. Practice involves helping people understand the problems they have in meeting their own social needs and adapting the social order to help people find ways of resolving their own problems.

The socialist-collectivist position questions the existing social order. It sees social problems as arising from failures of the social order to meet the legitimate social and personal needs of individuals because of fundamental injustices in the social order. Practice involves social action to change the injustices of the present social order and helping individuals question present social orders so that they may gain power to work collectively to achieve significant social changes.

The reflexive-therapeutic position rejects the importance of the problem of achieving social order. The crucial aim of practice is to enable people achieve the greatest possible human and personal development and to develop social structures which facilitate such personal development.

What potential relationships are there between these three positions? Are they incompatible and therefore always in opposition? Individualist positions reject socialist-collectivist positions as unrealistic. They say it is impossible for state employees whose role is concerned with individuals' social needs to oppose the social structures within which they work. Socialist-collectivist views reject individualist and reflexive positions because they do not adequately deal with the social origins of many social problems in inequality and injustice. Greater personal growth in consciousness can be criticised from an individualist position: greater personal growth is unlikely to help where there are psychological or social problems to be resolved. Moreover, it is difficult to define and account for achievements in psychological well-being. On the other hand, the socialist-collectivist position might be considered inhumane in giving priority to social issues rather than personal needs among clients.

Halmos (1978) counterposes the wish to provide personal help with the possibility that doing so might support a political system which itself creates the need for the help and should therefore be changed rather than supported. Thus, the apparently helpful merely promotes the damaging. Personal counselling seems inadequate when we are aware of widespread inequality and injustice. Only radical political action seems likely to have enough effect. However, this carries the risk that we would completely politicise social concerns and implies that there is no difference between social work and political action. Social work might then become a form of or instrument for political control and oppression. This can only be balanced by the individualist concern for meeting personal needs. Halmos argues, therefore, that social work action requires a constantly changing balance between collectivist and individualist action. The balance between these two approaches needs, in his view, to be constantly reconsidered and reargued. In more modern terminology, we might see this as an argument for constant participation in the discourse about social work. It relates to the assumption of this book, presented particularly in Chapter 1, that constant re-evaluation and exploration of our understanding of social work are essential to doing it.

The three approaches in the examples given above link together, but they are also in tension. When discussing social work and agencies, I noted how the basic reflexive-therapeutic position of social work is forced into relationship with individualist-reformist positions. I argued that they are compatible. This is because they share individualism and because reflexive personal fulfilment assumes a reformist view of social change because it seeks social change only through personal growth. Thus entwined, these perspectives stand in opposition to socialist-collective views. The opposition arises because socialist-collective views identify the oppression that arises from allying the power of personal and interpersonal work with social and political objective of élites mediated through agencies. In the following chapter, on the use of power, I showed how the reflexive aim of personal empowerment was harnessed to socialist-collective objectives of radical change through empowerment. In this case, it is individualist-reformist views which stand in opposition. Similarly individualist-reformist and socialist-collectivist positions combine in opposition to reflective-therapeutic ideas since the first two accept different structural analysis of society as the basis of their thinking while therapeutic views incorporate anti-structural views. So in crucial aspects of social work, tensions and alliances between these perspectives are readily apparent.

Social work needs them all. Let us start from the position that social workers are part of a profession. That is, among other things, they are employed to undertake their work. As the individualists recognise, this means that social workers must ultimately follow the purposes of those who have set up the agencies by which they are employed. Social work cannot be inherently revolutionary because it must implement the requirements of dominant élites in society. However, this does not mean that it needs to be completely uncritical. Particularly if it bases its critique of services on identified human needs, using research techniques and social analysis effectively, social work might play an influential role with political debate. This uses the particular strengths of its knowledge and work base, and justifies a focus on human experience and growth. Moreover, as Langan and Lee

(1989) propose, social work may have a defensive role by aligning its activities on behalf of oppressed groups. It also seeks to reduce the pressure of oppressive social structures by appropriate ethical behaviour. Trends to increased openness in social work practice, by enabling parents and young people to take part in case conferences affecting them, are an example. Similarly, efforts towards anti-discriminatory practice make worthwhile contributions.

For this reason, many social workers find feminist, anti-racist and empowerment approaches to their work effective. These approaches connect with important and powerful experiences in clients' lives. They aim to enable clients to take on greater responsibility for action on their own behalf. At the same time, they respond to agency requirements to move towards self-help and reduce clients' dependency. In all these ways, personal growth can be both an objective and a method. Another important feature of the nature of social work is the social problems and issues on which it focuses. Its role comes from the 'agency function', the politically sanctioned role that the agency has achieved or been given. Thus, social work's nature is constructed by its particular professional structure, by which it is carried out in an agency whose social role defines the nature and purpose of the work in terms of the social governance objectives of élites in society. That role inevitably reflects objectives of both altruism and social control. Also, pathways to the agency construct the focus of social work which clients and workers both experience (Payne, 1993b). In turn, that construction reflects social issues within the communities with which the agency works. A family problem might be defined as concerned with relationships, as a housing problem, an unemployment problem or a mental health problem. How it is defined derives partly from the function of the agency. Other relevant factors may be the experiences and social definitions of the problem which arise as the client moves through various social relationships on their pathway to the agency. At the interpersonal level, these derive from individual preferences and judgements. They also reflect powerful social influences permeating society which implement potentially or actually oppressive social ideas such as racism and ageism. And the wishes of powerful social élites define many controlling ideas of any society.

In this account of potential links between individualist, socialist-collectivist and reflexive views of the nature of social work, I started from social work as a profession. The argument has finished at the point of discussing a particular characteristic of that profession: its agency base. That base creates a context and sanction for action. The nature of social work's base and sanction may prevent a revolutionary role, but permits significant aspects of a social action role. Dixon (1992) argues that the radical literature demands political action but is pessimistic about its effect, while rejecting more individualist action for its failure to contribute to social change. She argues that realistic assessments of both social action and professional work must contain assessments of social and political forces as well as interpersonal ones. Crucial to social action is responsiveness to personal growth and individual need. Commitment to personal responsiveness is an essential justification for the invasion of personal space and individuality implied by seeing social work as a form of intervention in private domains for public purposes. Thus, the interpersonal nature of social work, if it is successfully implemented, counteracts and justifies its use of power in pursuit of social control.

Conclusion

Social work, then, necessarily includes the personal, professional and political. Its personal and interpersonal character and objectives justify its potentially oppressive political nature and carry out its potentially enlightened political purposes. It means, however, that it is always prone to overstep the mark in one or the other direction, according to the perception of others. The individualist-reformist will always be alert to ridiculous personal fulfilment and empowerment objectives or arrogant espousal of political change. The socialist-collectivist will seek to harness personal growth to social development ends and reject the covert oppression of the reformist. The reflexive-therapist will react against the limitations of managerialism and social power as they inhibit the therapeutic aims of social work, and ignore the generality of the social for the humanity of the personal.

But social work's character and organisation bring together, require and make possible its joint commitment to political and personal action. Without its commitment to social betterment, social work would be entirely personal and its objectives would be susceptible merely to political objectives - potentially to political oppression. As Sibeon (1992) argues, radical social theory is susceptible to repressive and authoritarian prescriptions for policy and practice, unless it is limited by including an element of reflexivity. Without its personal character, social work would have solely political objectives - potentially, again, politically oppressive aims. These two aspects of its character require a professional context in order to work together. A social worker develops a view of social work through practising it within a social context. That is, the contexts of its agencies, educational system, legislative basis, professional organisations and theoretical constructs. These were the bases of social work that I started from in Chapter 1. They form a way of understanding social interactions which are typical and characteristic of social work.

Throughout this book, I have been outlining and arguing for this way of understanding social work. I have argued that the nature of all social phenomena, such as social work, is ambiguous and changing. They all, including social work, contain interactions between different conceptions of themselves, and the different conceptions construct them. People's perceptions and analyses of social experiences within what they see as social work construct social phenomena such as social work. The worker's individual views affect and are affected by each of these contexts. Therefore agreed views arise but constantly change as social workers adapt their views to new experiences of social phenomena. It is this adaptation which forms the discourse that is social work. The discourse is between these three perspectives.

The methodology I have used, therefore, seeks to analyse both personal experiences and 'texts' and 'narratives' which provide accounts of the nature of social work. The implication of this methodology is that there cannot be any one statement about the nature of social work. We can, however, arrive at some understanding of its nature by examining its discourse and how that is formed. The content of our accounts of personal experience gives us ideas about the nature of social work practice. The content of our analysis of texts gives us ideas about how people within and around social work try to understand that practice.

What is professional social work? The answer will always be ambiguous and debated, particularly if we take a world view rather than a parochial one. Its boundaries will always be in negotiation, but its essence may be clearer. Social work is an activity and an occupational group which contains personal and interpersonal, political and professional aspects. Its discourse combines objectives and activities which seek social change, the betterment of social systems of welfare, and personal and interpersonal growth and development for people who become its clients. The motivations for its construction in societies are altruistic concern for welfare and social control and protection. Knowledge, skills and values concerned with understanding and developing personal and interpersonal human interaction in the pursuit of social justice form a significant focus of its learning, practice research and education. The social structures in which it is practised are organisations in close relationships with the State within societies where social work exists. Different interpretations of its purposes and methods combine emphases on meeting individuals' welfare needs, collective social provision and personal growth objectives.

In essence, then, social work is concerned with the connection between acting personally and interpersonally and social action. Its concern is practical: it is fundamentally about action, since it is a profession not a field of academic study. In constructing actions, though, it is also about social understanding and social criticism, since it is a field of academic study informing a profession, and understanding and criticism are required both for study and for action. It implements particular social understandings depending on the balance which workers achieve between the social objects of individualism, collectivism and personal growth, and the balance between social control, altruistic help and social development. Social work is thus also concerned with the connection between social understanding, personal, interpersonal and social action. This is because each action implies a social understanding, and in the analysis of each action we can identify an approach to understanding.

We need say no more by way of definition. This is an approach to definition which identifies the areas of debate that characterise social work, while acknowledging that they cannot be resolved in a constantly changing society. We can only really understand by thoughtful and critical participation in the daily negotiation of ideas and practices which accomplish current social constructions of the nature of the profession and activity of social work. Those constructions tell us about social work. They also tell us how people in society are thinking about social life and putting that thinking into action. Since views about social life are always in dispute, social work is always under strain. The strains identify conflicts in political debate about social life. These conflicts exist for all professions, as they try to act on understandings about social relationships. It is the burden and delight of social work that it brings together desires in society for action to achieve interpersonal fulfilment and social connection, but requires it to be constantly alert and critical in its defence of social and personal rights and its defiance of social oppressions.

Bibliography

Abrams, Philip, Sheila Abrams, Robin Humphrey and Ray Snaith (1989) *Neighbourhood Care and Social Policy* London, HMSO

Adams, Robert (1990) *Self-help, Social Work and Empowerment* London, Macmillan

Alexander, Leslie B (1972) 'Social work's Freudian deluge: myth or reality?' *Social Service Review* 46(4) pp517-38

Armstrong, Helen and Anne Hollows (1991) 'Responses to child abuse in the EC' in Malcolm Hill (ed) *Social Work and the European Community: the social policy and practice contexts* London, Jessica Kingsley

Askeland, Gurid Aga (1994) *Studium og klientarbeid: same arbeidsprosess?* Oslo, Det Norske Samlaget

Attlee, Clement R (1920) *The Social Worker* London, Bell

BAC (1993) *Code of Ethics and Practice for Counsellors* Rugby, British Association for Counselling

Baker, Sophie (1991) *Caste: at home in Hindu India* Calcutta, Rupa

Ball, Caroline, Robert Harris, Gwyneth Roberts and Stuart Vernon (1988) *The Law Report: teaching and assessment of law in social work education* London, CCETSW

Ballon, Eduardo (1992) 'The paradoxes of Latin America: challenges to pre-existent theories' in Hubert Campfens (ed) *New Reality of Poverty and Struggle for Social Transformation* Vienna, International Association of Schools of Social Work

Bamford, Terry (1989) 'Discretion and managerialism' in Steven Shardlow (ed) *The Values of Change in Social Work* London, Tavistock/Routledge

Barclay Report (1982) *Social Workers: their role and tasks* London, Bedford Square Press

Barker, Mary and Pauline Hardiker (eds) (1981) *Theories of Practice in Social Work* London, Academic Press

Bartlett, Harriett M (1970) *The Common Base of Social Work Practice* New York, National Association of Social Workers

BASW (1977) *The Social Work Task* Birmingham, BASW Publications

BASW (1986) *A Code of Ethics for Social Work* Birmingham, BASW

Beauchamp, Tom L and James F Childress (1994) *Principles of Biomedical Ethics* (4th ed) New York, Oxford University Press

Beddoe, Chris (1980) 'The Residential Care Association - a code of practice for residential social workers' in David Lane and Keith White (eds) *Why Care?* London, Residential Care Association Annual Review, 1980, pp152-7

Bell, Daniel (1974) *The Coming of Post-Industrial Society* New York, Basic Books

Beresford, Peter and Suzy Croft (1993) *Citizen Involvement: a practical guide for change* London, Macmillan

Beresford, Peter and Tessa Harding (eds) (1993) *A Challenge to Change: practical experiences of building user-led services* London, National Institute for Social Work

Biestek, Felix P (1961 - original USA publication 1957) *The Casework Relationship* London, Allen and Unwin

Boehm, Werner W (1958) 'The nature of social work' *Social Work* 3(2) pp10-18

Bose, A B and K D Gangrade (1988) *The Ageing in India: problems and potentialities* London, Asia Publishing House/New Delhi, Abhinav Publications

Brandon, David with Althea Brandon and Toby Brandon (1995) *Advocacy: power to people with disabilities* Birmingham, Venture Press

Brandon, David and Bill Jordan (1979) 'Introduction' in David Brandon and Bill Jordan (eds) *Creative Social Work* Oxford, Blackwell pp1-6

Braye, Suzy and Michael Preston-Shoot (1992) *Practising Social Work Law* London, Macmillan

Brearley, Judith (1995) *Counselling and Social Work* Buckingham, Open University Press

Brewer, Colin and June Lait (1980) *Can Social Work Survive?* London, Temple Smith

Britton, Bruce (1983) 'The politics of the possible' in Bill Jordan and Nigel Parton (eds) *The Political Dimensions of Social Work* Oxford, Basil Blackwell, pp130-45

Brown, Allan (1977) 'Worker-style in social work' *Social Work Today* 8(29), pp13-15

Brown, Hilary and Helen Smith (eds) (1992) *Normalisation: a reader for the nineties* London, Routledge

Brown, Kate (1994) 'A framework of teaching comparative social work' in Gerd Gehrmann, Klaus D Müller and Robert Ploem (eds) *Social Work and Social Work Studies: Co-operation in Europe 2000* Weinheim, Deutscher Studien Verlag, pp131-40

Bull, David (1982) *Welfare Advocacy: whose means to what ends?* Birmingham, BASW Publications

Bull, Rodney and Ian Shaw (1992) 'Constructing causal accounts in social work' *Sociology* 26(4) pp635-49

Bulmer, Martin (1986) *Neighbours: the work of Philip Abrams* Cambridge, Cambridge University Press

Bulmer, Martin (1987) *The Social Basis of Community Care* London, Allen and Unwin

Burkey, Stan (1993) *People First: a guide to self-reliant, participatory rural development* London Zed Books

Butrym, Zofia T (1976) *The Nature of Social Work* London, Macmillan

Cannan, Crescy (1972) 'Social workers: training and professionalism' in Trevor Pateman (ed) *Counter-Course: a handbook for course criticism* Harmondsworth, Penguin

Cannan, Crescy, Lynne Berry and Karen Lyons (1992) *Social Work and Europe* London, Macmillan

Bibliography

Cannon, M Antoinette (1928) 'Underlying principles and common practices in social work' in Fern Lowry (ed) (1939) *Readings in Social Case Work 1920-1938: Selected reprints for the case work practitioner* New York, Columbia University Press, pp14-21

Carkhuff, Robert R and Berenson, Bernard C (1977) *Beyond Counseling and Therapy* (2nd ed) New York, Holt, Rinehart and Winston

Carr-Saunders, Alexander M (1955) 'Metropolitan conditions and traditional professional relationships' in Robert M Fisher (ed) *The Metropolis in Modern Life* Garden City, NY, Doubleday, pp279-87

CCETSW (1975) *Education and Training for Social Work* London, CCETSW

CCETSW Working Party (1976) *Values in Social Work: a discussion paper produced by the working party on the teaching of the value bases of social work* London, CCETSW

CCETSW (1991) *Rules and Requirements for the Diploma in Social Work DipSW* (Paper 30, Second edition) London, CCETSW

Challis, Linda (1990) *Organising Public Social Services* London, Longman

Chan, Cecilia L W (1993) *The Myth of Neighbourhood Mutual Help: the contemporary Chinese community-based welfare system in Guangzhou* Hong Kong, Hong Kong University Press

Chau, Kenneth K L (1980) 'Notes on Chinese culture' in Peter Hodge (ed) *Culture and Social Work: education and practice in southeast Asia* Hong Kong, Heinemann Asia

Chow, Nelson W S (1987) 'Western and Chinese ideas of social welfare' *International Social Work* 30(1) pp34-41

Chu, Kimba Fung-Yee and Robert Carew (1990) 'Confucianism: its relevance to social work with Chinese people' *Australian Social Work* 43(3) pp3-9

Chung, Douglas K and Alphonso W Haynes (1993) 'Confucian welfare philosophy and social change technology: an integrated approach for international social development' *International Social Work* 36(1) pp37-46

Coleridge, Peter (1993) *Disability, Liberation and Development* Oxford, Oxfam

Collins, John and Mary (1981) *Achieving Change in Social Work* London, Heinemann

Comacho, Daniel (1993) 'Latin America: a society in motion' in Ponna Wignaraja (ed) *New Social Movements in the South: empowering the people* London, Zed Books, pp36-54

Commission on Social Justice (1994) *Social Justice: strategies for national renewal* London, Vintage

Compton, Beulah Roberts and Burt Galaway (1989) *Social Work Processes* (4th ed) Homewood, Ill., Dorsey Press.

Compton, Beulah Roberts and Burt Galaway (1994) *Social Work Processes* (5th ed) Pacific Grove, California, Brooks/Cole

Constable, Robert and Carmelo Cocozzelli (1989) 'Common themes and polarities in social work practice theory development' *Social Thought* 15 (Spring) pp14-24

Cormack, Una and Kay McDougall (1950) 'Case-work in social service' in Cherry Morris (ed) *Social Case-Work in Great Britain* London, Faber and Faber

Costa, Maria das Dores (1988) 'Social movements: a perspective for social rights and for social workers' professional practice' in Charles Guzzetta and Florence Mittwoch (eds) *Social Development and Social Rights* Vienna, International Association of Schools of Social Work pp142-50

Coulshed, Veronica (1990) *Management in Social Work* London, Macmillan

CSWE (1988) *Handbook on Accreditation Standards and Procedures* Washington DC, Council on Social Work Education

Dale, Jennifer and Peggy Foster (1986) *Feminists and State Welfare* London, Routledge and Kegan Paul

David, Gerson (1993) 'Strategies for grass roots human development' *Social Development Issues* 15(2) pp1-12

Davies, Martin (1994) *The Essential Social Worker: a guide to positive practice* (3rd ed) Aldershot, Hants, Arena

Davies Jones, Haydn (1994) *Social Workers, or Social Educators? The international context for developing social care* London, National Institute for Social Work International Centre

Day, Peter (1981) *Social Work and Social Control* London, Tavistock

de Schweinitz, Elizabeth and Karl de Schweinitz (1964) 'The place of authority in the protective function of the public welfare agency' in Shankar A Yelaja, (ed) (1971) *Authority and social work: concept and use* Toronto: University of Toronto Press

Dixon, Jane (1992) 'Practices for political impact and practice theories for profession building' *Australian Social Work* 45(4) pp9-19

Doel, Mark and Peter Marsh (1992) *Task-Centred Social Work* Aldershot, Hants, Ashgate

Dominelli, Lena (1988) *Anti-Racist Social Work: a challenge for white practitioners and educators* London, Macmillan

Dominelli, Lena and Eileen McCleod (1989) *Feminist Social Work* London, Macmillan

Downie, R S and Elizabeth Telfer (1969) *Respect for Persons* London, Allen and Unwin

Downie, R S and Elizabeth Telfer (1980) *Caring and Curing* London, Methuen

Dressel, Paula L (1992) 'Patriarchy and social welfare work' in Yeheskel Hasenfeld (ed) *Human Services as Complex Organisations* Newbury Park, CA, Sage, pp205-23

Eddy, David M (1984) 'Variations in physician practice: the role of uncertainty' in Jack Dowie and Arthur Elstein (eds) (1988) *Professional Judgement: a reader in clinical decision-making* Cambridge, Cambridge University Press

Ejaz, Farida Kassim (1989) 'The nature of casework practice in India: a study of social workers perceptions in Bombay' *International Social Work* 32(1) pp25-38

Ejaz, Farida Kassim (1990) 'The concept of familial duty in India: implications for social work practice' *Indian Journal of Social Work* 52(3) pp437-45

Bibliography

Eley, Ruth (1989) 'Women in management in social services departments' in Christine Hallett (ed) *Women and Social Services Departments* Hemel Hempsted, Herts, Harvester Wheatsheaf

Elliott, Doreen (1993) 'Social work and social development: towards an integrative model for social work practice' *International Social Work* 36(1) pp21-36

England, Hugh (1986) *Social Work as Art: making sense for good practice* London, Allen and Unwin

Estes, Richard J (1992) 'Models, social modeling and models of international social work education' in Richard J Estes (ed) *Internationalizing Social Work Education: a guide to resources for a new century* Philadelphia, PA, University of Pennsylvania School of Social Work

Etzioni, Amitai (ed) (1969) *The Semi-Professions and their Organization: teachers, nurses, social workers* New York, Free Press

Etzioni, Amitai (1975) *A Comparative Analysis of Complex Organizations: on power, involvement and their correlates* New York, Free Press

Evans, Estella Norwood (1992) 'Liberation theology, empowerment theory and social work practice with the oppressed' *International Social Work* 35(2), pp135-48

Fattahipoor, Ahmad (1991) 'The Malays' quest for a Muslim identity' in Sandra Sewell and Anthony Kelly (eds) *Social Problems in the Asia-Pacific Region* Brisbane, Boolarong Publications

Fink, Arthur E (1961) 'Authority in the correctional process' in Shankar A Yelaja, (ed) (1971) *Authority and social work: concept and use* Toronto: University of Toronto Press

Fisher, Jo (1993) *Out of the Shadows: women, resistance and politics in South America* London, Latin American Bureau

Fook, Jan (1990) 'Radical social casework: linking theory and practice' in Jude Petruchenia and Ros Thorpe (eds) *Social Change and Social Welfare Practice* Sydney, Hale and Iremonger

Fook, Janis (1993) *Radical Casework: a theory of practice* St Leonards, Australia, Allen and Unwin

Foren, Robert and Royston Bailey (1968) *Authority in Social Casework* Oxford, Pergamon

Foucault, Michel (1972) *The Archaeology of Knowledge and The Discourse on Language* New York, Pantheon

Freidson, Eliot (1970) *Profession of Medicine: a study of the sociology of applied knowledge* New York, Dodd, Mead

Freidson, Eliot (1986) *Professional Powers* Chicago, University of Chicago Press

Freire, Paulo (1972) *Pedagogy of the Oppressed* Harmondsworth, Penguin

Freire, Paulo (1974) *Education: the practice of freedom* London, Readers and Writers Publishing Co-operative

French, J R P and B H Raven (1959) 'The bases of social power' in Dorwin Cartwright and A Zander (eds) *Group Dynamics: theory and research* (3rd ed) London, Tavistock

Friedmann, John (1992) *Empowerment: the politics of alternative development* Cambridge, Mass, Blackwell

Furlong, Mark (1987) 'A rationale for the use of empowerment as a goal in casework' *Australian Social Work* 40(3) pp25-30

Galper, Jeffrey H (1975) *The Politics of Social Services* Englewood Cliffs, NJ, Prentice-Hall

Gargett, Eric (1977) *The Administration of Transition: African Urban Settlement in Rhodesia* Gwelo, Mambo Press

Garrett, Myra (1980) 'The problem with authority' in Mike Brake and Roy Bailey (eds) *Radical Social Work and Practice* London, Edward Arnold

Garvin, Charles (1985) 'Group process: usage and uses in social work practice' in M Sundel, Paul Glasser, Rosemary Sarri and Robert Vinter (eds) *Individual Change in Small Groups* (2nd ed) New York, Free Press

Garvin, Charles D and John E Tropman (1992) *Social Work in Contemporary Society* Englewood Cliffs, NJ, Prentice-Hall

George, Vic and Paul Wilding (1985) *Ideology and Social Welfare* London, Routledge and Kegan Paul

George, Vic and Paul Wilding (1994) *Welfare and Ideology* Hemel Hempsted, Herts, Harvester Wheatsheaf

Germain, C (1979) 'Introduction ecology and social work' in Carol B. Germain (ed) *Social Work Practice: People and Environments an ecological perspective* New York, Columbia University Press

Gibbs, Jocelyn, Moss Evans and Simon Rodway (1987) *Report of the Inquiry into Nye Bevan Lodge* London, Southwark Social Services Department

Giddens, Anthony (1993) *Sociology* (2nd ed) Cambridge, Polity

Gill, Robin (1992) *Moral Communities: the Prideaux Lectures for 1992* Exeter, University of Exeter Press

Gilligan, Carol (1982) *In a Different Voice: psychological theory and women's development* Cambridge, Mass, Harvard University Press

Glastonbury, Bryan, David M Cooper and Pearl Hawkins (1980) *Social Work in Conflict: the practitioner and the bureaucrat* London, Croom Helm

Goldstein, Howard (1988) 'Humanistic alternatives to the limits of scientific knowledge: the case of ethical dilemmas in social work practice' *Social Thought* 14 (Winter) pp47-58

Gordon, William E (1964) 'Notes on the nature of knowledge' in NASW *Building Social Work Knowledge* New York, National Association of Social Workers, pp60-75

Greenwood, E (1957) 'Attributes of a profession' *Social Work* 2(3) pp45-55

Gutiérrez, Gustavo (1992) 'Poverty from the perspective of liberation theology' in Hubert Campfens (ed) *New Reality of Poverty and Struggle for Social Transformation* Vienna, International Association of Schools of Social Work

Haines, John (1975) *Skills and Methods in Social Work* London, Constable

Hallett, Christine (1989) 'The gendered world of the social services department' in Christine Hallett (ed) *Women and Social Services Departments* Hemel Hempsted, Herts, Harvester Wheatsheaf

Halmos, P (1965) *The Faith of the Counsellors* London, Constable

Halmos, P (1970) *The Personal Service Society* London, Constable

Halmos, Paul (1978) *The Personal and the Political: social work and political action* London, Hutchinson

Hanmer, Jalna and Daphne Statham (1988) *Women and Social Work: towards woman-centred practice* London, Macmillan

Harcourt, Wendy (1994a) 'Introduction' in Wendy Harcourt (ed) *Feminist Perspectives on Sustainable Development* London, Zed Books

Harcourt, Wendy (ed) (1994b) *Feminist Perspectives on Sustainable Development* London, Zed Books

Hardin, Russell (1993) 'Altruism and mutual advantage' *Social Service Review* 67(3) pp358-73

Harrison, Jen (1990) 'Confessions of competent hoop jumper: becoming aware of unconscious conservative values' in Jude Petruchenia and Ros Thorpe (eds) *Social Change and Social Welfare Practice* Sydney, Hale and Iremonger

Hasenfeld, Yeheskel (1992) 'Theoretical approaches to human service organisations' in Yeheskel Hasenfeld (ed) *Human Services as Complex Organisations* Newbury Park, CA, Sage, pp24-44

Hollis, Florence (1970) 'The psychosocial approach to the practice of casework' in Robert W Roberts and Robert H Nee (eds) *Theories of Social Casework* Chicago, University of Chicago Press, pp33-75

Horne, Michael (1987) *Values in Social Work* Aldershot, Hants, Wildwood House

Horner, William C and Les B Whitbeck (1991) 'Personal versus professional values in social work: a methodological note' *Journal of Social Service Research* 14 (1/2) pp21-43

Howe, David (1986) *Social Workers and their Practice in Welfare Bureaucracies* Aldershot, Hnts, Gower

Howe, David (1994) 'Modernity, postmodernity and social work' *British Journal of Social Work* 24 (5) pp513-32

Howe, Elizabeth (1980) 'Public professions and the private model of professionalism' *Social Work* 25(5) pp179-91

Hu, Chi-Tse (1993) 'Some thoughts on psychoanalysis and Confucianism in China' in Louis Yang-ching Cheng, Fanny MC Cheung and Char-Niè Chen (eds) *Psychotherapy for the Chinese* Hong Kong, Department of Psychiatry, Chinese University of Hong Kong

Hugman, Richard (1991) *Power in Caring Professions* London, Macmillan

Hunt, Arthur W (1964) 'Enforcement in probation casework' in Eileen Younghusband (ed) (1966) *New Developments in Casework* London, Allen and Unwin

Husband, Charles (1991) ' "Race", conflictual politics, and anti-racist social work: lessons form the past for action in the 90s' in CD Project Steering Group *Setting the Context for Change* Leeds, Northern Curriculum Development Project, Central Council for Education and Training in Social Work

Imbrogno, Salvatore and Edward R Canda (1988) 'Social work as an holistic system of activity' *Social Thought* 14 (Winter) pp12-29

Imbrogno, Salvatore (1993) 'Dialectical discourse as a strategy for social development' *Social Development Issues* 15(2), pp14-28

Imre, Roberta Wells (1989) 'Moral theory for social work' *Social Thought* 15 (Winter) pp18-27

James, Ann (1994) *Managing to Care: public service and the market* London, Longman

Johnson, Louise C (1992) *Social Work Practice: a generalist approach* (4th ed) Boston, Allyn and Bacon

Jones, Chris (1976) *The Foundations of Social Work Education* Durham, Department of Sociology and Social Adminstration, University of Durham

Jones, Chris, (1979) 'Social work education, 1900-1977' in Noel Parry, Michael Rustin and Carole Satyamurti (eds) *Social Work, Welfare and the State* London, Edward Arnold

Jones, John F and Rama S Pandey (1981) *Social Development: conceptual, methodological and policy issues* Delhi, Macmillan

Jones, John F and Toshihiro Yogo (1994) *New Training Design for Local Social Development: the single system design for competency-based training; Vol. 1 Development of Training Curriculum* Nagoya, The United Nations Centre for Regional Development

Jones, Sandra and Richard Joss (1995) 'Models of professionalism' in Margaret Yelloly and Mary Henkel (eds) *Learning and Teaching in Social Work: towards reflective practice* London, Jessica Kingsley

Jordan, Bill (1990) *Social Work in an Unjust Society* Hemel Hempsted, Herts, Harvester Wheatsheaf

Kadushin, Alfred (1964) 'Assembling social work knowledge' in NASW *Building Social Work Knowledge* New York, National Association of Social Workers

Kandwalla, Pradip N (1988) *Social Development: a new role for the organizational sciences* New Delhi, Sage

Krill, Donald (1990) *Practice Wisdom: a guide for helping professionals* Newbury Park, CA, Sage

Kwhali, Josephine (1991) 'Assessment checklists for DipSW External Assessors' in (no editor named) *One Small Step Towards Racial Justice: the teaching of antiracism in Diploma in Social Work programmes* London, Central Council for Education and Training in Social Work

Laczko, Frank and Chris Phillipson (1991) *Changing Work and Retirement* Buckingham, Open University Press

Langan, Mary and Lee, Phil (1989) 'Whatever happened to radical social work?' in Mary Langan and Phil Lee (eds) *Radical Social Work Today* London, Unwin Hyman, pp1-18

Bibliography

Larson, M S (1980) 'Proletarianisation and educated labour' *Theory and Society* 9, pp131-75

Lee, Porter R (1929) 'Social work: cause and function' in Fern Lowry (ed) (1939) *Readings in Social Case Work 1920-1938: Selected reprints for the case work practitioner* New York, Columbia University Press pp22-37

Lees, Ray (1971) 'Social work 1925-50: the case for a reappraisal' *British Journal of Social Work* 1(4) pp371-80

Lewis, Harold (1973) 'Agology, animation and conscientization: implications for social work education in the USA' *Journal of Education for Social Work* 9 (Fall) pp31-8

Lewis, Harold (1982) *The Intellectual Base of Social Work Practice: tools for thought in a helping profession* New York, Haworth Press

Loch, Charles S (1883) *How to Help in Cases of Distress* (Facsimile ed, 1977) Plymouth, Devon, Continua

Lorentzon, Maria (1990) 'Professional status and managerial tasks: feminine service ideology in British nursing and social work' in Pamela Abbott and Claire Wallace (eds) *The Sociology of the Caring Professions* Basingstoke, Hants, Falmer Press

Lorenz, Walter (1994) *Social Work in a Changing Europe* London, Routledge

Lowe, Gary R (1987) 'Social work's professional mistake: confusing status for control and losing both' *Journal of Sociology and Social Welfare* 14(2) pp187-206

Lukes, Steven (1974) *Power: a radical view* London, Macmillan

Lurie, Harry L (1935) 'Re-examination of child welfare functions in family and foster care agencies' in Fern Lowry (ed) (1939) *Readings in Social Case Work 1920-1938: Selected reprints for the case work practitioner* New York, Columbia University Press, pp611-9

Malherbe, Madelaine (1982) *Accreditation in Social Work: principles and issues in context: a contribution to the debate* London, CCETSW

Marcus, Grace F (1935) 'The status of social case work today' in Fern Lowry (ed) (1939) *Readings in Social Case Work 1920-1938: Selected reprints for the case work practitioner* New York, Columbia University Press pp122-35

Martin, Elaine Wilson (1992) 'Themes in a history of the social work profession' *International Social Work* 35(3) pp327-46

Mason, J K and R A McCall Smith (1994) *Law and Medical Ethics* (4th ed) London, Butterworths

Mayer, John E and Noel Timms (1970) *The Client Speaks* Routledge and Kegan Paul

McDermott, F E (ed)(1975) *Self-determination in Social Work: a collection of essays on self-determination and related concepts by philosophers and social work theorists* London, Routledge and Kegan Paul

Midgley, James (1981) *Professional Imperialism: social work in the third world* London, Heinemann

Midgley, James, (1993) 'Ideological roots of social development strategies' *Social Development Issues* 15(1) pp1-13

Mondros, Jacqueline B and Scott M Wilson (1994) *Organizing for Power and Empowerment* New York, Columbia University Press

Morales, Armando and Sheafor, Bradford W (1992) *Social Work: a profession of many faces* (6th edition) Boston, Mass, Allyn and Bacon

Morris, Jenny (1993) *Independent Lives: community care and disabled people*, London, Macmillan

Morriss, Peter (1987) *Power: a philosophical analysis* Manchester: Manchester University Press

Mullaly, Robert P (1993) *Structural Social Work: ideology, theory and practice* Toronto, McClelland and Stewart

Mullender, Audrey and Dave Ward (1991) *Self-Directed Groupwork: users take action for empowerment* London, Whiting and Birch

Munson, Carlton E (1993) *Clinical Social Work Supervision* (2nd ed) New York, Haworth Press, Ch15

Mupedziswa, R R (1988) 'Popular participation as a strategy for empowerment and capacity building among underprividged groups: the case of Zimbabwe' in Charles Guzzetta and Florence Mittwoch (eds) *Social Development and Social Rights* Vienna, International Association of Schools of Social Work, pp100-112

Nagpaul, Hans (1993) 'Analysis of social work teaching materials in India: the need for indigenous foundations' *International Social Work* 36(3) pp207-20

Nartsupha, Chatthip (1991) 'The community culture school of thought' in Manas Chitakasem and Andrew Turton (eds) *Thai Constructions of Knowledge* London, School of Oriental and African Studies, University of London, pp118-41

National Association of Social Workers (1980) 'The NASW Code of Ethics' in Armando T Morales and Bradford W Sheafor (1992) *Social Work: a profession of many faces* (6th edition) Boston, Mass, Allyn and Bacon, pp234-40

National Association of Social Workers (1981) 'Working statement on the purpose of social work' *Social Work* 26(1) p6

NEA (1975) 'Code of ethics of the education profession' in Kenneth A Strike and Jonas F Soltis (1992) *The Ethics of Teaching* (2nd ed) New York, Teachers College Press

Netherlands Association of Social Workers Committee on Professional Questions regarding Social Work (1987) *Professional Profile of the Social Worker* Utrecht, 's-Hertenbosch

NUT Executive (1975) 'Union draws up code of professional ethics for teachers' *The Teacher* 14 November 1975

Ohlin, Lloyd E, Herman Piven and Donnell M Pappenfort (1956) 'Major dilemmas of the social worker in probation and parole' in Shankar A Yelaja, (ed) (1971) *Authority and social work: concept and use* Toronto: University of Toronto Press

Oliver, Michael (1990) *The Politics of Disablement* London, Macmillan

Oliver, Michael (ed) (1991) *Social Work: disabled people and disabling environments* London, Jessica Kingsley

Oppenheimer, M (1973) 'The proletarianization of the profession' in Paul Halmos (ed) *Professionalization and Social Change* Keele, Staffs, Sociological Review Monograph 20, pp213-24

Osei-Hwedie, Kwaku (1993) 'The challenge of social work in Africa: starting the indigenisation process' *Journal of Social Development in Africa* 8(1) pp19-39

Parad, Howard J (1965) 'Introduction' in Howard J Parad (ed) *Crisis Intervention: selected readings* New York, Family Service Association of America

Parker, Roy (1990) *Safeguarding Standards. a report on the desirability and feasibility of establishing a United Kingdom independent body to regulate and promote good practice in social work and social care* London, National Institute for Social Work

Parton, Nigel (1994a) ' "Problematics of government" (post) modernity and social work' *British Journal of Social Work* 24(1) pp9-32

Parton, Nigel (1994b) 'The nature of social work under conditions of (post) modernity' *Social Work and Social Sciences Review* 5(2) pp93-112

Payne, Malcolm (1979) *Power, Authority and Responsibility in Social Services: social work in area teams* London, Macmillan

Payne, Malcolm (1989) 'Open records and shared decisions with clients' in Steven Shardlow (ed) *The Values of Change in Social Work* London, Tavistock/Routledge, pp114-34)

Payne, Malcolm (1991) *Modern Social Work Theory: a critical introduction* London, Macmillan

Payne, Malcolm (1992) Psychodynamic theory within the politics of social work theory *Journal of Social Work Practice* 6(2) pp141-9

Payne, Malcolm (1993a) *Linkages: effective networking in social care* London, Whiting and Birch

Payne, Malcolm (1993b) 'Routes to and through clienthood and their implications for practice' *Practice* 6(3) pp169-80

Payne, Malcolm (1994a) 'Personal supervision in social work' in Anne Connor and Stewart Black (eds) *Performance Review and Quality in Social Work* London, Jessica Kingsley, pp43-58

Payne, Malcolm (1994b) 'Partnership between organisations in social work education' *Issues in Social Work Education* 14(1) pp53-70

Payne, Malcolm (1995) *Social Work and Community Care* London, Macmillan

Pearson, Veronica (1991) 'Western theory, eastern practice: social group work in Hong Kong' *Social Work with Groups* 14(2) pp45-58

Perkin, Harold (1989) *The Rise of Professional Society: England since 1880* London, Routledge

Perlman, Helen Harris (1957) *Social Casework: a problem-solving process* Chicago: University of Chicago Press

Perlman, Helen Harris (1979) *Relationship: the heart of helping people* Chicago, University of Chicago Press

Pieper, Martha Heineman (1989) 'The heuristic paradigm: a unifying and comprehensive approach to social work research' *Smith College Studies in Social Work* 60 pp8-34

Pincus, Allen and Anne Minahan (1973) *Social Work Practice: model and method* Itasca, Ill, Peacock

Pithouse, Andrew (1987) *Social Work: the social organisation of an invisible trade* Aldershot, Hants, Gower

Pithouse, Andrew (1990) 'Guardians of autonomy: work orientations in a social work office' in Pam Carter, Tony Jeffs and Mark Smith (eds) *Social Work and Social Welfare Yearbook 2 1990* Milton Keynes, Open University Press, pp42-53

Ragg, Nicholas (1980) 'Respect for persons and social work: social work as "doing philosophy" ' in Noel Timms (ed) *Social Welfare: Why and How?* London, Routledge and Kegan Paul, pp211-32

Ramsey, Richard F (1987) 'Social work's search for a common conceptual framework' in Yoko Kojima and Tetsuyo Hosaka (eds) *Peace and Social Work Education: Proceedings of the 23rd International Congress of Schools of Social Work* Vienna, IASSW, pp50-7

Rapoport, Lydia (1970) 'Crisis intervention as a mode of brief treatment' in Robert H. Nee (eds) *Theories of Social Casework* Chicago, University of Chicago Press.

Reamer, Frederick G (1990) *Ethical Dilemmas in Social Service: a guide for social workers* (2nd ed) New York, Columbia University Press

Reamer, Frederick G (1993) *The Philosophical Foundations of Social Work* New York, Columbia University Press

Rees, Stuart (1975) 'How misunderstanding occurs' in Roy Bailey and Mike Brake (eds) *Radical Social Work* London, Edward Arnold

Rees, Stuart (1991) *Achieving Power: practice and policy in social welfare* Sydney, Allen and Unwin

Reeser, Linda Cherrey and Irwin Epstein (1990) *Professionalization and Activism in Social Work: the sixties, the eighties and the future* New York, Columbia University Press

Reynolds, Bertha C (1935) 'Social case work: What is it? What is its place in the world today?' in Fern Lowry (ed) (1939) *Readings in Social Case Work 1920-1938: Selected reprints for the case work practitioner* New York, Columbia University Press, pp136-47

Richmond, Mary E (1917) *Social Diagnosis* New York, Free Press (1965 reprint of the 1917 edition, published by the Russell Sage Foundation)

Richmond, Mary E (1922) *What is Social Case Work?* New York, Russell Sage Foundation

Roberts, Robert.W and Nee, Robert H (1970) *Theories of Social Carework* Chicago, University, Chicago Press

Robertson, Geoffrey (1993) *Freedom, the Individual and the Law* London, Penguin Books

Robertson, Roland (1992) *Globalization: social theory and global structure* London, Sage

Rogers, Carl R (1951) *Client-Centred Therapy: its current practice, implications and theory* London, Constable

Bibliography

Rojek, Chris (1989) 'Social work and self-management' in Chris Rojek, Geraldine Peacock and Stewart Collins (eds) *The Haunt of Misery: critical essays in social work and helping* London, Routledge, pp173-88

Rooff, Madeline (1957) *Voluntary Societies and Social Policy* London, Routledge and Kegan Paul

Rooney, Ronald H (1992) *Strategies for Work with Involuntary Clients* New York, Columbia University Press

Rorty, Richard (1989) *Contingency, Irony and Solidarity* Cambridge, Cambridge University Press

Rose, Stephen M and Bruce L Black (1985) *Advocacy and Empowerment: mental health care in the community* Boston, Routledge and Kegan Paul

Rosenfeld, Jona M (1984) 'The expertise of social work: a cross-national perspective' in Charles Guzzetta, Arthur J Katz and Richard A English (eds) *Education for Social Work Practice: Selected International Models* Vienna, International Association of Schools of Social Work, pp111-18

Satyamurti, Carole (1979) 'Care and control in local authority social work' in Noel Parry, Michael Ruston and Carole Satyamurti (eds) *Social Work, Welfare and the State* London, Edward Arnold

Schön, Donald A (1983) *The Reflective Practitioner: how professionals think in action* (place of publication not stated), Basic Books

Schriver, Joe M (1987) 'Harry Lurie's critique: person and environment in early casework practice' *Social Service Review* 61(3) pp514-32

Schwartz, Barry (1993) 'Why altruism is impossible . . . and ubiquitous' *Social Service Review* 67(3) pp314-43

Scott, W Richard (1975) 'Professional employees in a bureaucratic structure: social work' in Amitai Etzioni (ed) *The Semi-Professions and their Organization: teachers, nurses, social workers* New York, Free Press, pp82-140

Seipel, Michael M O (1994) 'Disability: an emerging global challenge' *International Social Work* 17(2) pp165-78

Shardlow, Steven (ed) (1989) *The Values of Change in Social Work* London, Tavistock/Routledge

Shulman, Lawrence (1991) *Interactional Social Work Practice: toward an empirical theory* Itasca, Ill, F E Peacock

Sibeon, Roger (1990) 'Social work knowledge, social actors and de-professionalisation' in Pamela Abbott and Claire Wallace (eds) *The Sociology of the Caring Professions* Basingstoke, Hants, Falmer Press

Sibeon, Roger (1992) 'Sociological reflections on welfare politics and social work' *Social Work and Social Sciences Review* 3(3) pp184-203

Silavwe, Geoffrey W (1995) 'The need for a new social work perspective in an African setting: the case of social casework in Zambia' *British Journal of Social Work* 25(1) pp71-84

Simpson, Richard L and Ida Harper Simpson (1969) 'Women and bureaucracy in the semi-professions' in Amitai Etzioni (ed) *The Semi-Professions and their Organization: teachers, nurses, social workers* New York, Free Press, pp196-265

Sinha, Durganand and Henry S R Kao (1988) *Social Values and Development: Asian perspectives* New Delhi, Sage

Siporin, Max (1989) 'The social work ethic' *Social Thought* 15 pp42-52

Skidmore, Rex A Milton G Thackeray, and O William Farley (1994) *Introduction to Social Work* Englewood Cliffs, NJ, Prentice-Hall

Smalley, Ruth E (1967) *Theory for Social Work Practice* New York, Columbia University Press

Smalley, Ruth E (1970) 'The functional approach to casework practice' in Robert W Roberts and Robert H Nee *Theories of Social Casework* Chicago, University of Chicago Press

Solomon, Barbara Bryant (1976) *Black Empowerment: social work in oppressed communities* New York, Columbia University Press

Statham, Daphne (1978) *Radicals in Social Work* London, Routledge and Kegan Paul

Stevenson, Olive (1973) *Claimant or Client? A social worker's view of the Supplementary Benefits Commission* London, Allen and Unwin

Strike, Kenneth A and Jonas F Soltis (1992) *The Ethics of Teaching* (2nd ed) New York, Teachers College Press

Studt, E (1954) 'An outline for the study of social authority factors in casework' in Shankar A Yelaja (ed) *Authority and Social Work: Concept and Use* Toronto, University of Toronto Press

Teare, R. J. and McPheeters, H. L (1970) *Manpower Utilization in Social Welfare: a report based on a Symposium on Manpower Utilization in Social Welfare Services* Atlanta, Georgia, Social Welfare Manpower Project, Southern Medical Education Board

Tesfaye, Andargatchew (1987) 'Social welfare programmes and social work education in Ethiopia' *Indian Journal of Social Work* 47(4) pp363-77

Thomas, Edwin J (1970) 'Behavioral modification and casework' in Robert W Roberts and Robert H Nee *Theories of Social Casework* Chicago, University of Chicago Press

Thomas, Terry and Joan Forbes (1989) 'Choice, consent and social work practice' *Practice* 3(2) pp136-47

Tilbury, Derek E F (1977) *Casework in Context: a basis for practice* Oxford, Pergamon Press

Timms, Noel (1983) *Social Work Values: an enquiry* London, Routledge and Kegan Paul

Tolfree, David K (1980) 'Objectives and values' in David Lane and Keith White (eds) *Why Care? A volume of articles on the values underlying residential work* London, Residential Care Association

Toren, Nina (1969) 'Semi-professionalism and social work: a theoretical perspective' in Amitai Etzioni (ed) *The Semi-Professions and their Organization: teachers, nurses, social workers* New York, Free Press, pp141-95

Toren, Nina (1972) *Social Work: the case of a semi-profession* Beverly Hills, Sage

Truax, Charles B and Carkhuff, Robert R (1967) *Toward Effective Counseling and Psychotherapy: training and practice* Chicago, Aldine

Turner, Bryan (1987) *Medical Power and Social Knowledge* London, Sage

UKCC (1985) *Advertising by Registered Nurses, Midwives and Health Visitors* London, United Kingdom Central Council for Nursing, Midwifery and Health Visiting

UKCC (1987) *Confidentiality: an elaboration of clause 9 of the second edition of the UKCC's Code of Professional Conduct for the Nurse, Midwife and Health Visitor* London, United Kingdom Central Council for Nursing, Midwifery and Health Visiting

UKCC (1991a) *Midwives Rules* London, United Kingdom Central Council for Nursing, Midwifery and Health Visiting

UKCC (1991b) *A Midwife's Code of Practice* London, United Kingdom Central Council for Nursing, Midwifery and Health Visiting

UKCC (1992a) *Code of Professional Conduct for the Nurse, Midwife and Health Visitor* (3rd ed) London, United Kingdom Central Council for Nursing, Midwifery and Health Visiting

UKCC (1992b) *Standards for the Administration of Medicines* London, United Kingdom Central Council for Nursing, Midwifery and Health Visiting

UKCC (1993) *Standards for Records and Record Keeping* London, United Kingdom Central Council for Nursing, Midwifery and Health Visiting

Vernon, Stuart, Robert Harris and Caroline Ball (1990) *Towards Social Work Law: legally competent professional practice* London, CCETSW

Verma, Ratna (1991) *Psychiatric Social Work in India* New Delhi, Sage

Wakefield, Jerome C (1993) 'Is altruism a part of human nature? Toward a theoretical foundation for the helping professions' *Social Services Review* 67(3) pp406-58

Walton, Ronald G and Medhat M Abo el Nasr (1988) 'Indigenization and authentization in terms of social work in Egypt' *International Social Work* 31(2) pp135-44

Waring, Mary L and Gerald O'Connor (1981) 'The domain of social work: what is it?' *Journal of Social Work and Social Welfare* 8(4) pp698-709

Watson, David (ed) (1985a) *A Code of Ethics for Social Work: the second step* London, Routledge and Kegan Paul

Watson, David (1985b) 'What's the point of A Code of Ethics for Social Work?' in David Watson (ed) *A Code of Ethics for Social Work: the second step* London, Routledge and Kegan Paul

Weale, Albert (1978) *Equality and Social Policy* London, Routledge and Kegan Paul

Weick, Ann (1990) 'Knowledge as experience: exploring new dimensions of social work inquiry' *Social Thought* 16(3) pp36-46

Weissman, Harold H (1990) 'Play and creativity' in Harold H Weissman (ed) *Serious Play: creativity and innovation in social work* Silver Spring, MD, NASW

Whittaker, James K and Tracy, Elizabeth M (1989) *Social Treatment: an introduction to interpersonal helping in social work practice (2nd ed)* New York, Aldine de Gruyter

Wignaraja, Ponna (ed) (1993) *New Social Movements in the South: empowering the people* London, Zed Books

Wilding, Paul, (1982) *Professional Power and Social Welfare* London, Routledge and Kegan Paul

Wilensky, Harold L (1963) 'The professionalisation of everybody' *American Journal of Sociology* 70, pp137-58

Wilensky, Harold L and Charles N Lebeaux (1965) *Industrial Society and Social Welfare* New York, Free Press

Wilkes, Ruth (1981) *Social Work with Undervalued Groups* London, Tavistock

Witkin, Stanley L and Shimon Gottschalk (1989) 'Considerations in the development of a scientific social work' *Journal of Sociology and Social Welfare* 16 pp19-29

Wood, Gale Goldberg and Ruth R Middleman (1989) *The Structural Approach to Direct Practice in Social Work* New York, Columbia University Press

Woodroofe, Kathleen (1962) *From Charity to Social Work: in England and the United States* London, Routledge and Kegan Paul

Wootton, Barbara (1959) *Social Science and Social Pathology* London, Allen and Unwin

Wuthrow, Robert (1993) 'Altruism and sociological theory' *Social Service Review* 67(3) pp344-57

Yasas, Frances Maria and Vera Mehta (eds) (1990) *Exploring Feminist Visions: case studies on social justice issues* Pune, India, Streevan/Ishvani Kendra

Yelaja, Shankar, A (1965) 'The concept of authority and its use in child protective service' in Shankar A Yelaja, (ed) (1971) *Authority and social work: concept and use* Toronto: University of Toronto Press

Yelaja, Shankar A (ed) (1971) *Authority and social work: concept and use* Toronto: University of Toronto Press

Yelloly, Margaret A (1980) *Social Work Theory and Psychoanalysis* Wokingham, Berks, Van Nostrand Reinhold

Young, Katherine P H (1983) *Coping in Crisis* Hong Kong University Press

Author Index

Subject Index